TQM: QUALITY TRAINING PRACTICES

Also available from Quality Press

TQM: Leadership for the Quality Transformation
Richard S. Johnson

TQM: Management Processes for Quality Operations
Richard S. Johnson

TQM: The Mechanics of Quality Processes
Richard S. Johnson and Lawrence E. Kazense

TQM: A Step-by-Step Guide to Implementation
Charles N. Weaver, PhD

A TQM Approach to Achieving Manufacturing Excellence
A. Richard Shores

An Approach to Quality Improvement That Works, Second Edition
A. Donald Stratton

Management Excellence Through Quality
Thomas J. Barry

Total Quality Management: Performance and Cost Measures
Dorsey J. Talley

To request a complimentary catalog of publications, call 800-248-1946.

TQM: QUALITY TRAINING PRACTICES

RICHARD S. JOHNSON

Sponsored by the ASQC
Quality Management Division

Volume IV of the ASQC
Total Quality Management Series

ASQC Quality Press
Milwaukee, Wisconsin

TQM: Quality Training Practices
Richard S. Johnson

Library of Congress Cataloging-in-Publication Data

Johnson, Richard S.
   TQM: quality training practices/Richard S. Johnson.
      p.   cm.—(ASQC total quality management series: v. 4)
   Includes bibliographical references and index.
   ISBN 0-87389-234-8
   1. Employees—Training of. 2. Total quality management.
I. Title.   II. Series
HF5549.5.T7J527   1993
658.3'12404 — dc20   92-42759
                                                         CIP

10987654321

ISBN 0-87389-234-8

Acquisitions Editor: Jeanine L. Lau
Production Editor: Mary Beth Nilles
Marketing Administrator: Susan Westergard
Set in Palatino by Linda J. Shepherd. Cover design by Wayne Dober.
Printed and bound by BookCrafters.

For a free copy of the ASQC Quality Press Publications Catalog, including ASQC membership information, call 800-248-1946.

This book follows lesson plans for the TQM process by Quality America, Inc. of Mechanicsburg, PA.

Printed in the United States of America

Printed on acid-free recycled paper

ASQC
Quality Press
611 East Wisconsin Avenue
Milwaukee, Wisconsin 53202

Contents

Acknowledgments

There is an obvious debt to hundreds of authors who have provided the works I studied over the past 30 years. Their thoughts are evident throughout and credit is provided wherever possible. Many of these people are listed in the bibliographies. However, these are only a few of the many authors who have inspired my ideas over a lifetime of study. Often one cannot remember the source of an idea, but knows it came from somewhere.

An even greater debt is owed to the U.S. Navy and the men and women who serve her. As a member of this outstanding organization, I was fortunate enough to attend several lengthy train-the-trainer type programs. Many of the ideas in this book are founded in the knowledge that was accumulated during these formal periods of study and later supplemented by self-study initiatives. Perhaps even more information was acquired and subsequently added to this volume through the input of the thousands of students I have worked with over the years. In so many cases, the trainer learns more in training sessions than the trainees. Many fine leaders added substantially to this book over the years. I have been tempted to name some of them, but would undoubtedly forget someone and that would be unfair.

Many leaders and managers from corporations and the government have added to this effort. In my training and consulting activities, I am in constant contact with dedicated professionals in many organizations. Their thoughts and practices also are a part of the ideas and concepts presented herein.

Members of the American Society of Training and Development (ASTD) also had a part in this effort. Our meetings, training sessions, and Train America's Work Force efforts all provide substantial knowledge and information for the training professional.

Four other people must be recognized for their contributions over a great many years. My grandmother, Irene C. Lewis, was a trainer who provided ongoing instruction on subjects ranging from the Bible to nature. My parents, Richard and Ada Johnson, provided considerable training, much of which did not take during earlier years. That wasn't because of any training deficiency— rather it was an application problem. Finally, and most important in my adult life, my wife, Sandy, has put up with years without vacations, supported a never-ending string of all-night projects that resulted in this effort, typed, edited, and encouraged the effort of which I have been a part in the last 25 plus years. Thanks, Sam.

–R. S. Johnson

Preface

It is becoming increasingly difficult to read major newspapers or business journals without coming across articles lamenting the state of organizational training in the United States. Various statistics show that this country's major competitors outspend U.S. businesses, often by considerable amounts.

While the level of spending must increase to maintain competitiveness, training efficiency and effectiveness also must be improved. The total quality management (TQM) process requires considerable training to implement and continual training to ensure continuous process, product, and personnel improvements. Performance improvements don't just happen, well-trained personnel cause them to happen. Therein lies a problem. Many organizations are strapped for cash, the number of bankruptcies is high, and global competitiveness requires a sharpened pencil when figuring costs to maintain or grow markets. When cuts must be made, training dollars often are the first to go, usually with predictable results.

In many organizations, a disproportionate amount of training dollars is spent on management training while the people who produce products and services often receive little. This factor shows up in undertrained workers producing inferior goods—a major problem when competing in a global marketplace. It also is one source of the we–they attitudes between management and work force personnel that trouble many organizations.

These situations pose a dilemma, but it is a dilemma with answers. Training efficiency and effectiveness can be enhanced with the use of additional in-house training through a broadened base of instructors. TQM achieves maximum effectiveness when led from the top down. Most executives and managers have considerable knowledge that is a required part of all improvement efforts. Cascade training—training where leaders train their subordinates—has proven most rewarding. Utilizing these management assets, subject matter experts, and other in-house resources greatly expands training capabilities. Simultaneously, the working environment is improved because workers see the commitment and efforts from the top down. These training activities support management efforts to get involved in the processes for which they are responsible.

Workers also can be used in the training equation. No one knows more about a process than the people who work there. Many of these skilled people thrive on training opportunities when they are provided train-the-trainer training and afforded the opportunity to use it. Workers want to be members of quality organizations and they want to be a part of improving their operations. It makes sense to provide those opportunities.

This book is designed to support professional in-house training activities in order to initiate TQM successfully. Each chapter is a stand-alone subject that addresses particular aspects of training. At the same time, each chapter builds on the information provided in the preceding chapter, progressing in an orderly fashion to Chapter 17 which ties training requirements to customer needs.

Checklists, charts, comparisons, questionnaires, and survey samples from many different sources provide information to support all training efforts. Examples of various situations are included because they help the reader identify with problems occurring in their personal organization.

This book is designed to support organizational goals. Every TQM requirement ultimately goes back to the main reason the organization exists—"*The Goal.*" For business, this ultimate goal is to produce a profit; for educational systems the goal is educated graduates; for government it is cost-effective service that constituents cannot provide for themselves; for nonprofit organizations it is services that government doesn't provide; and for the military it is the ability to win wars when they cannot be prevented. No concept is more important to TQM than understanding what the goal is.

Training is tied to the bottom line in order to support the quest to meet "The Goal" or bottom line, because every organization is tied to fiscal constraints. The procedures required for the development of an effective in-house program are presented in detail. Chapter bibliographies provide additional sources to further study each subject. A composite bibliography is provided at the end of this book listed by subject matter to support additional research.

Finally, this book is written in a manner to support the studies of every employee from the work force to the CEO. It is hoped that your organization will include members from these levels and every other level in between in its training efforts.

Introduction

Business does not stand alone in the global marketplace. All types of organizations are intertwined together, and they must learn to work together and support each other to change the way we conduct our business as a nation. There is no other choice for an America bent on recovery of its standard of living as it builds into tomorrow.

Enter training. Change is impossible without the solid training efforts which make successful change possible. People cannot work and do things differently if they don't know how to change. Change is required in every organization if America is to survive as a world leader. As a people, we aren't prepared for anything less. Like it or not, every individual is in this improvement effort together. There can be no other way.

This book was developed to assist the broad range of trainers and training skills that must be involved in a TQM training program. Often organizations have excellent technical personnel who lack training and development skills. These subject matter experts (SME) can rapidly increase their training skills through the proper use of the information in this book.

In this book and other TQM books in this series, individual organizations are never discussed in the context of problems they might have. It would be a breach of trust to recognize these situations and would satisfy no need. Conversely, organizations that stand out in positive ways are recognized where appropriate. It is important for readers to know that there are organizations with excellent systems and most of them are supportive of other organizations beginning TQM initiatives.

Training programs that provide the instruction crucial for success in the TQM process and quality training in itself are discussed simultaneously.

For that reason the terms often are considered synonymous in successful programs.

Standard training programs are developed to support all types of training situations. These are then applied to an on-the-job training program. Following this, the potential problems that can hinder training success are discussed and additional training concepts are covered.

CHAPTER 1

Understanding the Need

Performance improvement is the single biggest challenge facing the United States as it struggles to remain competitive in the global market. Gains in both aspects of performance—productivity and quality—must be equal to or greater than our competition's or we face a freefall into a second-rate economic power. Although necessary to maintain world stability, our military might will not increase our standard of living. Only performance improvement can do that.

Productivity improvements must continue to increase. Contrary to what many might have you believe, however, the American manufacturing worker is still the most productive worker in the world. The annual productivity increase in the manufacturing sector stood at almost 4.0 percent over the past decade. This is approximately equal to our two greatest competitors—Germany and Japan.

During this same period, American quality increased for many manufacturers. Unlike the productivity factor, this improvement for most companies is a catch up process. Having fallen from a place where "Made in USA" stood for quality at its best, the United States is struggling to regain its place at the pinnacle. Regrettably, by itself, this will not be enough to keep the American standard of living from slipping further.

The reason for this is that only about 20 percent of all Americans are employed in manufacturing positions. Although their performance improvements are absolutely essential to remain competitive, the performance of all other American workers must improve dramatically if we are to remain competitive as a nation. The service sector which has, by far, the most workers must improve its performance dramatically. This means that equal or greater attention must now be placed on these workers so that organizations, and in turn the United States, can become more productive.

The numbers of administrative workers, computer and data processing personnel, managers, and other nonmanufacturing personnel have grown rapidly, but output per person has not kept pace with that of the manufacturing counterpart. It is not a matter of not receiving support in terms of equipment because expenditures for these areas often rival that received in manufacturing. Part of the problem is based in administrative rules, procedures, checks, and so forth, which strangle the nonmanufacturing employees where they are coming under review in the manufacturing operations. It also is caused because little attention is paid to process improvement off the manufacturing floor.

Although times are changing, organizations in the United States typically focus on the processes directly involved in producing the end product or service and pay little or no attention to all the supportive processes unless they impact significantly on production. A major problem exists here. By the time supportive operations impact on production, the work force is upset, customers are threatening everything from cancelling orders to lawsuits, and vendors complain they don't know what is expected of them.

Waste must be searched out and eliminated in every process. Training functions generally have more than their fair share of opportunities for improvement. Larger operations including state and federal governments have major training departments supporting individual bureaus with little sharing of ideas, training plans, or programs. The wheel is invented and reinvented in every individual training department. Another significant waste is the cost of developing in-house training plans and programs when canned programs already are available at a cost far below what in-house development would cost. These plans tend to be proven in practice and upgraded over time.

Another major waste is training developed by the training department and presented to other departments in the "Here is what you need—take it and use it wisely" mode. It is seldom what the managers or workers at the receiving end perceive the training need to be, and until their perceived need is satisfied, the training department's perceptions of training will have little positive affect.

Most departments have problems that seriously impact on performance and customer service, and the correct training could alleviate these problems. As an example, customer relations or customer service training is provided to correct customer dissatisfaction when the problem is caused by faulty process.

Not long ago the performance improvement process was being discussed with a training manager for a major insurance company. This organization was in the process of raising its rates to meet rising costs which was the subject that had triggered the conversation. The training manager was asked if his company had flowcharted its various processes so it could systematically attack bottlenecks and waste prior to increasing rates. His reply was staggering, "I'm not sure anyone knows what all the processes are, let alone how to improve them." This would indicate a major problem in any organization, especially when the comment was made by someone responsible for training employees, presumably to improve their performance through such sessions as process and process control.

The Training Need

Performance improvement is achieved through skilled, knowledgeable, and committed workers who want to make their organization better. Most people want to do a good job. They often lack the skills necessary to operate to their true potential, a problem that may arise over time as technology and new processes are introduced into the organization.

Some employees welcome innovation and new ways of doing things—most do not. One office manager did a commendable job running the administrative function until computer systems were introduced. She was reluctant to learn word processing operations, spreadsheet applications, automatic costing, tracking and reporting systems, and computer-based filing systems. When training was held, she always seemed to have some emergency she had to handle personally or was on planned time off. At the same time she felt her job was threatened because the system was bypassing her. Fortunately for all involved, the basis for her fear was discovered and overcome through training that was need-based for her.

Management skill deficiencies also can impact heavily on employee performance in much the same way. Many senior managers lack the computer skills, quality knowledge, and technical information to make TQM happen, yet they don't mention it because it could impact on everything, including job security.

Every organization faces these situations. Too often the problems are diagnosed as employees who have suddenly developed an attitude or employee burnout. Correct assessment of need is most important.

Organizational security and, in turn, employment security depends on continuous training/retraining evolutions so that employees can thrive in a quality system, meet the technological requirements of emerging business opportunities, and satisfy the customer. In turn, employment security promotes employee loyalty and increases commitment to TQM.

Training is becoming increasingly important to success. There are many reasons for this and most of them reside in the necessity for TQM as a system for success. Strong leadership coupled with quality training and training for quality are the factors that cause quality environments to happen, and therefore, they must become an integral part of all TQM processes.

Well-trained and highly motivated work teams are essential for TQM, performance improvement, organizational stability, and long-term success. Quality will not come from cheerleading sessions, rah-rah speeches, or decree. Quality requires hard work and continued effort over the life of the organization. As many have noted, an organization cannot expect improved performance in any area by doing things the same way they have always done them.

Change must take place. Failure to recognize the external challenges that impact on the organization can prove disastrous. Neglecting to make the changes necessary for the organization to remain a competitive, growing entity is one of the major factors impacting on American quality. Well-planned and well-executed training must lead change or ability to survive world competition is questionable.

Behavioral changes and performance improvement require solid training designed to need. Training that is not need-based wastes time and assets while it demotivates most people who are involved.

Organizations face a host of other training requirements. New employees will require indoctrination training to bring them up to speed on their jobs, TQM, performance, and customer service requirements. Ever-increasing numbers of entry-level employees join the work force requiring long-term training to make up for the differences between the product put out by the secondary education system and organizational needs in advanced technological environments. Fast-changing markets spawn training requirements almost beyond imagination. Many of the advanced skills needed within organizations are not found in the available pool of workers. Additionally, various training and apprenticeship programs are important tools in an organization's efforts to meet Equal Employment Opportunity goals.

Well-trained employees must become a foremost concern of every member of an organization. Nothing less will do because every member must become a strong performer, capable of carrying his own weight. The time is long past when organizations can remain competitive and successful without a strong emphasis on training their work force.

Unions recognize the need for skilled workers in terms of their ability to successfully compete. They are placing even more emphasis on training. A recent GM-UAW contract specifies that so much money for every worker hour be placed in a training fund. The union in turn administers a highly sophisticated program that provides worker training in all phases of their work lives. This certainly has to play a large part in the recent resurgence of quality in GM products.

Organizational leadership also must assume increasing responsibility for training. Telling workers to do something and showing them how to do it so they can successfully complete the task(s) themselves in the future are two different things; the latter being the method that promotes quality.

Dynamic training, structured to need, is mandated to meet the changing demands placed on each organization by the ever-increasing pace of global competition. This requires that two goals be met: (1) the work force must be trained to continually improve performance so the organization can survive, and (2) they must be trained in quality and problem-solving skills so they can be empowered to produce the important, long-term change necessary to become true quality organizations. These skills coupled with participative and delegative leadership skills are foundations for self-management teams.

Emphasis on quality also requires organizations to change the way they view their people. Employees can no longer be viewed as assets that can be quickly discarded as the needs of the organization outpaces their current skills. Dedicated and skilled employees are long in demand and short in supply, and the supply problem is becoming more alarming as our high schools turn out graduates ill-prepared to function in modern organizations. Solid employees must be retained and trained for the long term. Retraining the current work force is almost always more productive, less expensive, and considerably more positive in terms of employee morale.

Performance improvement requires additional changes in the way organizations tend to view their training operation. Training has been viewed as a means to overcome immediate problems or changes, such as those caused by equipment or process changes. Forward-looking training must be provided that prepares employees to change their work environment and processes before a crisis develops. This is far removed from the panic training held for mere survival. The different basic requirements for training will be discussed in greater detail in the chapters that follow.

Quality also demands leadership from the top down with every person in every leadership position understanding the operation and being able to assess training needs in his or her area of responsibility. These leaders also must be trained to provide training to meet quality needs. The odds are against improvements in quality in any organization where the leader doesn't understand the jobs of those immediately under him and cannot provide those people with the training they require.

This is not to say the leader must personally provide all the training received by his group, but certain kinds of training must be handled by the leader for effectiveness. This criterion produces an immediate problem because most leaders have not learned how to be effective trainers. Through this course, the organizational leader will acquire skills to ascertain when there is a training requirement and have a system to provide high payoff training that promotes performance improvement.

Problems

Let's look at where we are now. America is in a quandary of sorts. Ever-improving quality is demanded to remain competitive in both the domestic and world markets. Americans and the world demand it. The basic foundations for these improvements must come through continuous, improved training that is designed to meet performance needs. Emerging technology also mandates improved training and increased training emphasis as viewed by increased executive commitment and expenditures.

At this time of increased need, there are deficiencies in our secondary educational systems that make it more difficult to train current graduates who are now entering or are projected to enter the work force. The American secondary education system has no method to deliver individuals trained to the specific skills needed in organizations. The 70 percent of youth who do not go on to complete college programs are not prepared to enter the work environment.

Simultaneously, many of the people who do go to college complete programs with no specific end job in mind. This puts the United States at a disadvantage in global competition with countries such as Japan and Germany. These countries have comprehensive programs to meet their current demands and are preparing for emerging requirements. It also places an increasing economic and time burden on organizations to train their incoming work force to make up for these shortages.

Training dollars are not getting any easier to come by with business and industry now outspending secondary educational institutions in the United States. Organizations often feel compelled to reduce training commitments because of economic reasons even though many studies prove solid training programs are a required investment that does not cost—it pays. Ask our foreign competitors. They are greatly outspending American organizations on both a per capita cost basis and on an annual hours of training per individual basis.

Statistics reveal that U.S. companies invest approximately 1.4 percent of payroll in training while Japanese and European companies based in the United States spend three to five times as much for employee training. Compounding the situation, training reaches only 10 percent of the American work force—mostly management-level personnel. Even worse, the training is not part of a long-term, well-thought-out program based on need, rather it is a little bit of this and a little bit of that without much application or follow-through evaluation.

To meet the new era competition, the following five training requirements are vital:

1. Training directed to all levels of the organization.

2. More productive need-based training.

3. Innovative ways to train the now entering work force who have been found lacking in basic educational skills.

4. More effective, yet cost-efficient training that pays off in terms of performance improvements and/or an improved quality of work life.

5. Increased training investments.

The program presented in this book satisfies the first four requirements while it works toward improving the environment for the fifth one. A more productive work force generates more profits which allows more funding availability for training.

It isn't that employers are not currently spending money on training. They invest about $30 billion annually on training. The American Society for Training and Development (ASTD), through their national TRAIN AMERICA'S WORKFORCE CAMPAIGN, recommend this dollar amount be increased to 2 percent of payroll or $44 billion near term, which it is estimated will reach another 5 percent of the employees, or 15 percent total. The ultimate ASTD goal is 4 percent of payroll, which would increase the current outlay for training to $88 billion.

Increased funding is only part of the cure. Focused, effective training is required. This means a change in the way training is approached. Figure 1.1 illustrates an approach that has proven successful in application.

Figure 1.1 points out several important considerations.

1. All training should be focused toward the goal. Each organization must understand exactly what their goal is before training programs are discussed. For example, the goal of business is profit through focused customer service. Customer service by itself is of little value. Goals of schools must be educated students prepared to meet the challenges of their follow-up plans in terms of college, work, or the military. Every organization must make this same determination of what the goal is before focused training can be planned.

2. Exact need to meet the goal must be ascertained in terms of each hierarchical level of the organization in order to provide economical training that contributes to the bottom line, regardless of what that bottom line is. Economical training or training based on a need that is not focused on the end goal does not support performance improvement or the premises of TQM.

3. The training determination includes decisions that ascertain the most effective and efficient way to promote the required learning experience in terms of the required end result.

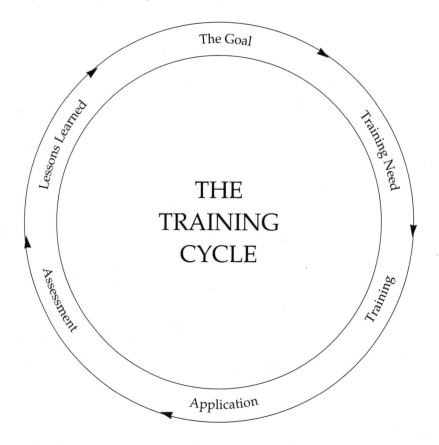

Figure 1.1 Training Cycle

4. Application to the work situation is essential. Training that is not applied is time and assets wasted and leads to employees placing reduced importance on all training.

5. Application must be followed closely by assessment for effectiveness. Excellent training that does not accomplish the stated objectives is a problem. Assessment reveals where changes and improvements can be made to improve follow-up sessions.

6. The lessons learned are discussed with plans made to build on the strengths and overcome any problem areas. Application to other situations and operations always is a part of the "Lessons Learned" step. This prevents reinvention of the wheel, while it promotes overall organizational performance improvement.

Payoff

Can American organizations afford this level of funding for training? That is a difficult question to answer. Perhaps the question should be, Can the United States survive as an economic power without a considerable increase in training dollars?

Money is not the only ingredient in training payoff. Organizational training must be more than a simple process; it must become the way of life. The dividends can be enormous because training pays off in so many ways. It opens the door for maximization of employee ability. Most employees have a great capacity for training and education that is never tapped. Training meets self-development needs while it provides the organization with trained personnel capable of being advanced. Training must lead the way as more and more tasks are delegated to lower organizational levels. There is one way to tap the great reservoir of human potential through solid training programs.

Training supports the organization's performance management program. It is seldom possible to hire a person with the exact skills needed, especially at a competitive salary. Trained technical and quality personnel are becoming scarcer commodities in the pool of available workers. It is estimated that need will mandate America import technical workers during this decade just the way they now import doctors and nurses. Training can relieve much of the need for new hires for special skills.

Training also provides an excellent communications vehicle. Organizational quality commitment can be inserted and must be evident in every phase of the training program. Performance improvement feedback can be provided to participants concerning the successes and contributions fellow employees are making in the TQM process. The organization vision, along with goals and strategies, can become standard parts of training sessions. Training provides an opportunity to recognize participants who have made contributions to TQM success in yet another setting.

The knowledge and skills required to improve performance in terms of both quality and production can be effectively acquired only through some sort of training program. It is a means to enhance teamwork and promote quality customer service.

Employee benefits from solid training programs are numerous. Training provides the feeling of being a professional while it increases job security. Training provides the knowledge and skills required for high performance and workers strongly desire to produce quality efforts of which they can be proud. These factors improve the potential for both increases in compensation and promotion. Training also provides the material to build a personal resumé which increases an employee's value in the organization, builds self-image, and provides a measure of personal security.

Summary

1. Organizational in-house training is becoming increasingly important to success in the 1990s.

2. Well-trained and highly motivated work teams are essential for TQM, organizational stability, and long-term success. This migration to quality environments mandates strong training programs.

3. A poorly prepared entering work force, retraining requirements brought on by new technology, the focus on quality, the TQM environment, and human relations requirements are among the many situations that must be supported through training.

4. Solid training programs pay great dividends in every area of an organization.

5. Employees receive a great many benefits through training. Some of these benefits include improved job security, increased professionalism, and the potential for compensation increases and promotion opportunities.

Bibliography

Abella, K. T. *Building Successful Training Programs*, Reading, MA: Addison-Wesley, 1986.

Asionian, C. B. and Brickell, H. M. *Americans in Transition: Life Changes As Reasons for Adult Learning*, New York: College Entrance Examination Board, 1980.

Bienvenu, B. J. *New Priorities in Training*, New York, NY: American Management Association, 1969.

Brinkerhoff, R. O. *Achieving Results from Training*, San Francisco: Jossey-Bass, 1987.

Cassner-Lotto, J. and Associates. *Successful Training Strategies: Twenty-six Innovative Corporate Models*, San Francisco: Jossey-Bass, 1988.

Cooper, S. and Heenan, C. *A Humanistic Approach*, Boston: CB Publishing Company, 1980.

Friedman, P. G. and Yarbrough, E. A. *Training Strategies from Start to Finish*, Englewood Cliffs, NJ: Prentice-Hall, 1985.

London, M. *Managing the Training Enterprise*, San Francisco: Jossey-Bass, 1989.

Rogoff, R. L. *The Training Wheel*, New York: John Wiley and Sons, 1987.

The Learning Enterprise, Alexandria, VA: The American Society for Training and Development, and Washington D.C.: U.S. Department of Labor, 1991.

Put Quality to Work—Train America's Workforce, Alexandria, VA: The American Society for Training and Development, 1991.

Workplace Basics: The Skills Employers Want, Alexandria, VA: The American Society for Training and Development, and Washington D.C.: U.S. Department of Labor, 1991.

CHAPTER 2

Organizational Requirements

TQM, process understanding, continuous performance improvement, and focused customer service—organizational life is changing and training requirements follow. What are the training requirements of today's organizations—my organization in particular? How do I find out what requirements we should address? How do I know what my needs really are?

These important questions must be correctly answered before the first training session is ever considered. Those who have journeyed through Volumes I through III in this series have an idea of all the topics which should be addressed over time. The volumes also include the basic information required to tackle each subject. How should you attack your situation? What is best for you?

Like the answers to other organizational questions, the answers to these queries also can be complicated. There are many reasons for this. People are involved. Employers see things one way, employees another. Education plays a significant part. College-educated individuals see things at one level, high school grads judge from another level, and nongrads, well, let's just say our work is cut out for us there. Executives have one look, managers another, and the work force yet another.

Within the work force, professionals, administrators, customer service personnel, and salespeople see different needs. Don't kid yourself about sales personnel—every organization has them. If you think of yourself as a successful leader, you are a successful salesperson or you won't be successful as a leader. This discussion is not meant to complicate your life, it is to provide an understanding of all the factors that must be addressed in order to develop a quality training program that pays dividends on the investment, instead of being more money down the drain.

The United States is extremely rich in natural resources. We have metals, minerals, forests, and rich farmland. These resources provide us with advantages other nations envy, yet we waste much of what we have. The most productive farmland in the world is routinely paved over to provide parking space for shopping centers. Our landfills bulge with wasted metals, plastics, glasses, and paper that can all be recycled. This waste, however, is trivial when placed with the greatest of all wastes—the waste of human resources.

Japan, Korea, and Nationalist China (to name three tough competitors) have few natural resources other than their people. Yet these nations are rapidly making inroads into markets that traditionally were ours. They use our raw materials such as logs and produce finished products that take away our markets. They are grabbing market shares in industries we invented. Some industries have been totally taken over by foreign entities. They have discovered the value of their people and are investing in their training to a degree most American organizations find unbelievable.

How can these nations invest the money to provide two to three weeks of training annually for individual employees? The answer is simple; they believe they have no other choice. If they are to remain competitive, they must use the only real natural resource they have in abundance—their people.

The remainder of this book is dedicated to providing answers to the questions raised in this chapter. There are ways American organizations can provide the training needed, at the level needed without putting every organization in the red.

Employer–Employee Needs

The growing deficiency between workplace skill and knowledge requirements, and the level of those skills and knowledge which exist in the pool of potential workers, can be considered alarming at best. Many organizations including the U.S. military are going through dumbing down exercises to provide training and materials for individuals who are not prepared to the same educational competencies achieved by people just a decade ago. Many predict that before the 1990s fall behind us, America will be forced to import technical workers from abroad the same way we now are importing people for the medical professions. Scary? You bet it is, but it doesn't have to end this way.

Many individuals believe there are too many highly trained people who cannot find the technical jobs for which they worked so hard. This is only half true. There are highly educated people who cannot find jobs, but in general, they are not technical people, they are those with degrees in subjects such as sociology, psychology, police science, and so forth, where there are more than enough people to fill the jobs available. Engineers, technicians, and other technical specialists readily find employers who demand their skills. This suggests organizational needs must be better understood by those in the education business so that education is not just great information to know, but also supports the search for and placement in a fulfilling job.

For now, we must shift to using the products turned out by the various education systems and work for change to those systems over time. What skills and knowledge, then, do employers require of their employees?

Employer Needs

The first need of employers consists of the three Rs—reading, 'riting, and 'rithmetic. Many professional groups have come out with employer desires in this area, "Give me people who can read and write with the ability to handle basic math and I can train them for the work I do." These basics are the prerequisites for all other learning. Basic knowledge by itself is not enough, the employee must be able to use these skills in the context of the workplace. The concepts of quality tools, process, and so much more demand the mastery of these subjects beyond the level at which most high schoolers currently are able to function. It is important to remember that it is not only entry-level employees who may have problems, long-term employees also may need refreshers or even initial training in these areas.

By themselves these skills are not enough. Communicating, listening, interpersonal relations, problem-solving, and decision-making skills are becoming more important. Workers at all levels from entry level to seasoned employee must become well versed in these skills.

This is not to say that employees without these skills will not find work—it lets us know that all employers must face the increasing prospects of these people being a growing percentage of their work force for at least the immediate future. Although it is a difficult problem, it is not hopeless.

In a radio broadcast a couple of years ago, Tom Peters used Quad/Graphics printing as an example of a company that successfully employed a large portion of non-high school grads in their work force. However, their education immediately took on great importance upon entry into the Quad/Graphics organization. They received eight or so hours of training every week in addition to their work hours. Much of this time was unpaid time, a price to pay to be part of this team. Every employee also was expected to become a trainer over time. There is nothing wrong with that. It is an outstanding way of doing business—the way the Navy has operated successfully over the past 200+ years.

Two other skills are invaluable: the ability to learn and the ability to develop life goals. These two subjects should be mandatory parts of all freshman high school curriculums. Those who don't learn to learn (and there are a great number of people in that category) struggle their entire life trying, often unsuccessfully, to master the most basic principles. You have to know how to learn before you can learn.

The second course on setting life goals is equally important. The lack of this kind of program is the singular greatest reason why our youth graduate from high school and wonder what they are going to do next. They attend and complete college still wondering the same thing. This is much of the reason why so many students change majors during college and then end up working in a field outside their education. It is a noble idea that college provides the foundation for learning, but wouldn't it be better if it also was the basis for a person's lifetime career choice?

Establishing goals has an importance beyond what many believe. If all freshmen had a research project designed to make them investigate career fields and set career goals in terms of their skills and interests, expected salary, educational requirements, job locations, and so forth (information readily available in the Labor Department Bulletin 2250), there would be additional incentive to remain in school and succeed. Students would be more productive in school, better prepared for life after school, and a more valued employee when they enter the work force. They would also have the foundation for establishing career goals that would benefit both themselves and the employer. Since most people entering the work force don't have this skill, the employer would do well to provide it.

At one organization all new employees fill out a goals sheet that covers personal, career, and organizational goals in some detail. These goals are discussed with management as the final step of the check-in process. A senior engineering manager reported it was the first time in his 35-year work career that he had been forced to write down his goals, and it had been both a trying and rewarding experience. Goals are important for everyone.

The following discussion provides an overview of subjects which employers must consider in their initial training efforts. As in all training, some areas will need more effort than others, depending on the employees and the work they do. Some areas will be covered again in more detail later in the chapter.

Learning to learn begins with a knowledge of how employees acquire information. Visual, auditory, and tactile skills are all discussed later in this book to facilitate the learning process. Teaching those individuals how to learn is a prerequisite for all other training. This is one area where package training programs often are the answer because learning to learn is a subject common to all mankind and is not organization specific.

The three Rs is a second area where packaged training plans serve organizational needs well. Computer-based training (CBT) programs are available, as well as programs assisted by audio and video tapes. These programs make learning a variety of subject matter possible outside of normal work hours. Most organizations are surprised by the number of personnel willing to work through training programs on their own time in order to qualify for other jobs, raises, and promotions.

Self-management becomes increasingly important. Employers who desire high performance work teams cannot overlook training on goal establishment, self-training programs, self-esteem, self-motivation, and career action planning.

Communications has long been important, but is generally overlooked. Because most performance improvement projects depend on team efforts, communication becomes extremely important. Talking isn't enough. Listening and being able to comprehend and act on what has been said becomes all important.

Team skills such as teamwork, interpersonal relations, personal negotiations, problem solving, the use of quality tools, and basic leadership skills also are crucial to the development of empowered employees who can transform the workplace.

Each of these subjects is developed in stand-alone sections in Volumes I to III in this series.

Employee Needs

What does the employee need? Many employee needs will be taken care of when the previously described employer needs are met. Many other needs are not necessarily the responsibility of the employer, although the employer may benefit from them in the long run. College courses that do not directly transfer to the workplace benefit the employee in terms of completion of work required for a degree, but their benefit to the employer is questionable. Most employers do not assist with these types of programs.

The employee needs a job, job security, career potential, and the opportunity to make a decent living. This involves learning skills that directly apply to the workplace. Employees soon learn that as their skills increase, their value to the organization increases, which brings promotions, pay raises, bonuses, and so forth. Most employees like that.

Education and training programs benefit both the employee and the employer. The employee prepares for career improvement and the many benefits that accrue from making oneself more skilled. The employer retains an employee with higher skills that add to organizational performance improvement efforts and increase competitiveness. As mentioned earlier, the trained employee is any organization's most valuable asset.

Skill enhancement programs can be provided in many ways. Apprenticeship programs are especially valuable. Those programs approved by state and federal agencies carry program content, time per subject, and course requirements that support the employee's training cycle. Completion certificates confirm that the person successfully completed the material necessary to become a journeyman or some other such designation, which in turn increases the value of his service.

There are all kinds of other approaches to skills training. Some use CBT with interactive video and supportive material. This may be combined with classroom exercises and on-the-job training sessions. Each of these is a valuable method of improving employee skills.

One method that is gaining considerable favor consists of the programs provided by CBT. These programs can be utilized during off-work hours through a computer log on process that automatically allows entry by designated employees. It records portions of training correctly completed and enters information on computer personnel records when a program is successfully completed.

These programs are extremely effective when correctly applied and used by people who want to learn. They require little monitoring, instructors need not be present, and they are cost effective. Technical skills are readily learned through this medium. Because each step of the process is reinforced by the next step, and because the trainee cannot get past efforts incorrectly answered, the exact level of accomplishment is easily ascertained. The employee benefits because she spends additional time only with areas of personal difficulty.

Need by Structural Hierarchy

Those occupying each level of an organization have separate and distinct needs which depend upon their function, the roles assigned to that function, the technical expertise required to correctly perform that function, and the relationships each level has internal and external to the organization. Technical professionals tend to receive, by far, the most training, followed by nontechnical professionals, technicians, management support specialists, general managers, mechanics, and other repair personnel.

Within the work force itself, there is a wide disparity in the application of training to solve performance problems and improve service. Laborers, service workers, and machine operators tend to receive little training, and they are the people that produce the products and services in every organization. The demands of TQM, continuous performance improvement, and customer-focused service require considerable additional training efforts for these production personnel. Every performance area of each employee's work processes must be analyzed and training provided so that the employee can correctly handle his job.

For example, learning how to operate a cash register correctly is not sufficient training for a cashier. Of equal, and perhaps greater, importance is the need to satisfy customer needs through professional customer relations and strong interpersonal skills.

Figure 2.1 exhibits how different levels of the organization work together to make a whole. Three levels were chosen for simplicity. Managers and supervisors are grouped together as managers; all personnel who are not executive managers or managers are grouped together as work force. When work force training is discussed, several different types of workers and their associated needs will be covered.

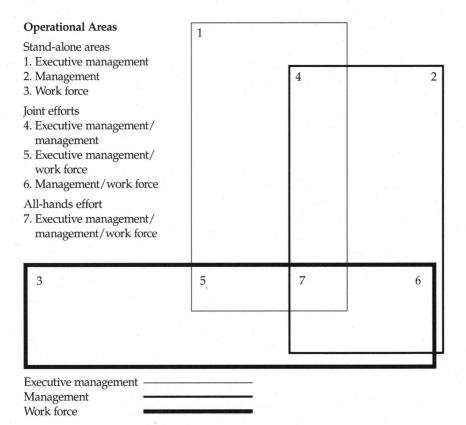

Operational Areas

Stand-alone areas
1. Executive management
2. Management
3. Work force

Joint efforts
4. Executive management/
   management
5. Executive management/
   work force
6. Management/work force

All-hands effort
7. Executive management/
   management/work force

Executive management
Management
Work force

Figure 2.1 Organizational Structure for TQM

Structural Interrelationships

Training requirements vary according to the organizational structure as it is depicted in Figure 2.1. Some training adapts well to all or most levels of the organization. Other efforts pertain to only one or two areas, while still other efforts would cover areas where two areas of the organization must work together. The areas are depicted of equal size because they are equally important to the success of all TQM/performance improvement initiatives.

Stand-alone areas depicted in this model include areas: 1–executive management, 2–management, and 3–the work force. Each of these areas has specific tasking requirements that demand training specific to that level.

Joint efforts include areas where two segments of the organization work together. These are depicted by areas: 4–executive management/management efforts, 5–executive management/work force efforts, and 6–management/ work force efforts. The duties in area 4 generally are well-known. Planning and operational duties require these two segments of the organization to work in close harmony for many evolutions. Area 5 may be practically nonexistent in many organizations, other than an occasional cursory visit or guided guest tour by an executive. TQM, however, requires more than that. This area denotes the time organizational leaders invest walking through work areas, listening to employees, and discovering what is happening in the work force in terms of their own perspective without the various shading which occurs as information is passed through a chain of command. Area 6 is considerably larger in this figure than it often is in reality. Again, TQM requires changes here. Management must get out of the office and onto the work floor. Team initiatives, team meeting time, and "how goes it" time on the work floor will take this much time.

All hands efforts are those outlined by area 7 where all segments of the organization come together in teaming efforts. These efforts could be training efforts, problem-solving initiatives, general quality briefings, and so forth. Work force professions often are required to meet with management and executive management to sort out details for new products, overcome problem areas, and the like. Some work force personnel attend executive management/management meetings in their roles as subject matter experts or internal consultants.

Executive Training Needs

Executives make up about 2 percent of the American work force of 120 million people. Over the years, they generally receive considerable training as they climb the organizational ladder. Most individuals who reach this level in any organization have been carefully selected based on performance, knowledge, skills, and other such criteria. They have proven themselves or they wouldn't be in the position.

This does not mean they know it all. Training in strategic issues such as planning, benchmarking, and change management are especially applicable. The executive is responsible for benchmarking in two ways: benchmarking the competition to prepare combative plans, and benchmarking quality organizations to better understand the level of quality that can be achieved. Strategic planning is based in part with the information discovered through benchmarking exercises while change management is important to properly carry out strategic plans.

Sessions on an overview of quality, organizational structure for quality, and implementation are especially important. Other quality subjects, including visioning, leadership, performance management, process control, problem solving, and quality tools, are especially important at the executive level. Training on emerging technology also is important. The executives interests are best served when the training takes an innovational use perspective rather than an operational perspective more applicable to lower management and the work force.

Organizational development becomes another vital training subject for the executive who must ensure intra-unit relationships that support process improvement throughout the organization. Without cooperation throughout, there is little chance of the overall improvements occurring that are necessary in order to experience major successes in performance improvement efforts. Job design efforts are required to ensure management, supervision, and worker positions are aligned to support the needs of TQM fully.

Work sessions on administration and the reduction of unnecessary rules and requirements is another subject of importance for all managers. Programs to improve performance management and human resource planning are similar subjects that precede efforts at realignment of organizational structure to meet the competitive challenges faced by global competition, new technology, and economics.

Because the executive position requires work with both managers and work force personnel, team training and interpersonal skills training will be most supportive of their position and their quality efforts. Contact with external entities makes the subject of customer service an appropriate one.

Career development is important as a training subject for all those who serve in management positions, regardless of level. There should be several people in training for promotion to the next level at all times. Those people chosen must be apprised of the opportunities, challenges, and requirements of promotion. They need assistance with personal educational programs and other career guidance. Mentoring, coaching, and counseling skills are essential to management success, and all managers and supervisors must receive appropriate training and hone these skills.

Management Training Needs

Approximately 4 percent of all working Americans are in the manager ranks and a like number are included in the supervisory work force. Although most managers begin with a solid education profile including college, they still receive the lion's share of money for training, especially when the amount of money is compared against the percentage of employees. Supervisors tend not to have the same education backgrounds in many work areas. Manufacturing supervisors and their counterparts in other operations tend to come up through the work force and often have a limited education. Employees in this level may need more specific training than managers. Supervisors generally receive little training on their supervisory duties or the new skills required in their leadership and management functions. Somehow they are supposed to have gained these skills through osmosis on the work floor. Unfortunately, this is a major reason why many newly appointed personnel fare poorly as supervisors. You can't do that which you don't know.

Leadership training is mandatory. Too many managers have had little exposure to the concepts of leadership, and it shows when they attempt to gain commitment to the changes required in performance improvement efforts. TQM demands much more in the way of leadership skills because it is an interactive process that depends on employees doing more than they were previously accustomed to doing. Training also is required in general topics such as managing meetings, communications, and dealing with difficult people.

Management training subjects would include the organizational development, job design, human resource planning, and performance management subjects taken by executive managers because management must assist with planning and carry out the changes. Interpersonal skills such as coaching, mentoring, questioning, negotiating, and communicating are also training subjects that should be included in the manager's training plan.

Management in a quality environment includes training on such subjects as teams and team building, problem-solving, quality tools, performance management, budgeting, strategic planning, and training skills. Training skills are becoming increasingly important as managers are called on to train lower level managers and workers in a great many quality and quality-related subjects.

All managers should receive training in the business competencies. Important topics include business practices, cost-benefit analysis, organizational structure, personnel development, and behavior studies, financial applications, project planning, and project management.

Technical training is becoming more important for the manager who must spend more and more time in the work areas. You cannot serve on quality teams and not know the technical aspects of the job. Innovative use of technology requires training in the application of technology to the workplace. These are vital areas for managers truly bent on performance improvement.

Customer service, customer relations, community relations, and interpersonal skills training also are important subjects for today's manager. The manager must be adept at working with people internal and external to the organization.

In broader terms, the manager must know those things her people know so that she can assist them in their efforts to improve the organization. Managers well versed in leadership and quality principles are a key to success in TQM.

The Work Force Training Needs

It goes without saying that workers need to know how to do their jobs correctly. This requires technical and process training to the level required because of the complexities of their individual operations. Performance improvement requires training on process, process control, recording and graphing information, troubleshooting, quality tools, and problem solving.

Many workers will be used in various training applications so train-the-trainer efforts will be required for them as well as managers. Application of technology in both training and working situations also is appropriate.

Team, interpersonal, and communications skills training are applicable for the work force also. Team efforts demand it and work areas become quality environments because of it. Computer literacy is becoming an important subject in many organizations as spreadsheets, planning evolutions, monitoring processes, and recording various information becomes a work force level function in many operations.

Direct quality subjects include quality awareness subjects appropriate to particular work stations, an introduction to TQM, implementing quality in the workplace, impact of quality on the work force, working in a quality environment, the importance of quality including organizational survival, and "what's in it for me" subjects.

Specific Needs of Work Force Specialists

In addition to the generic needs previously listed, specialists will require additional training particular to their fields. The following were chosen as guides for types of training that would serve chosen groups.

Technical professionals including technicians will find specialty training in their field absolutely essential. Much of this initial training will be received external to the organization although a cadre can receive the training and then train others within the organization. Every technical field is witnessing advances occurring so rapidly that it becomes difficult to keep up with them.

Computer and data processing personnel are in the same boat as other technical specialties. Programs, languages, applications, and equipment tend to change rapidly. Training skills will be important because operators throughout the organization must be trained as computer-based operations keep pace with the technological improvements available. No part of a manufacturing operation or most service operations is immune from the need for computers and computer training.

Clerical personnel require training in word processing and computer systems because of the rapid advances in information technology. Spreadsheet operations, planning and scheduling programs, and so forth are finding increased use by clerical personnel. Paperless administrative systems lurk on the horizon. Significant performance improvement can come through computerization of operations if it is handled correctly.

Customer service personnel are growing rapidly in numbers. Product knowledge, customer service, customer relations, dealing with difficult people, and interpersonal relations are all mandatory training requirements.

Educators require training in several fields that often are neglected during their professional education. Leadership (especially classroom leadership), interpersonal relations, dealing with difficult people, and various communications skills are training subjects that could well be annual topics for those involved with education. One can never know too much about any of these subjects.

Trainers require expertise in leadership and managerial skills as their department importance is elevated to the level of reporting to executive management in many organizations. They also need skills and knowledge of the latest training equipment and technology so they can choose which is most effective for their organization at a cost they can afford. Trainers must continuously update their quality knowledge and be able to tie training to the bottom line. Those requirements listed under the educator are equally applicable to the trainer.

Program Need

Needs based with the employer, employees, and the structural levels of individuals provide guidance as to the subject material and depth of training for given subjects. A third look is necessary before the actual training program can be determined—the needs of a successful TQM process. This need outlines a time frame approach so that priorities become a part of the training decision. Three phases of training are easily identified: awareness, mechanics, and job function specifics.

Awareness

Awareness training kicks off the program. People cannot commit to something they don't understand. During the initial stages of the TQM process, awareness will consume most of the training energy and assets. All employees must be aware of the program as it pertains to "The Goal" and how the successes which can be expected will benefit them. Initially, the following subjects should be considered.

1. *TQM and resulting benefits*–Describe the TQM process in terms common to hierarchical structure and the resultant benefits that can be expected in terms of "the real benefit to you is . . . ."

2. *The quality vision*–Make every employee aware of what the vision is, how it was defined and why, and how that vision relates to the goal.

3. *Define the infrastructure*–Provide details of the TQM council, how that council ties into the organizational structure, who leads the council, and how employees fit into that chain of command for performance improvement efforts.

4. *Assess the work force*–Conduct employee surveys to determine their knowledge level of TQM; their current commitment to such a program; and how committed they *perceive* the organization, executive managers, managers, supervisors, and employees are to the TQM process. Perceptions initially must be dealt with because they are largely responsible for the level of effort individuals will invest in making TQM a reality.

Mechanics

The second phase of TQM training provides individuals with the mechanical skills and knowledge factors necessary to operate TQM. Any number of subject breakouts are possible in this area. Those mentioned must be considered for any such list.

1. *Quality teams*–A main premise of TQM is team development and utilization to solve process and performance problems. Each individual must know the mechanics of teams and his part in making teams productive.

2. *Quality environment*–Solid teams develop in a quality environment. Each person must understand what a quality environment is and the part she shares in making such an environment become reality.

3. *Customer focus*–Employees must realize what customers are, who the internal and external customers are, and how they are best served.

4. *Process*–Employees must understand a process before they can be expected to improve it.

5. *Audits*–The audit is used to determine how the processes operate against the way they are supposed to operate and the problems that exist in each process.

6. *Problem-solving process*–Identified problems must be solved, which requires each employee to be literate on problem-solving methods.

7. *Quality tools*–Many useful tools exist to support performance improvement efforts. Employees must be knowledgeable of applicable tools and how to apply them in practice.

8. *Statistical process control (SPC)*–Processes must be under control before performance problems can be correctly detected. Once process improvements are made, the process must then be controlled to the new level. SPC provides the method necessary to detect problems and control process.

Job-Specific Training

The third phase is job-specific training to the exact employee need. Each employee must know his overall process, each step of his operation, and how his effort fits into the larger process.

Knowledge is only the first step. The second step is skill development so that knowledge can be effectively and efficiently applied to the work effort. Step three is performance analysis. Several questions will help determine training needs at this point.

1. Do problems exist and if so, what are they?

2. How often do problems occur?

3. How many employees appear to have problems?

4. What knowledge factors appear to be missing?

5. What skill factors appear to be missing?

6. What attitude factors compound knowledge and skill factors?

7. Is it possible that the problem is work avoidance rather than training?

8. What solutions appear to be appropriate?

Putting It All Together

An organization training checklist is a good place to start. The list is comprehensive, but there is good news. With the exception of the technical training required, virtually all of the subjects are covered in detail within this four-volume text.

This list is utilized by placing the group (such as management, production worker, and so forth) in the space provided adjacent to the title.

Training Checklist

Group	*Title*	*Group*	*Title*

Leadership Subjects

____ Quality America–Where Are We? ____ Directing and Coaching
____ TQM–Getting Started ____ Participative Leadership
____ TQM as a Leadership Environment ____ Delegative Leadership
____ Leadership vs. Management ____ Power and Influence
____ Leadership by Choice ____ Empowerment
____ Leadership Styles ____ Visioning

Management Subjects

____ TQM–A Management Overview ____ Planning for Quality
____ Organizational Structure ____ Implementation
____ The Quality Culture ____ The Quality Manual
____ Performance Management ____ Managing Change
____ Correct Hiring Practices ____ Management Ethics
____ Performance Appraisal

Quality Mechanics Subjects

____ Audits ____ Problem-Solving Process
____ Quality Goals ____ Making Decisions
____ Understanding Process ____ Quality Tools
____ Understanding Productivity ____ Statistical Process Control
____ Improving Productivity ____ Process Control
____ Graphical Display

People and Quality Subjects

____ Meetings ____ Difficult People
____ Quality Teams ____ Personal Side of
____ Quality Environment Communications
____ The Customer Defined ____ Formal Side of
____ The Customer Served Communications
____ Conflict Resolution ____ Time Management

✳ **Training Subjects**

____ Understanding the Need ____ The Training Decision
____ Organizational Requirements ____ Preparing Solutions
____ Training and the Bottom Line ____ Constructing Training Materials
____ Training as Change Management ____ Training in Action
____ In-House Training ____ On-the-Job Training
____ Developing a Program ____ The Adult Learner
____ Assessing Training Need ____ Training Sins
____ Analyzing the Data ____ Additional Training Concepts

Summary

1. Determining organizational training requirements can be difficult. The problem must be reviewed in various ways: employer–employee, executive manager, manager, or work force, professional or nonprofessional. Each will require different topics and often different approaches to the same topics.

2. Employers need employees well-schooled in the three Rs—reading, 'riting, and 'rithmetic. They also need workers who know how to learn.

3. Employees need training that improves their job skills, which in turn improves their value to the organization, their promotability, and their self-esteem.

4. Executives require quality training from a strategic viewpoint. Training, benchmarking, and visions become important subjects. They also are interested in performance management, organizational development, technical innovation, and broad-based quality subjects.

5. Managers need to learn how to lead and work with and through people, especially with those individuals serving on quality teams. Interpersonal relations, communications, quality concepts, mechanics, process control, performance management, and people subjects are important training topics.

6. Need determination based on the TQM process requirements assists with the prioritization of training. Three steps are outlined: awareness, mechanics, and job-specific training.

7. Work force personnel need to know how to correctly perform their job, process, process control, quality teams, troubleshooting, problem solving, quality tools, and the overall quality picture in terms of TQM and continuous performance improvement.

Bibliography

Brinkerhoff, R. O. *Achieving Results from Training*, San Francisco: Jossey-Bass, 1987.

Broadwell, M. M. *The Supervisor as an Instructor*, Reading, MA: Addison-Wesley, 1970.

Craig, R. L. (Ed.) *American Society for Training and Development, Training & Development Handbook*, New York: McGraw-Hill, 1976.

Craig, R. L. (Ed.) *Training and Development Handbook*, New York: McGraw-Hill, 1976.

Deming, W. E. *Out of the Crisis*, Cambridge: Massachusetts Institute of Technology, Center for Advanced Engineering Study, 1982.

Juran, J. M. *Juran on Planning for Quality*, New York: The Free Press, 1988.

King, D. *Training Within the Organization*, London: Tavistock Publications, 1964.

London, M. *Managing the Training Enterprise*, San Francisco: Jossey-Bass, 1989.

Odiorne, G. S. *Training by Objectives*, New York: The Macmillan Company, 1970.

Put Quality to Work—Train America's Workforce, Alexandria, VA: The American Society for Training and Development, 1991.

The Learning Enterprise, Alexandria, VA: The American Society for Training and Development and Washington, D.C.: U.S. Department of Labor, 1991.

Workplace Basics: The Skills Employers Want, Alexandria, VA: The American Society for Training and Development and Washington, D.C.: U.S. Department of Labor, 1991.

CHAPTER 3

Training and the Bottom Line

Victory in any war is achieved through people. Granted, advanced weapon systems must be employed, but it is people who develop, build, repair, and operate weapons. A major factor in winning World War II was the ability of American industries to outproduce the enemy with superior weapons and materials.

As technology complicates wars such as the recent Persian Gulf War (Desert Storm), the level and quality of training provided must increase for those who use and repair the instruments of war. The nations aligned against Iraq had a decided advantage because of the state of readiness achieved through the well-trained personnel they had in their forces.

The global economic war now being waged will be won or lost through people—the winners will have the trained personnel to take advantage quickly of emerging opportunities through the employment of advanced technology; the losers won't. For some reason, many Americans have not yet seen the truth in this statement although our competitors readily recognize the training need and are doing something about it.

This is not to say that no American organizations have recognized the value of increased expenditures on training because many have. They also tend to be competitive in the global market. It has been reported that IBM–Rochester now spends approximately 5 percent of payroll annually on training, and other organizations approach this. While working with a company for a training article, it was discovered that they too spend well over 5 percent annually on training, and it shows in their performance and safety records.

Two things are important here: The amount of money does not necessarily translate to the value of training, and all companies cannot begin with a level of training investment at 5 percent of payroll or many would go broke. However, training focused to need will pay dividends, a part of which must be invested in additional levels of training if organizations are to leverage themselves into a competitive position in the only market remaining—the global market.

The important criteria is that training be both future focused and on immediate need. To accomplish this, each organization must ensure that they achieve the most bang for the buck with every training evolution, so that maximum investment payoff is achieved. This also requires some method of determining the investment payoff.

How do you know ahead of time what training will meet these criteria? This chapter presents a method to tie training to the bottom line so there will be a payoff. Organizational training strategies must be aligned with organizational strategies in order for true payoff to be achieved in terms of asset utilization toward meeting the bottom line. Training cannot stand outside the strategic organizational planning process and still maximize payoff. That just won't happen.

Training and Organizational Structure

The training department often is considered as a pseudo stand-alone unit tied to the organization through the training budget. Many trainers like that. They have semiautonomy to produce the training on which they decide, develop it to meet needs as they see them, and provide to the people they choose using the format they prefer. Similar to the way Americans sold merchandise before the TQM customer focus, the training department designs training, develops a slick promotional package, and sells the customer on the need when primarily it should be the customer who determines the need.

Some training provided through such systems is exactly what the doctor ordered and pays handsome dividends. Other efforts are enjoyable for attendees, but have little potential payoff; still others are despised by those forced to attend and instead of a payoff, there is a long-term negative impact.

The problem in these negative situations lies not with the trainers, but the way the training department is managed. Too much is left to chance when training is handled in this manner.

Strategic planning is becoming a recognized necessity in most organizations of any size. Considerable time is spent on planning evolutions that generate solid plans for the future. These plans are good as far as they go, but they don't form a closed loop function with continuous input, which promotes strategic changes, nor do they include training as a strategic initiative.

Throughout these topics, the importance of the goal and customer focus has been stressed repeatedly. Given their importance, how are these crucial factors tied to training in your organization? Is there a closed loop system that assesses customer needs and wants, and then ties them to strategic planning so that those desires are incorporated into the training program? Are annual business results tied to the customer and the training program? Are training results routinely assessed and automatically fed back into the system so both near- and long-term training programs are improved to meet the need? Is training both now- and future-focused so current needs and emerging opportunities can be addressed. Is training tied to the bottom line?

If the answer to any of these is "no" or "maybe," training tied to the bottom line is in doubt. Figure 3.1 depicts a closed loop organizational system with the training function outlined as an operational part of the system.

The Planning Process

Planning for training is an extension of strategic planning efforts which support TQM and continuous process improvement efforts. It must be tied into this closed loop system and become an organizational entity designed to support the goal.

Strategic Planning

Strategic planning is the determination of the desired future of the organization based on the vision and resulting mission goals and objectives coupled with the action steps required to make that future occur as it is visioned. This planning effort must be a dynamic action continuously updated to take advantage of emerging opportunities which are identified as a result of various assessments and benchmarking activities. Although one person may compile inputs from all available sources, the planning evolution itself should not be the responsibility of one person. Inputs from vendors, clients, internal management, various assessments, and the annual business results are all useful information sources.

Strategic planners must then use this information to focus on two customer bases: their current customers' future needs and the needs of potential customers who will be available in the future marketplace because of the production of products and services designed and planned now to meet their future needs. Both of these customer bases must be considered in the strategic training plan.

Organizations may respond to the planning need in the following three ways.

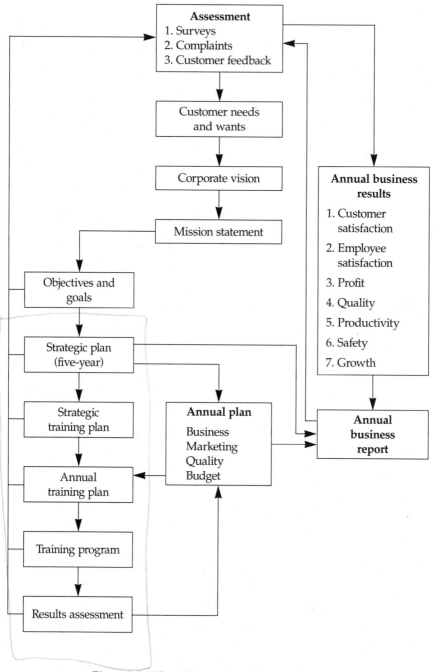

Figure 3.1 Closed Loop Organizational System

1. They can ignore it and hope it works out by itself. The odds for this are about the same as they are that a person will leave a haphazard, low-performance work environment one evening and report to a high-performance, customer-focused work environment the next morning without changing organizations.

2. They can be reactive firefighters who tackle the problems and situations as they turn up. The reactive planner promotes a stressful, low-quality work environment without a future in today's competitive world.

3. They can be visionary planners and prepare strategic plans based on the desired future, benchmarking, and projected opportunities based on technology, internal technical breakthroughs, research and development, and so forth. The visionary approach doesn't require all the resources and knowledge up front before starting. Much of the technology required for our Apollo moon landing program was not available when this ambitious program was visioned. That technology was developed and produced in response to the need created by the vision.

Strategic planning evolutions require contingency plans which tend to reduce or eliminate short-term crisis. Many of the changes that occur without strategic planning can be anticipated and eliminated when focus plans are constructed and carried out.

Strategic Training Plan

The strategic training plan is designed to look into the future using the strategic plan as a vehicle, determining what the future training needs will be for both internal and external customers. At the same time it considers current training requirements, which will be considerable with the emphasis on TQM. This look allows the training department to develop programs to cover future and current needs alike.

The individuals involved with the strategic plan should work on the strategic training plan—the two should not be separated. The same inputs from internal and external clients and customers are required so it makes sense to cover training as a joint effort also. The elevation of the training department to a position reporting directly to executive management makes this department's input into both plans a necessity and becomes a most helpful addition to organizational bottom line training payoff.

Problems can be expected in this area. Since it is impossible to nail down the future in exact terms, training goals get hazier as they extend further out into the future. However, as experience increases in the strategic area, the ease with which projections can be accurately made will increase also, usually quite dramatically after initial attempts. Benchmarking exercises provide considerable support in these long-range planning efforts because a solid understanding of possibilities is acquired through such efforts as long as the organizations chosen have made significant advances in the areas being benchmarked.

Strategic training plans prevent many of the fires that occur in organizations not prone to such planning efforts. A caveat must be applied—the plans must be based on reality including asset availability, and these plans must be carried out.

Zero-based planning has merit in this case. This does not mean that any programs not completed are discarded—it means that with each planning cycle all plans are reconsidered and prioritized according to need. Without such priorities, every program has equal value and the tendency is to succumb to pressures like the squeaky wheel or the person with the most organizational horsepower.

Annual Training Plan

The annual training plan is a one-year extension of the strategic plan. It endeavors to meet the needs which exist between the required knowledge and skills level and the current level of knowledge and skills in the workplace. This knowledge and skill gap receives the highest priority in the annual plan.

The introduction of new products or services will require both internal and external training considerations. These should have been considered in strategic plans over time so the annual plan will be simple.

Projected employee turnover creates another need that must be considered and met. This is also true for new vendors and customers that are projected to become part of the team during the next business year. Each of these areas must be addressed in the annual plan.

By themselves, these sources are not enough. Managers and supervisors must have input and be accountable for the training their people receive. After all, they are responsible for the performance of their people, and training or lack thereof has significant impact on performance. If it didn't have this impact, there would be little reason to hold training.

Managers and supervisors cannot be the sole input, employees also should have input into the training plan. It is their knowledge and skills we are endeavoring to upgrade through training. Who knows their need better as it pertains to their on-the-job performance. They can provide valuable insight into training deficiencies.

A caution is in order. This input must be carefully weighed against the goal. Often employee input includes nice-to-have training at the exclusion of more difficult must-know subjects.

The annual budget is the final input considered. Money talks. Once the level of money designated for training purposes is known, prioritizing training needs begins.

In the past, trainers prepared budget requests based on guesstimates that were highly questionable and with no ties to strategic plans. Sure, all of us involved in this operation developed figures and proof of need that seemed plausible. There almost always was a fallacy, however, it wasn't tied directly toward meeting the bottom line or goal.

When the training budget was received, the question became "What can we get for our money?" This is not good enough and the training planners cannot be allowed to take this approach. A better approach is to answer the question, "How can we provide the training we need to meet our goal with the money that has been allotted?" Every manager must provide answers for the same questions because training is crucial to performance improvement. Throughout the later chapters, ideas are presented that will stretch those budget dollars to increase training opportunities.

Planning Training Efficiencies

Improved training efficiency can save considerable amounts of money in most organizations. Considerations include utilizing more in-house personnel, ensuring training content and the delivery medium match, and adapting prepared material instead of creating new programs. At times, using actual equipment during slack periods instead of models or aids can save money. At other times simulators prove cost efficient over actual equipment (for example, using aviation simulators rather than expensive flight time). The important concept is that potential efficiencies should always be discussed as part of the budgeting process, cost planning, resource utilization, and training program development efforts.

Cost avoidance is another way to stretch money. A local firm developed a CBT program that replaced two instructors who had previously handled the training using various aids and equipment. The instructors were able to devote full time to the implementation of their quality program, and the CBT program was available for use when employees had slack periods or after hours. It utilized less space, reduced salary expenditures for trainers, was self-paced and could be accomplished in convenient segments instead of all at one time. Each of these savings were easily calculated, and the equipment and package were paid for over the first several months of operation. This training also proved to be more effective in this application.

Another cost avoidance area that must be considered is the costs avoided when rework efforts and scrap are reduced or eliminated. Too often these are not projected, and they are figures that put training costs into another

Cost Avoidance

perspective when proper training reduces or eliminates scrap or rework, which it so often does. Cost of training and cost avoidance are not difficult to determine. The following charts serve as guides to develop projections based on the actual work environment.

Cost Avoidance Through Training

Labor costs = number of employees × hours × wages × benefits = total labor costs for rework efforts   _____

Equipment costs   _____

Energy costs   _____

Material costs   _____

Cost associated with lost capacity because of rework   _____

Cost associated with waste   _____

Cost of late or lost orders   _____

Cost of service calls, recalls, and replacement   _____

Cost of lost customers   _____

Total cost avoidable through proper training   _____

Training Costs

Performance analysis cost: hours × salary and benefit cost per hour = total cost   _____

Course development costs: hours × salary and benefit cost per hour = total cost   _____

Instructor costs: hours × salary and benefits   _____

Costs per hour   _____

Space   _____

Equipment   _____

Materials   _____

Outside trainer/consultant costs   _____

Student costs: number of students × hours × cost of wages and benefits   _____

Total cost of training   _____

Many other cost avoidance and training cost figures could be added based on the type of organization using them, but these serve the purpose of examples. In-house training provides cost avoidance by itself. Travel, lodging, and meal costs are eliminated while at the same time, the in-house training personnel are gaining proficiency.

Training costs should be prorated and charged back to the appropriate departments. Managers and supervisors become more cost conscious, and it tends to make them cognizant of who should attend training for what reason so assets will be effectively and efficiently utilized.

The managers involved in training must become horse traders of sorts. It always is important to negotiate a deal with those in power at the top concerning prorating a percentage of the money saved or profit created through training, back into the training program. This provides incentive for all to ensure the correct training is planned and executed and that proven results can be documented because of the training effort. Most executives will approve of such a plan when it is properly presented because it ties training directly to the bottom line.

Return on Investment

"Was the training we did worth the price we paid?" The payoff achieved must be tracked to determine training effectiveness. Assessment is an absolute necessity without which this all-important question cannot be answered. The value of past training and the need for future training is little more than a crystal ball evolution which cannot support claims of training effectiveness without assessment.

Some organizations use student hours or student days per month per instructor as a measure of sorts, but this tells nothing more than how many hours classrooms were utilized. Several methods of measuring training effectiveness will be presented, all of which have validity. The best course of action is the use of a combination of sources because all are important.

Performance Improvements

These measures tend to be given greater credibility by managers tasked with reviewing training effectiveness, as they should. They are real-world measures that relate to the bottom line in terms everyone understands.

In most cases, the measures discussed here can be extracted from data that is routinely recorded as organizations track performance improvements. These are not discussed in detail because they are organization specific. A few of them require additional test or surveys, but these are not difficult or expensive to administer. Each of these measures is a reflection of some type of performance improvement when posttraining operations are compared to pre-training data. They are listed in no particular order.

1. Increased profit
2. Production improvement
3. Quality improvement
4. Rework reduction
5. Waste reduction
6. Fewer equipment malfunctions
7. Reduced maintenance costs
8. Increased percentage of operating time
9. Reduction in operating costs
10. Few personnel performance problems
11. Sales increases
12. Increased market share
13. Process time reductions
14. Less warranty work
15. Fewer service calls
16. Fewer customer complaints
17. Less returned merchandise
18. Less employee turnover
19. Reduced absenteeism
20. Fewer disciplinary problems
21. Improved performance on posttraining tests when they are compared with pretest results
22. Increased cleanliness of facilities
23. Improved customer satisfaction based on survey results
24. Increased SAT scores (school systems)
25. Higher graduation rate (school systems)
26. More honor students (school systems)

It is entirely possible to compare these measures against the cost of the training that produced them. Managers responsible for training may show initial hesitancy to have their training efforts measured against some bottom line standard such as profit increases. Their fears are founded to some degree.

Leaders responsible for work force performance have a major impact on training effectiveness and how training will be utilized. The abilities of these leaders and their use of the training must be concurrently evaluated in order for performance improvement to occur to the level that is ultimately possible.

Student Opinion Surveys

Student surveys provide insight into student perceptions of training effectiveness. They cannot be considered exact because some students are super critical while others don't want to hurt anyone's feelings. All in all they are solid informational sources.

Some considerations are required to ensure a level of validity to these surveys. Questionnaire respondents must remain anonymous so trainees aren't hesitant to answer them truthfully, and confidentiality must be maintained for the results so trainers don't try to skew them.

The following sample questionnaires are composites of many that are used. There are many variations of this form. Some allow for comments after each question. At times a second copy is sent to the student after the course was presented, often six months later, and the two responses are compared.

Your Opinion Is Requested

Course title _____ Completion date _____

Instructors _____

_____

Please read the following questions carefully. Circle your response in the block you believe is appropriate.

    SA = Strongly agree
    A   = Agree
    N   = Neither agree nor disagree
    D   = Disagree
    SD = Strongly disagree
    NA = No opinion or the question doesn't apply

1. The course description was accurate. SA A N D SD NA

2. Enrollment procedures were handled correctly. SA A N D SD NA

3. Facilities supported learning. SA A N D SD NA

4. Training aids supported learning. SA A N D SD NA

5. Handouts were appropriate. SA A N D SD NA

6. Course materials will be useful on the job. SA A N D SD NA

7. Course objectives were met. SA A N D SD NA

8. Course content matched my needs. SA A N D SD NA

9. Topics were presented in a logical order. SA A N D SD NA

10. Training was presented in a learner-centered manner. SA A N D SD NA

11. Students were involved in all aspects of training. SA A N D SD NA

12. Ample time was allotted to cover each topic. SA A N D SD NA

13. Questions were encouraged and answered to my satisfaction. SA A N D SD NA

14. Practice time was sufficient. SA A N D SD NA

15. In-class exercises aided learning. SA A N D SD NA

16. Examples aided learning. SA A N D SD NA

17. The instructor was knowledgeable of the subject. SA A N D SD NA

18. The instructor maintained interest. SA A N D SD NA

19. The instructor presented the material clearly and in an effective manner. SA A N D SD NA

20. The instructor respected me as an individual. SA A N D SD NA

21. This training will improve my job performance. SA A N D SD NA

22. This training will help me off the job. SA A N D SD NA

23. I will recommend this training to others. SA A N D SD NA

24. Your recommendations for improvement: _____
_____
_____
_____

Supervisor Opinion Surveys

Occasionally, student opinions of the value of the training and the way the supervisor views the value will be different. Input from supervisors provides valid information for this question.

A sample supervisor opinion survey follows.

Your Opinion Is Requested

Course title _____ Completion date _____

Instructors _____

_____

Please read the following questions carefully. Circle your response in the block you believe is appropriate.

SA = Strongly agree
A   = Agree
N   = Neither agree nor disagree
D   = Disagree
SD = Strongly disagree
NA = No opinion or the question doesn't apply

1. Student performance indicates course objectives were met.
    SA A N D SD NA

2. Student work skills improved as a result of this training.
    SA A N D SD NA

3. Student job knowledge improved as a result of this training.
    SA A N D SD NA

4. Student production increased as a result of this training.
    SA A N D SD NA

5. Student work quality improved as a result of this training.
    SA A N D SD NA

6. The course materials the student received benefited other members of the work force. SA A N D SD NA

7. This training program will pay off in improved performance.
    SA A N D SD NA

8. I am satisfied with the results of this training. SA A N D SD NA

9. I will send other workers to this training. SA A N D SD NA

10. Your recommendations for course improvement: _____
    _____
    _____
    _____

Other Measurements

Trainer effectiveness also can be measured in terms of preparation time required, training improvements submitted, ability to handle new material, and so forth. Trainer performance should be routinely appraised during training sessions. Nothing supports training excellence more than this practice.

Summary

1. Training has been important in the past but its importance in the future is considerably greater. The main function of training is to support the bottom line or the goal.

2. Training often has been considered as a stand-alone item apart from the mainstream of the organization. This must change. Training must be included in the strategic planning evolution as part of a closed loop system.

3. The strategic training plan takes its shape from the strategic plan. It looks at both future and near-term training and provides the information necessary to formulate an annual training plan.

4. The annual training plan endeavors to reduce or eliminate the gap between the level of skills or knowledge required and the present level of skills or knowledge.

5. The expected payoff for training can be projected prior to training through a comparison of projected training costs against the cost avoidance which can be expected because of training.

6. Several methods are provided to determine the return on investment. This is important because it promotes effective training, encourages training to be used wisely, and proves the value of training for improving the bottom line.

Bibliography

Abella, K. T. *Building Successful Training Programs,* Reading, MA: Addison-Wesley, 1986.

Brinkerhoff, R. O. *Achieving Results from Training,* San Francisco: Jossey-Bass, 1987.

Cassner-Lotto, J. and Associates. *Successful Training Strategies: Twenty-six Innovative Corporate Models,* San Francisco: Jossey-Bass, 1988.

Craig, R.L. (Ed.) *American Society for Training and Development, Training & Development Handbook,* New York: McGraw-Hill, 1976.

———. *Training and Development Handbook,* New York: McGraw-Hill, 1976.

Davis, L. N. and McCallon, E. *Planning, Conducting and Evaluating Workshops,* Austin, TX: Learning Concepts, 1975.

Friedman, P. G. and Yarbrough, E. A. *Training Strategies from Start to Finish,* Englewood Cliffs, NJ: Prentice-Hall, 1985.

Hamblin, A. C. *Evaluation and Control of Training*, New York: McGraw-Hill, 1974.

Juran, J. M. *Juran on Planning for Quality*, New York: The Free Press, 1988.

Kirkpatrick, D. L. *Evaluating Training Programs*, Madison, WI: American Society for Training and Development, 1975.

London, M. *Managing the Training Enterprise*, San Francisco: Jossey-Bass, 1989.

Mitchell, G. *The Trainer's Handbook*, New York: American Management Association, 1987.

Phillips, J. J. *Handbook of Training Evaluation and Methods*, Houston: Gulf Publishing, 1982.

Wedel, K. R. and Brown, G. *Assessing Training Needs.* Washington, D.C.: National Training and Development Service, 1974.

CHAPTER 4

Training and Organizational Change

Dramatic changes are taking place in the global market forcing businesses to rethink their strategies to remain competitive. The importance of organizational training expands geometrically as new technologies, concepts, and customers tax the ingenuity of training teams. Most organizations face budget constraints that require training effectiveness to increase as the need for training increases.

American business organizations do not stand alone in this global marketplace. Other groups impact heavily on business operations which, in turn, affects how well business can compete. The manner in which a business carries out its efforts and the kind of neighbor each business is, impacts on the organizations which are intertwined with business. Figure 4.1 provides a look at these relationships.

At different times, the organizations with the greatest effect on business, or that are affected the greatest by business, also change. For example, government impacts heavily when a company is designing and building a new steel mill, schools and colleges impact when people are being hired or trained to operate the plant, and unions impact when they are negotiating contracts. Families, religious organizations, and community organizations impact when the mill is assuming an organizational culture. Each of these groups ultimately is impacted because the ultimate source of funding, like it or not, comes from this mill and other such businesses.

As businesses change, the service organizations that control, guide, and tax these businesses also must change, developing customer-focused goals and trained personnel to support these changes. The educational systems that supply the labor force must reconsider their goal, the product they produce,

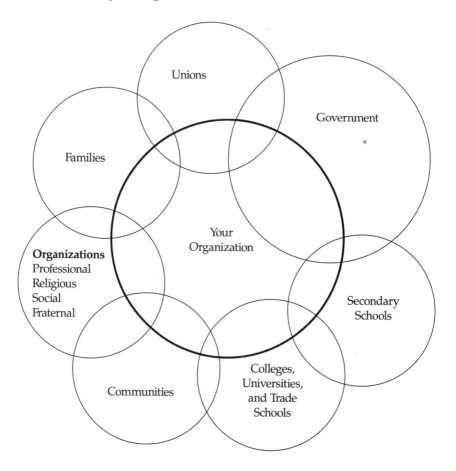

Figure 4.1 Organizational Relationships

and the customer they serve in order to produce the product that best meets the needs of their various customers. Schools with excellent facilities and superb athletic teams are just so much waste if they aren't turning out students educated to conduct the nation's business.

A first review of the statistics contained in the ASTD program, Train America's Workforce (listed in the bibliography), gives reason to pause and think. For example, it takes four or five years to design and build a new blast furnace in the United States, while it takes only three years in Japan and two years in Korea. How could this be?

If you have ever been a member of a building committee for a new building you realize how much time can be spent on nonproductive activities. It can take as long to complete the environmental impact studies and obtain the various permits from township, county, and state governmental departments as it does to design and build a million-dollar church. How much time must an American steel company invest to gain approval for a multibillion-dollar blast furnace? Certainly the United States, which had one company (Kaiser) that completed a Liberty ship every day to support World War II, could design and build a blast furnace in less than four years if it weren't for the bureaucratic hoops through which they are forced to maneuver.

This is not to say the environment isn't important, or that various permits aren't necessary. The point is that the procedures to get the permits and the apparent lack of urgency of many in bureaucratic positions must be changed to support our businesses if they are to remain competitive. It appears that agencies tend to bend, fold, and mutilate applications or they disappear into a black hole never to reappear. They must then be resubmitted for any number of reasons.

Anyone who deals with various governmental agencies has probably heard some of the following: "Vivian just left for her two-week vacation and nobody—I mean *nobody*—fools with Vivian's department. I'm sorry but you'll just have to wait." or "Mr. Ross is out of town on a business trip and he took your business application with him to look it over." or "We never work that quickly on any proposal. There are a good many hoops it has to go through and they all take time. Yours is not the only application that gets reviewed around here," or "We're short-staffed around here and everybody has to wait," or "Perhaps you don't understand how the system works."

All of these excuses have some validity, but every operation is a process that can and must be improved. The emphasis must be placed on customer service because each organization's existence depends on it. Government agencies must develop goals to support their customers and then focus their efforts in that direction.

The school situation must be addressed in a nonthreatening, non-finger-pointing forum. Recently a highly respected science teacher was discussing education and the reasons why it is so difficult to improve our school systems and the quality of education. His answer gives pause for reflection. "There isn't any real pressure to change the education system. Our principal would get more flack if the football field wasn't ready on Friday night than he would if the average SAT scores dropped by 200 points."

Our educational systems will not improve to the degree necessary until they develop visions of educational excellence with customer centered goals which everyone works to achieve. Everyone means every administrator, teacher, student, secretary, janitor, and bus driver must be committed as if their future depends on it because *it does!* Without such effort, educational reform cannot occur.

About now, many readers should agree that changes must be made, but may wonder how that ties to training. It's simple—training must become a change agent to lead organizational improvement instead of an entity that reacts to current need.

In Chapter 3, strategic training plans were discussed as part of the overall organization strategy. Strategic training signifies that the organization with such planning efforts is looking into the future to determine the training needs that reside there. This preview is necessary in order to plan the training necessary to get there, and when that future time becomes the present, the training must be ready to lead the organization forward.

Is your organization's training program equipped to act as a change agent? Answers to the following questions will help determine how supportive your organization is to long-term payoff training.

1.   Does your organization have a published vision and mission statement which is posted to guide all employees?

2.   Does your organization have a strategic plan based on the vision and mission statement?

3.   Is this strategic plan customer focused?

4.   Does your organization have a strategic training plan based on the strategic plan?

5.   Are the strategic plans supported by the annual business, quality, training, and marketing plans plus the budget?

6.   Are the strategic and annual training goals and objectives need-based and in place to support strategic plans?

7.   Are training results evaluated to ensure that goals and objectives are met?

8.   Are the results fed back into the strategic planning cycle?

9.   Can the goals and objectives of each training program be considered subsets of the organization goals and objectives?

10. Is the goal discussed as part of every training evolution?

There are those who immediately kiss these questions off as a pie-in-the-sky, nice-to-shoot-at dream system. They are not. Such closed loop systems are reality in guiding many competitive organizations. They are considered a must for every TQM organization dedicated to production, quality, and customer service improvement.

One organization I recently wrote an article about has an impressive training system which is an investment worth about $30 million, complete with expensive simulators. One would assume the training program would be driven by the simulators, but that would be a mistake. They are tools within a needs-driven, strategically planned operation. This company's total vision and the plan to reach it is neatly outlined and posted throughout the operation for everyone to see.

Their strategic plans are considered dynamic think pieces that describe where they are today and where they intend to be five years down the road. They cover conceivable eventualities and the training that will be required to meet emerging requirements. This training program definitely is designed as a change agent.

The nature of an organization's work methods, the attitude of its people, and the environment in which they toil will not change unless training changes. Being tied to the vision and strategic plans is not enough. The training provided, the way training is conducted, and the people who provide training must all change if training is to have the impact necessary to bring about continuous performance improvement. Training and trainers must continually exhibit a focus on "The Goal" or they face considerable difficulty getting the people focused to use the training provided. Employees strongly desire to do a good job and most realize that quality training is the key to their performance improvement.

The Trainers

Employees at every organizational level must be trained in their processes and the latest technology, knowledge, and skills that are available to improve those processes. Their supervisors must acquire the same knowledge and skills so they can lead the performance improvement efforts.

The trainers who assess need, must design, develop, and provide training. The leaders of the operations where people put their training to work, control the effect of training whether it be positive or negative. Both trainers and leaders must be quality individuals. The best leader without trained people and well-trained workers without solid leaders are formulas for disaster.

The results received from training will be about as good as the people who provide it. Excellent material is worth nothing if the instructors who present it aren't of equal caliber. Therefore, the selection of training personnel is a critical step in the creation of an environment where continuous performance improvement becomes a way of life. Great trainers tend to create great training programs that work.

Potential Mistakes

A large sales-based organization provided training for its managers and sales force at the home office. Training was primarily of the motivational type. Field personnel enjoyed going to the headquarters for week-long programs because they were fun and provided a break from routine work efforts. After these training sessions, students departed feeling good about themselves. However, when they returned to their jobs, that motivational high soon wore off when they faced their tasks with no new skills to make that work easier.

A new manager arrived and decided to change training directions, to make it more skill enhanced and less motivational. He believed that people who learn to do their jobs more proficiently will be motivated to some degree, especially when they also learn to do it easier. That belief proved true in actual practice to a degree far beyond what was expected.

A subsequent meeting with the training personnel on the staff met with considerable resistance. They were totally against this change. This was a difficult position to understand, especially when these individuals had previous field experience doing the work or managing such efforts.

The decision was made to check out their previous field experience to determine if a reason could be found for the resistance. A problem was immediately evident. These individuals had not been chosen because of excellent field records. In fact, the opposite was true; they had been chosen because they were good communicators. They also had poor production records and removing them from the production environment would not negatively affect production because they weren't performing well in their positions.

These trainers were opposed to skills-type training because their personal track records reflected skill deficiencies in several key areas. It is difficult to train people to do something at which you are not skilled, especially when people determine one's skill level at the job they are training others to do. Credibility is vital to training excellence.

New Directions

The decision was made to call for volunteers who would like a training assignment as an interim position for three years. The volunteers had to be recognized as outstanding production-oriented people with solid communications skills. They also had to be people who had the potential for advancement.

The training positions then became stepping-stones for promotion. Field personnel came to the training team and honed their training skills. They developed better training methods and programs which they provided to operational activities. Their successes were measured against increases in bottom line performance improvement.

Operational managers and workers were queried on any ongoing basis for suggested improvements. These turned into course improvements, new programs, and so forth. Various training packages were developed to aid operational supervisors in their on-the-job training initiatives. Each of these paid dividends in terms of performance improvement.

After three years in a training status, successful trainers reported back to operational activities in management positions above their pretraining level. Each was better prepared for the leadership and technical management roles they assumed.

Many organizations are headed in similar directions. They are moving away from a general education approach to training and now focus their initiatives to support strategic corporate goals and objectives. Training assignments are used as a path to management assignments. Sales specialists rotate through training assignments where the extensive training programs enhance their sales skills. Their management-related skills (such as leadership, communications, and public speaking) improve greatly as they become polished through their training evolutions. After training assignments they rotate to management positions where this training experience pays real dividends.

In cases such as these, the payoff for solid training performance is a known factor for participating individuals when they accept training assignments. These trainers work harder and put more into the training assignment. Payoff from training increases dramatically. People with solid track records from operational assignments bring knowledge, skills, and credibility to the training team. They understand the need and how to present training that meets operational requirements. It is a positive cycle that definitely enhances the quality initiative.

Selecting Trainers

Obviously everyone won't be able to handle such training evolutions. What criteria should be supplied to select trainers correctly to work in the systems just outlined?

1. *Promotable*–If the training assignment is going to prepare people for promotion, they must be promotable. Organizations have promotions standards and the people selected for training programs must meet these standards.

2. *Capable*–The person must be knowledgeable of his entire process and be capable in terms of problem solving, process control, and use of quality tools.

3. *Experienced*–The person must have the experience level and skills common to her operation. Trainers should have both technical and supervisory experience, unless of course, he is not yet in a supervisory position. Trainers must know what they are talking about and have proper skills to succeed.

4. *Credible*–Peers and subordinates must know that the person selected is the right choice for the training position based on performance in his current job. Without this track record, the trainer will be less effective.

5. *Communications ability*–Those who cannot communicate make poor instructors. Trainers do not necessarily have to be polished speakers, although it helps. They must be interested and interesting, capable of getting their points across to their students in an effective, efficient manner.

6. *The goal*–Trainers must know what the goal is and train students so they can support the organization's attempt to meet that goal. Those who do not fully support the organizational vision and the goal should never be chosen for leadership of training positions. Above that, they should probably float resumés so they can become a member of an organization they can support.

7. *Customer service*–Trainers must be properly oriented toward both internal and external customers. Training must satisfy the customers' skill and knowledge needs.

Training Methods

No organization can stick with old training methods and materials and expect new and improved results. It doesn't happen that way. Changes must occur if training is to become a strong positive force in organizational change plans. Training is developed to meet changing organizational needs and to change the organization. Technology provides cheaper methods of training with improved results, but also requires new training skills and knowledge to correctly adapt technology to the workplace where it is used.

Those individuals who guide training efforts and the development of goal-focused training that meets customer needs must have a solid understanding of the organization's vision and strategic plans. Only when this understanding is reached, will goal-focused training result.

Training is in the process of changing from providing training based on trainer desires and response to management initiatives. Internal and external customer need is becoming the basis for the development of training programs. Organizations such as AMP, Inc. complete surveys on customer and employee perceptions of customer service and quality. These needs become the basis for training determinations as they strive to enhance areas where they are good and improve training to upgrade performance in areas that are not that strong.

Building on strengths is essential. Organizations grow because of their strengths; they must use and improve these strengths if they are to continue to improve performance. At the same time, weak areas cannot be ignored. Each of them provides an opportunity for significant performance improvement. Employees and customers can pinpoint areas that require improvement and will do so if they are asked.

Performance-Based Training

The basis for performance-based training is in solid job and task analysis (developed in Volume II). Each job must be broken down into its component parts. The steps required to complete each of these components are developed into procedures for completing that particular part of the process. Standards are then developed stating how well each step must be performed.

The steps that must be completed and the standards that designate how well they must be accomplished provide the guidelines for performance-based training. Training objectives ensure that each of these criteria will be completed satisfactorily and that each trainee will be able to meet those objectives. Some form of testing must follow to determine if the correct skill level has been achieved through the training program.

A simple but effective four-step process for achieving satisfactory results in skill type training is to:

- Show participants the process.
- Have them show you.
- Drill to develop skills.
- Test for satisfactory performance.

Training Teams

At one large company, training teams consist of training, production, and management personnel who work to solve problems. Workers with solid performance track records are selected to work on the training solutions. In the process, they are schooled in training, problem-solving, and production procedures. Training is need-driven and occurs in the workplace whenever possible.

This way of conducting training has several advantages for all involved. The training is readily accepted because it is solving a production problem for the work force. The trainer is viewed as "one of our own" because she was a member of that production team or effort. Once the training initiative is completed, the trainer returns to that work group with added knowledge, improved skills, and increased self-esteem, ready to support ongoing training and performance-improvement initiatives.

Managers improve their knowledge and skills of the technical aspects of their job, hone their leadership skills, and develop closer working relationships with their people. Trainers broaden their knowledge and develop greater understanding of the processes and operations that make up the organization. Everyone wins!

Working as a member of such training teams also reinforces the knowledge of "The Goal" and what that means in terms of individual employee goals, job security, and quality work-life. The value of this aspect of such team training evolutions should not be underestimated.

Team Training

The complex relationships common in today's organizational environments require several different ways of providing training. Team training is one method that takes advantage of these relationships and produces surprisingly positive results when groups of employees must work together to complete a process or operation.

Performance improvement can happen only when all members of the team are working to transform their operation. This is another example of a company's being no stronger than the weakest link. The best way to develop effective work teams is through team training initiatives.

Football or basketball teams could not be expected to perform as a team on game day if all their training sessions centered on individual skill enhancement. Certainly there is a place for individual training (such as when new members are brought on the team), but team skills must be developed for team performance.

Team training forces communications between individual members because each player must know what the other is thinking and doing. Since they are working closely together, each member receives the same information, uses the same types of skills, and works together to meet the same standards. As they work together, an understanding develops of their individual roles and how these roles make up the team role. The skill level of each member is increased as he or she works together with others.

Team members quickly accept responsibility for helping team mates who struggle with some aspect of the operation. They realize the team will not become a proficient, well-honed work group until each member is capable of pulling his own weight. On a more selfish note, they also realize that someone will be forced to do more than her fair share when another member isn't carrying his load. This factor increases the desire to help everyone be their best. Those who have served in combat have probably experienced this.

Cross-Training

Work force versatility is becoming increasingly important as organizations strive to become more competitive. Cross-training is the most effective way to increase people's ability to handle multiple job assignments.

There are significant benefits to this method of work force operation. Cross-trained personnel can be employed where the need is greatest. Just-in-time production becomes more of a reality when workers can handle several different operations.

An even greater organizational benefit results. As workers are cross-trained, their understanding of the entire process or operation is broadened. They can stand in for employees on vacation. They also have a much greater impact on performance improvement efforts because they have acquired this broader knowledge of the way things work. At times they become their own customers when they take the place of others and can envision how their product or service impacts the next person. A number of process changes occur in this manner.

Job security increases as workers learn additional jobs. Each employee becomes a more capable, and thus more valuable, member of the organization. It also assists in the effort to train employees for supervisory positions. The individual who understands the whole process before promotion to supervisor is considerably more prone to success in such positions.

Training Quality Assurance

Instituting these training initiatives is not enough, they must be continually audited for effectiveness and efficiency. Effectiveness answers the question: Is this the correct training for this process or operation? Efficiency answers the question: Is this the best and most cost-effective way of meeting the training need?

Training quality assurance strives to answer the following:

1. Was the training plan developed to need?
2. If followed, will the training plan meet the goals outlined in strategic and annual plans?
3. Is the training plan performance oriented?
4. Has the training plan been implemented as planned?
5. Are the training objectives accomplished as scheduled?
6. Are all people receiving training as planned?
7. Is the training utilized in the workplace?
8. Do training assessments indicate additional training is required?

9.   Does management support training initiatives?

10. Are personnel better able to perform their jobs as a result of the training?

11. Is training tracked to the bottom line?

Ideas presented in Chapter 3 support a solid audit system. The results of training audits should be produced in report form and made available at the end of each training year, more often when deemed appropriate. Everyone should know the successes that were achieved. The weak areas also should be understood so that all employees can take the opportunity for improvement.

Training and Change

Organizations are discovering that training, when correctly developed and properly utilized, is an essential tool in their efforts to insert quality procedures and continuous performance improvement into their culture. Training is about change—change in the knowledge and skill levels, change in the way skills are utilized, change in the way processes are completed, change in interpersonal relations, and change in culture. Training must lead organizational transformation to the ways of excellence.

Several factors must automatically become natural parts of every training session. Some of these are repeats from other text sections but apply here.

1.   Every training session must be an outcome of the strategic plan and support organizational vision and the goal. If it can't be proven to support the goal there are probably more important areas for the training dollars. Organizational goals should be discussed as part of the objectives so students realize why they are learning what they are learning. There should never be a doubt about the value of training sessions or how the material applies to the efforts expended to reach the goal.

2.   Changes required as a result of training must be known at the beginning of each session. Students must know what actions are expected as the result of the training they will receive.

3.   All training must be customer focused to meet the needs of the internal customers who will receive the training so they can, in turn, improve their performance to support the external customer.

4.   All training should be audited against the bottom line. Training that does not relate to the bottom line in a traceable way probably is not the best use of training assets.

5.   Every training session will be a stern test of the trainer's leadership ability. This means the trainer must be prepared to lead the training effort in

whatever method is required to best assist the students to meet their training objectives.

6. All training must be conducted in a professional manner. Few things are more detrimental to long-term training efforts than poorly handled training exercises.

Getting It Together

At the top, executives and managers must learn how to use leadership styles that range from directive to coaching, participative to delegative. They must learn power styles from positional power to empowerment to accompany these leadership styles. These events must occur before the work force can progress from awareness of quality through involvement, commitment, and ownership, changes that are required so that self-led and self-managed work teams can occur.

This education is a change in itself. Too often, executives and senior managers mandate training for managers and the work force, but refuse to attend it themselves because "I'm much too busy." They have little or no idea what the employees receiving training actually learn and then wonder why little occurs as the direct result of training. The comment often put forth in these organizations is "Training never works around here. We should place our money into something with a payoff."

Those organizations led by executives with no intention of learning the skills required in a quality environment, or who are not about to change the way they personally operate, should save the assets they would place on quality initiatives and use them to survive as long as possible. They cannot remain competitive in the new world order unless they are willing to change. Those who labor in governmental organizations and educational systems face the same problem—change or the customer will change you. There is a growing movement to demand what the customer believes is her money's worth.

Work force and technical personnel training will be geared to those things that can affect the quest for performance improvement. If it requires technical skills training, that training becomes important; if it requires computer literacy, that is important. The idea is that the training will be need-based.

Training flexibility is a high priority so emerging needs can be quickly met. Some scheduled training may lose importance as more vital needs materialize. Flexibility also is important in the selection of training methods. Different subjects require different approaches. In fact, some sessions may require a method change during the session if the trainer detects a student understanding problem.

One last change is important for the training enterprise. Training should be designed to help people understand and become more supportive of their organization. In this context, discussions are awareness tools concerning organizational culture, strategies, requirements for employee success, and the employees' part in reaching the goal. These need not be separate sessions; they should be woven into all training sessions so they appear as supportive information rather than propaganda.

Summary

1. The global marketplace is changing dramatically, which alters the way businesses must operate to survive. All other organizations also must change because organizations are intertwined, and ultimately all of them depend on business for survival.

2. Training acts as a change agent to lead the quest for excellence when it is tied to the vision and strategic plans. Every person involved with training must understand what the goal is and how training applies to the efforts to achieve that goal.

3. Trainers control the effect training will have on performance improvement. They must be carefully selected and correctly trained.

4. Trainers should be accepted for their training assignment based on several criteria: promotability, capability, experience, credibility, communications ability, attention to the goal, and customer focus.

5. Training methods also must change. It must become performance-based and audited for results.

6. Many new methods of training occur in forward-thinking organizations. Team training, training teams, and cross-training all gain importance.

7. Training programs should have their own quality assurance program which determines effectiveness and efficiency. Training audits provide the means to make these determinations.

8. Training truly becomes a change agent when everyone in the organization is willing to change through training and to train for change. Change will not occur unless this willingness is evident from the top of the organization down.

Bibliography

Asionian, C. B. and Brickell, H. M. *Americans in Transition: Life Changes As Reasons for Adult Learning*, New York: College Entrance Examination Board, 1980.

Brinkerhoff, R. O. *Achieving Results from Training*, San Francisco: Jossey-Bass, 1987.

Cassner-Lotto, J. and Associates. *Successful Training Strategies: Twenty-six Innovative Corporate Models,* San Francisco: Jossey-Bass, 1988.

Cohen, W. A. *The Art of the Leader,* Englewood Cliffs, NJ: Prentice-Hall, 1990.

Cooper, S. and Heenan, C. *A Humanistic Approach,* Boston: CB Publishing Company, 1980.

Craig, R.L. (Ed.) *American Society for Training and Development, Training & Development Handbook,* New York: McGraw-Hill, 1976.

Deming, W. E. *Out of the Crisis,* Cambridge: Massachusetts Institute of Technology, Center for Advanced Engineering Study, 1982.

Friedman, P. G. and Yarbrough, E. A. *Training Strategies from Start to Finish,* Englewood Cliffs, NJ: Prentice-Hall, 1985.

London, M. *Managing the Training Enterprise,* San Francisco: Jossey-Bass, 1989.

Mitchell, G. *The Trainer's Handbook,* New York: American Management Association, 1987.

Pfeiffer, J. W. and Jones, J. E. *A Handbook of Structured Experiences for Human Relations Training* (Volumes I–VI). LaJolla, CA: University Associates, 1974–1979.

Rogoff, R. L. *The Training Wheel,* New York: John Wiley and Sons, 1987.

———. *The Learning Enterprise,* Alexandria, VA: The American Society for Training and Development, and Washington, D.C.: U.S. Department of Labor, 1991.

———. *Put Quality to Work—Train America's Workforce,* Alexandria, VA: The American Society for Training and Development, 1991.

———. *Workplace Basics: The Skills Employers Want,* Alexandria, VA: The American Society for Training and Development, and Washington, D.C.: U.S. Department of Labor, 1991.

CHAPTER 5

The In-House Training Program

In-house training becomes increasingly important as organizations strive to develop work forces to meet competitive challenges. Cost control and organizational specific needs places further emphasis on training efforts.

This chapter begins the development of an in-house training program through a discussion of a quality training program and methods to find the part-time trainers necessary to augment training operations for such a program. The benefits of an in-house program are discussed along with some of the possible drawbacks. In this way the benefits can be maximized while the drawbacks are minimized or alleviated altogether.

Outlining a Training Program

Improving the quality of training and training for quality, two distinct and separate entities, must become the highest priorities. Quality training requires a sound training system, qualified trainers, solid training materials and methods, and emphasis on training from the top down. Training for quality demands an understanding of the broad range of quality subjects with the training geared to the needs of each particular level of the organization.

Since much of the training required for performance improvements will take place in the work centers, a strong on-the-job training (OJT) program supported by classroom training and self-paced training available in computer-based training (CBT) systems, interactive video (IV) systems, and audio/video programs is extremely valuable. This type of program can overcome many of the problems inherent when OJT, classroom type sessions, or self-paced sessions are used as stand-alone methods. Combination training programs provide thorough, long-lasting training that pays off in performance improvements.

OJT probably is the least effective and most poorly organized of all training efforts in most organizations. This subject is fully developed in Chapter 13. Suggestions are offered to help overcome the deficiencies that typically inhibit OJT so that it can become the dynamic change agent that it has the potential to be. This requires a review of the requirements for solid training programs with specific application to OJT.

No one standard training program is recommended because each organization is a unique entity. A successful program will be a blend of in-house efforts and outside help. The exact mixture depends on the extent of training assets within the organization and the needs of the people who serve that organization. Flexibility is a key concept in this area. Needs assessment is vital to training payoff and is discussed in detail in Chapters 7 and 8.

A caution is necessary at this point. Like TQM, the training program that supports quality is not a once-and-done affair. It is a long-term part of the process and is critical to success. As each performance improvement begins to pay off, new areas needing improvement emerge and gain prominence, each requiring additional assessment and more training. The payoffs from performance improvements will shortly generate additional profits and/or services that pay for the additional training many times over.

The Base for Quality Trainers

In many organizations, training departments that are not a part of the strategic structure provide much or all of the training provided by their organization. Although this may provide a measure of control and promote expediency, it tends to support generic rather than customer-specific training. In many small and midsize organizations, there is no training program. Perhaps the resources were not available or the need was not readily apparent prior to the decision to begin a quality program.

There are solutions to both of these situations. The base for quality trainers must be expanded to include all subject matter experts (SMEs) within the organization. These highly skilled, knowledgeable people are the most under-utilized assets in most organizations. Often with little additional training the SMEs will be serving as highly productive trainers in the quality program.

SMEs with the feel for particular work centers can greatly magnify the productive results obtainable from training efforts. There is an added benefit. Most SMEs enjoy training and helping others. They feel honored to be chosen for training duties. As they help develop their particular programs, their value to the organization increases, which supports them during performance and promotion reviews. This factor makes this training method a true benefit for all who participate.

There are many ways SMEs can assist in the quality program. Most important, they can conduct all of the training for some parts of the quality program. They can assist others in the development of their training programs through technical or organizational input and research. They also can attend or be available for certain parts of training sessions to provide technical expertise.

How can these SMEs be identified? Some years ago I served as site manager for an engineering, logistics, and technical research operation. We were in the beginning stages of implementing a TQM program. Both necessity and desire made us want to use our own personnel to the maximum extent possible.

The ensuing process became an eye-opener in many ways. It turned out that as an organization we didn't know very much about our people, and their resumés didn't provide the information we needed. At that point the decision was made to complete an assets survey. Figure 5.1 was used with considerable success.

The results were phenomenal. We were sitting on top of a personnel gold mine (I suspect most other organizations are, too). Not only did these people have talents, knowledge, and skills far beyond what we had perceived, it was evident that most of them were anxious to use these attributes to help fellow employees and the organization.

The following steps are recommended to get your arms around the talent available in your operation.

1. Construct a quality assets survey sheet. Figure 5.1 proved successful in actual application.

2. Distribute the survey to the employees. We recommend mandatory completion by managers, supervisors, and others in leadership positions. Each of these individuals was chosen for his special skills and should be asked to share those skills with others through training. All employees should be encouraged to complete a survey. Some workers, however, may feel they have no special skills, and they should not be embarrassed by forcing them to complete a sheet.

3. Review the survey sheets to determine what assets are available. Analyze them carefully. Often those things people tend to forget may be just as important as the ones they choose to include.

4. Interview potential trainers and instructors with the required experience or the desire to contribute. Remember, actual classroom training experience is not a must. Effective train-the-trainer instruction can be provided which will help most interested people become proficient enough to train successfully. Besides, much of the training for quality and process improvement takes place on the work floor where the workers may possess considerable experience.

We are currently in the process of developing a total quality management (TQM) program. It is our desire to use in-house assets where possible. Nobody knows more about this company than the people working here. Please fill out this questionnaire and return it to your supervisor by _____ .

1. Please list your consulting, coaching, training, and mentoring experiences:

2. Please check the subject areas on the following list in which you have knowledge or experience. Additional areas can be added on the reverse side of this form.

____ Training concepts	____ Vision
____ Total quality management	____ Quality goals
____ Supervisory training	____ Planning for quality
____ Management training	____ Implementing quality processes
____ Technical management	____ Quality awareness
____ Project management	____ Employee empowerment
____ Leadership	____ Customer service
____ Team development	____ Sales/marketing techniques
____ Meeting dynamics	____ Management role in quality
____ Change management	____ Work processes
____ Quality environments	____ Process control
____ Conflict resolution	____ Statistical process control
____ Difficult people	____ Performance improvement
____ Participative leadership	____ Job task analysis
____ Delegative leadership	____ The cost of quality
____ Problem solving	____ Quality audits
____ Decision making	____ Drafting a quality manual
____ Using quality tools	____ Others (list on reverse)
____ Communications	

3. Please list any areas where you are willing to serve:

____ Quality teams	____ Program development
____ Trainer/instructor	____ Quality research
____ Researcher	____ Other (list on reverse)

4. Please list any other ways you are willing to support a total quality management program:

NAME _____ WORK CENTER _____

Figure 5.1 Quality Assets Survey

5. It is imperative that the person coordinating or directing the quality training program join other managers to negotiate the use of their people. Most will provide the assistance as long as it does not seriously impact on their operational performance. The terms under which other managers support the external use of their people must be clearly understood from the onset. Written confirmation of the agreement should be sent to each manager as a matter of record.

6. Management support encourages most SMEs to work in the program. The roles and responsibilities of the SME in the quality program must be developed before training is initiated. Professionalism must be high on the discussion list. Such sessions are a good time to point out the benefits provided by serving as a trainer.

7. Provide train-the-trainer instruction. Obviously this is an essential evolution. If there is no person available who is capable of holding this instruction, outside assistance should be obtained. Organizations such as ASTD and local colleges may provide this training. Many training and consulting firms also provide seminars on this subject. This is one area where penny-pinching can severely limit your ongoing program.

8. Match trainers to the topics that will be taught and get them started on the development of their part of the training materials. Standardized lesson plans and solid handouts should be a mandatory part of every training session. Without them, the trainer is winging it and the potential to leave out important information, critical steps, or safety procedures can prove disastrous.

9. Review program assignments with SMEs and other trainers at selected intervals to ensure that the development of their training material is on track and that they will be ready on the date they are scheduled to train. There is a human tendency to procrastinate on the development of lesson plans, handouts, and other required training materials. Progress follow-up is necessary. Periodic reviews ensure that the course material for related subject sessions meshes correctly and the information that is being issued in the training sessions matches organizational objectives.

Payoffs from an In-House Program

There are a host of payoffs that accrue from a solid in-house program. These should be understood because the determination between internal and external programs must be carefully weighed. The following factors should be considered.

1. *Cost*–The first and most obvious payoff is program cost. Properly used, internal training resources produce a distinct cost advantage. However, if the training that results from an internal program does not meet organizational performance improvement requirements, the end cost could become monumental. This program will help you ensure the cost decision is correctly made.

2. *Orientation*–The training program will be oriented to the goal. Internal trainers have more knowledge and a significantly higher degree of concern for their organization's vision and strategic plans. This knowledge and concern provides significant support for quality and performance improvement efforts.

3. *Commitment*–A successful TQM program demands commitment from the entire work force. Nothing completes the personal transition from awareness to involvement, commitment, and ownership faster than being a part of the internal training team. As members invest their personal time to prepare training, hold classes, and coach people, they become owners of the training program and the TQM process. As owners, they now have a personal stake in the program's outcome. It becomes theirs. They will invest the necessary effort to ensure they receive a payoff. That is pride of ownership coming through.

4. *Self-education*–There is no better way to learn a subject than by an assignment to instruct it. The background research, time behind the podium, and interchanges with participants cement ideas. No one learns more in a training situation than the instructor if that instructor truly desires to learn.

5. *Leadership ability*–One of the greatest tests of leadership, and one of the biggest builders of leadership skills, is service as an instructor, a teacher, or a trainer. Virtually every communication skill is tested and improved. Human relations skills are enhanced continually in ways limited only by the imagination. One soon learns to take charge of the classroom if there is to be a positive outcome.

6. *Known quantities*–The people within an organization have known capabilities, personalities, and track records. The complete range of these items is unknown until an assets survey is completed, but they are a known quantity to some point. These workers relate to the training needs because they are part of the team that needs training. This factor often makes management more comfortable getting started on quality training because "they are our own people. They think like us because they are us." Team members have a personal stake in the training's outcome. Additionally, trainees relate to these internal trainers because "they are us."

7. *Program standardization*–An in-house program has everybody playing off of the same sheet of music because it is developed for that institution. This precludes "quality guru chasing" when one part of the organization follows the dictates of one guru and another follows the dictates of someone else. Those who study the precepts of the various quality experts soon realize they all are in agreement on the need, but are not all in agreement on how to best meet that need. It also limits the tendency to "guru hop" when the program of one individual is started and before it can provide results the decision is made to switch to another program. Both of these tendencies are extremely detrimental to long-term performance improvement.

8. *Organizational fit*–An internal program is designed to meet the needs of that organization. Time is not wasted on elements that are not needed within the operation. However, a caution is in order. Program coordinators must ensure they are programming training to meet all needs. Important areas can be overlooked through ignorance or personal agenda. Both must be guarded against. In Chapter 2, a comprehensive list of recommended subjects is provided as a guide for a quality curriculum. The Quality Assets Survey (Figure 5.1) also provides a checklist for this purpose.

9. *Personal fit*–Three universal criteria exist for successful training programs. These must be job-performance related, trainee centered, and (when possible) individually paced. Trainees learn best when they understand how the training relates to the goal and enhances their performance on the job. After all, that performance determines such things as job security, pay raises, promotions, and self-satisfaction. Because it is job related, there is an immediate application of the knowledge and skills which reinforces the training.

   All training should be trainee centered. This topic is covered in detail in Chapter 14. People learn best from what they do and not from what the trainer does. It is imperative that the trainee be actively involved in the training to the maximum extent possible.

   Trainee-paced training is desirable when it is at all possible. This allows each individual to master the material before proceeding on to the next step. This criteria is met through on-the-job training, computer-based training, interactive video, and self-paced lessons.

10. *Personal growth*–This final benefit answers the eternal question, "What's in it for me?" Every individual in every organization should be expanding a resumé. This is not to say that everyone should be continually job hunting. Quite the contrary. Resumé building is important as a career development tool in the organization currently being served.

Training experience and the resultant leadership, communications, human relations, and other skill improvements have a positive effect on virtually everyone who ever tackles the job. Every organization has room for leaders with training experience. Potential value within the organization is enhanced greatly because successful training provides a visibility individuals probably would not have otherwise. The value of this benefit should be stressed from the program's onset because it assists greatly in the quest for volunteers when one is first launching a TQM training program.

Drawbacks to Using Internal Training Sources

There are two sides to every coin and an organization embarking on the quality trip must be aware of potential drawbacks when using internal training sources. These can be overcome and, as they say, "forewarned is forearmed."

1. *Hesitant training departments or training personnel*–Not everyone will heartily endorse quality training initiatives. This can be true of almost anyone in the organization, including those involved in training. Many people resist change, especially to an unknown, which TQM usually is. There also may be a hesitancy to share training duties with those outside of the training department. Some folks involved in training may have personal agendas they would rather pursue. Embarking on a new process involves a considerable amount of hard work, which initially can frighten some fainthearted souls.

2. *Short on training skills*–As mentioned earlier, in-house personnel may have the required technical skills, but lack training skills. This is not an insurmountable problem. Some organizations, however, are not willing to incur the required investments to help their people acquire the necessary training skills. The problem results in ill-prepared trainers who dilute the results of good training material. In some cases, these people do not have the know-how to develop solid lesson plans and materials. This creates an even bigger problem.

3. *Lack knowledge of latest quality or technical developments*–In-house personnel concentrate on those technical developments and quality subjects they perceive as applying directly to their jobs. After all, no one can be expected to know everything about everything. The problem rears its ugly head when the training does not include the latest innovations and knowledge, which puts the organization one step to the rear at the outset. Outside training organizations make it their business to keep abreast of the latest developments. It is their competitive edge.

4. *Ineffective ways of completing their efforts*–There are untold examples of people doing things the way they have always done them even though new equipment and technology provides vastly improved methods for increased performance. A large machine shop serves as an excellent example of this situation. It had recently changed ownership. The new owner was walking through the shop on an initial visit after acquiring it. He noticed several people using an outmoded method of machining an item and proceeded to show them an alternate method which cut production time from 10 hours to a little over an hour and a half. That section's supervisor later discussed this situation with us. He had over 20 years of service with the organization, and in that time they had never had outside training. Processes were learned on the job from employees with more seniority. No one ever investigated new techniques. However, the new owner mandated it. He subscribed to several publications, brought in a person skilled in the latest technology and methods, and installed a quality training program. The employees love it.

5. *Lack time for research and program development*–There is only so much time available in each employee's work day. When training responsibilities are added, something must be subtracted. In many cases there is enough wasted time to allow for these activities. However, management cannot automatically assume employees can make time in their schedules for these new assignments and correctly perform all of their old functions, too. Perhaps some of their efforts can be delegated. Other tasks can be eliminated altogether when the situation is analyzed. Solid training will pay off over time with improved performance. This allows more time for training, but it won't happen at the start of the program.

6. *Lack commitment to excellence*–At the onset of quality programs there usually is some hesitancy to commit to the effort. Older workers watched other programs come and go and they are not that interested in putting considerable additional energy into something that will disappear in six months or a year. It is strongly recommended that personnel who are not committed to the quality program never be used for instructors at any level. Those who have suffered through training tragedies put on by people who did not believe in the information they were putting out and made a point to prove this program wrong at every opportunity, realize how devastating these people can be. A quality program cannot stand this sort of experience.

Rather than presenting obstacles or barriers that cannot be broached, most of these situations tend to be initial learning opportunities that disappear rather quickly given time, management effort, and leadership from the top. Most individuals soon climb on the quality express when the engineer is

Mr. Big Boss from the ivory tower. The advantages of being part of the performance improvement efforts are immediately visible to all in these cases.

Summary

1. Quality training and training for quality are both required to support organizational leadership in their TQM journey.

2. There is no standard training program that fits all organizations. Effective training is need-based and is a combination of OJT, classroom, and self-paced instruction. It is important to remember that training is an ongoing evolution and not a once-and-done quick fix.

3. Every organization has an internal base for quality instructors. Subject matter experts can provide much of the training in any quality training program if they are properly coached. A quality assets survey sheet will assist with the identification and training of personnel as potential trainers.

4. An in-house program has great potential. Cost savings, increased commitment, self-education possibilities, and improved leadership skills are all organization builders. Internal employees are known quantities who will customize the quality training program to the organization's exact needs. Dedicated employees support the efforts to match the needs of the organization and its people to the requirements of a quality training program. In turn, all participants benefit from the experience.

5. There is a potential for problems with an internal program that can be largely sidestepped by the knowledge of their existence. Training departments may not fully support new training initiatives that involve personnel outside their group as trainers. Some personnel with needed quality skills may be short on training and program development experience. They also may lack the time for research and development of materials and may believe they don't possess sufficient knowledge of the latest quality and technical developments. These problems may be compounded by the lack of initial commitment to the program because of previous negative experience with similar projects.

Bibliography

Abella, K. T. *Building Successful Training Programs*, Reading, MA: Addison-Wesley, 1986.

Brinkerhoff, R. O. *Achieving Results from Training*, San Francisco: Jossey-Bass, 1987.

Broadwell, M. M. *The Supervisor and On-the-Job Training,* Reading, MA: Addison-Wesley, 1986.

———. *The Supervisor As an Instructor,* Reading, MA: Addison-Wesley, 1970.

Cassner-Lotto, J. and Associates. *Successful Training Strategies: Twenty-six Innovative Corporate Models,* San Francisco: Jossey-Bass, 1988.

Craig, R.L. (Ed.) *American Society for Training and Development, Training & Development Handbook,* New York: McGraw-Hill, 1976.

Friedman, P. G. and Yarbrough, E. A. *Training Strategies from Start to Finish,* Englewood Cliffs, NJ: Prentice-Hall, 1985.

Kirkpatrick, D. L. *Evaluating Training Programs,* Madison, WI: American Society for Training and Development, 1975.

London, M. *Managing the Training Enterprise,* San Francisco: Jossey-Bass, 1989.

McLagan, P. A. *Helping Others Learn,* Reading, MA: Addison-Wesley, 1978.

Mitchell, G. *The Trainer's Handbook,* New York: American Management Association, 1987.

Proctor, J. H. and Thorton, W. M. *Training: A Handbook for Line Managers,* New York: American Management Association, 1961.

CHAPTER 6

Developing a Training Program

An organization's people have been widely recognized as the key ingredient for success. This means all the people in the organization from top to bottom. It also includes the extended family of vendor, supplier, and customer. Never has this been more true than it is in the new global marketplace. The ultimate effectiveness of any organization depends on the knowledge, skills, and commitment of this performance team. The end success of this team depends on training—the right people assigned to the right jobs receiving the right training. People can perform only to their highest level of skills and knowledge—the level to which they have been trained.

Training is one of the most talked about yet least productive processes in many organizations. Too often training boils down to what a person picks up by being on the job. Odds are against anyone acquiring the correct, most productive way of completing any work objective using this method. Nor will this method develop the skills necessary for a successful TQM process in any organization.

Training of this sort is much like the way many of us learned to swim. I was conned into the water at the old swimming hole with the promise of being taught to swim. Two larger boys grabbed me, one by the ankles and the other by the wrists. As they began swinging me, one yelled, "On the count of three, let 'em go." Sure enough, shortly after the word "three" rang out, I came up in a near panic, gasping for breath, stroking wildly, and coughing out water at the same time. All the other kids stood around yelling encouragement while it was up to me to sink or swim. After considerable splashing I made it to a shallow area where I could stand, and everyone cheered. Training was successfully completed.

When I headed for the creek that day I didn't know if I could swim and hadn't been in water over my head. When the "trainers" talked about teaching me to swim I was trusting without knowing. I entered the water with no plan for the training process or knowledge of the potential ramifications of this training exercise. I wanted to learn to swim right then. This story contains several implications for training endeavors, and they all begin with planning.

1. Determine your subject knowledge and compare that to what you should know before considering the training plan.

2. Plan training in advance with consideration for Murphy's law, performance issues, the customer, and safety related issues.

3. Consider the training need, the methods available to meet this need, and which training method best matches the need with the least potential for problems before beginning the exercise.

4. Evaluate potential trainers, look for hidden agendas, think through their motives, and consider what benefit they will derive from the training session before determining to use their services.

In the aforementioned incident all four areas were overlooked. Many current training programs negate their potential effectiveness because one or more of these criteria are overlooked during the planning stage. The program presented here is designed to alleviate these problems by providing a complete system approach that produces results. Outcomes have high predictability before the training commences. Professionally conducted training must be goal oriented and promote respect for training, emphasize safety, increase success and payoff, and reduce cost in terms of assets expended and time utilized.

Planning for Training

Effective training has its basis in the performance management system discussed in Volume II. Manpower requirements, hiring procedures, job/task analysis, work and process standards, performance appraisal, and performance improvement efforts are each important considerations of the training decision.

The first decision must answer the question, "Whose responsibility is the training evolution?" If the answer is the training department, work supervisors then have a handy excuse to hang any performance problems on: "Don't blame me—that's the way training taught them to do it." If the answer is management, training is provided an out: "Don't blame us. They received the training, but their supervisor won't let them use it." Either way the organization and its people lose and nobody wins. This represents the ultimate failure.

People and their performance are ultimate responsibilities of their supervisor. Therefore, ensuring people are trained is a supervisory responsibility that is shared to some degree with the individual. Each person also has a responsibility for self-training performance improvement efforts.

Training is the responsibility of line management and not the training department. However, management, the training department, SMEs, and the individuals involved must develop training as a team if it is to be effective. The programs used must be signed off by both operations and training management before they are used. The actual training department should be an independent, high visibility unit that reports directly to an executive. This increases training accountability while it is a check to ensure management is providing the required training. The system works. Many competitive organizations are proving it every day through performance and customer service improvements.

Potential Problem Areas

Consider for a moment all of the training programs with which you have been involved, including any current programs within your organization. Then check the statements that apply to training you have received. The following list provides a basis for understanding the extent of problems inherent in training programs.

_____ 1. Employee training was given a low priority by the management team.

_____ 2. Participants didn't receive advanced notice that training would be held.

_____ 3. A training agenda was not promulgated with the subject, time, and place.

_____ 4. The trainer waited until the last minute to prepare for the training exercise.

_____ 5. Training objectives were unclear.

_____ 6. Training quality was adversely impacted by poor preparation.

_____ 7. Training aides were of poor quality or missing altogether.

_____ 8. The trainer was disorganized before or during training.

_____ 9. The trainer didn't support the subject, and this attitude impacted on the quality and effectiveness of training.

_____ 10. The trainer did not appear to have the necessary skills or background knowledge to conduct the training.

_____ 11. Training conflicted with previous training sessions and the problem was evident during training.

_____ 12. The trainer's presentation contradicted program handouts, current processes, or accepted procedures.

_____ 13. Management seldom attended training sessions.

_____ 14. Training occurred without advanced planning.

_____ 15. Training held a low priority and was cancelled when scheduling conflicts occurred.

_____ 16. A long-range training plan was not evident.

_____ 17. Training did not appear to have ties to strategic, annual, business, or marketing plans.

_____ 18. Quality and customer satisfaction related subjects were accorded a lower priority than productivity related topics.

_____ 19. Individual and organizational training records were not maintained.

_____ 20. Training seemed to be the first item cut when funding problems arose.

Each of these statements is indicative of the importance of preplanning training exercises and fencing training budgets. Training is so important to long-term performance improvements and, in turn, organizational survival that little should be allowed to interfere with it. Training dollars and time should be fenced so that organizations force themselves to comply with this need.

Factors to Consider in the Training Process

The number of factors that could be considered in the training decision is as limitless as the number of different organizations. However, there are some factors considered extremely important to every organization and these are included in this section.

Quality standards–It would be difficult to conceive there are individuals who do not believe quality is important. They want to buy quality goods and services and they desire to provide the same. The problem begins when one tries to determine what the quality standards are because everyone tends to have their own definition of quality. This problem has roots within many organizations because the organization has not spelled out their quality standards. It is hoped that this will not be the case here because earlier volumes helped define what the quality standards should be. The following are some of the questions that could be asked in the determination of current quality standards:

1. What is the acceptable level of performance (ALP) for this process or function?

2. What are the established quality standards for this process or operation?

3. Are these standards the basis for go/no-go decisions?

4. Are any errors acceptable and, if so, which errors are and are not permitted?

Training quality requirements–It would be unrealistic to assume that all training regarding a particular subject would be of the same level and quality. Therefore, when building the program, the determination must be made if the in-house training assets will achieve the level of performance desired. If they will, that's fine. If they will not, outside help will be required. This may be achieved through any number of sources. Outside trainers and consultants might be used or new personnel may be hired. The situation dictates the solutions to this question.

The quality vision–The quality vision provided at the onset of the quality program provides many of the broad organizational requirements for the training plan. Each must be addressed in order to bring that vision to reality.

Organizational plans–Every organization has or should have strategic plans to guide it. A business might have a budget, business plan, marketing plan, and quality plan providing operational guidance. The training plan must dovetail with each of these. In this case the budget would designate funds available for training purposes, the business plan might outline new knowledge that would be required, the marketing plan could outline new customer-directed attitudes that would be needed, and the quality plan might provide direction for new skill requirements. Each of these would be consulted before drafting the overall training plan and individual initiatives.

Goals–There are many goals that must be considered when developing training. What are the organizational goals as outlined by the quality vision and other sources? What management goals must be considered? Each layer of management tends to have goals that impact on the training decision. What are the goals of the individuals within the organization? There would be immediate conflict if an organizational goal was to train every employee to some high level when a majority of the work force didn't desire to attend any additional training.

Assets–Organizational assets including personnel, funds, equipment, and plant facilities must all be considered when building a training plan. Grandiose plans are of no use if the assets are not available to carry them out, or that level of training commitment is not required.

Needs–Ultimately, all training should be need-based. This is determined by the six previous areas of consideration that were just discussed. Each of these provides certain needs that must be a part of all training considerations.

Conditions for learning–There are at least eight conditions for learning that should be considered during the development of any training program. These conditions follow.

1. *The need to learn*–This need is the other side of the coin from organizational needs. Participants learn more and faster when the job or situation provides a strong need. This need should be highlighted early in the program for added effect. Should the need be difficult to project, the decision to train should be reconsidered. The training may not be required.

2. *The benefits of learning*–If there are no benefits, the training isn't required. The potential benefits for the organization are performance improvement and increased customer service which help them reach their goal. Potential benefits for the participant include increased performance, improved job security, potential promotions, and perhaps bonuses resulting from increased performance.

3. *Performance incentives*–The trainer must acknowledge all positive performance in the classroom. Training participants should be recognized along with any success they have that can be attributed to the training they received. Disincentives should be considered and alleviated. A prime example is working yourself out of a job because training assisted with performance improvement.

4. *Professionalism*–Trainers and training programs must be professionally handled or limited learning takes place. There is little excuse for nonprofessional training sessions. Proper preparation and attention to the details generally prevents nonprofessional training activities.

5. *Trainer–trainee relationships*–There is no stronger reason for screening potential trainers than that of ensuring the person can relate well to participants. Extremely knowledgeable people can be poor trainers if they do not relate well to people. Human relations skills are extremely important and can make up for some deficiencies in the knowledge area.

6. *Prevalent attitude toward training*–Organizational and participant attitude toward training are important considerations. The organization must strongly support training at all levels or a negative message is transmitted to the troops. Likewise, the troops must carry a positive attitude about training or they will gain little from it. Their attitude will be built through successful training plus the payoffs on the job from training.

7. *Training fundamentals*–Three training fundamentals reign supreme in program development. All training should be job related, trainee centered, and (as much as possible) individually paced.

8. *Learning environment*–Most people are apprehensive about training. Will I be able to handle the program? Are they telling me I don't know how to do my job well enough? Are they training me so they can tighten

down the production screws? These and many more potential participant concerns should be considered when building a program.

An Improved Process

Quality training must be a well-planned and well-executed evolution—not a
hit-or-miss process. Training cannot be haphazard. All training efforts should
feature a structured approach designed to meet specific objectives.

In Chapter 2, Figure 2.1, a training wheel was presented that relates the
training need to the goal. Every organizational training decision must question how particular training programs relate to the goals and objectives, but
there's more. Training also must relate directly to individual operations and
processes. Every process must be examined individually and then in terms of
the whole operation while seeking ways to improve both process and operation. This requires a more detailed approach to the assessment of training
requirements.

A five-step approach is presented and should be considered as part of
every training decision. Each of the five steps is a separate and distinct action,
yet they operate as one interconnected system. The process can be considered
as a five-part circular evolution where one proceeds from one step to the next
around the circle until a problem is encountered. When problems occur the
process requires returning to the place where the effort was on track and
proceed again using the new information. This approach is presented in
Figure 6.1.

All training should begin with a training needs assessment, or a training
audit if you prefer that term. The data is then analyzed and reported out so
the correct training decision can be made. Solutions are developed and action
taken to carry out those solutions utilizing whatever training may be required.
An outline of the procedure follows.

Assessment of Need

1. What is the current process?

2. Do workers understand the process?

3. Is the process correct?

4. If not, what should the process be?

5. What is the perceived attitude of the players toward this process and
   any potential performance improvements?

6. What skills and knowledge are required to complete the processes
   correctly?

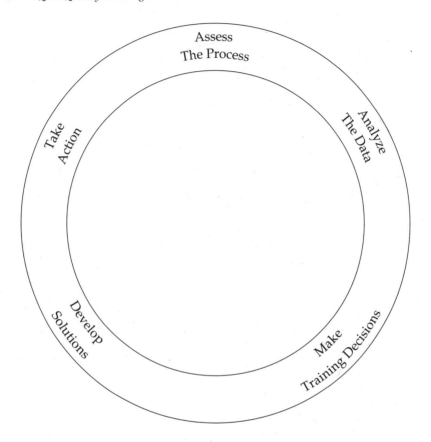

Figure 6.1   Five-Step Training System

7. What method of assessment will be used to audit the organization's needs?
8. Who should complete the assessment and why should they be chosen?
9. Will the assessment consider the goal?
10. Will results be tied to the bottom line?

Analyze the Data

1. How should the data be organized?
2. What different categories of information should be considered?

3. How should the analyzed data be formatted for a report?

4. Who should receive the report?

5. Was the process correct?

6. Was the process followed?

7. Was training conducted previously?

8. Was training used effectively?

9. What are the known deficiencies?

10. Were workers or their supervisor aware of the deficiencies that were discovered?

The Training Decision

1. Are noted deficiencies a training problem?

2. Who needs the training?

3. What do they need to know?

4. What do they currently know?

5. Do they have the background knowledge to learn the difference?

6. What performance issues are involved?

7. What should be the training objectives?

8. How should these objectives be developed?

9. Who should provide the training?

10. What time constraints should be considered?

Develop Solutions—The Action Plan

1. Define the correct process.

2. Determine the training need.

3. Select and train the training team.

4. Determine the appropriate training format.

5. Decide where the training should be conducted.

6. Develop a training program to meet the need.

7. Produce the materials such as handouts and training aids required to support the program.

8. Complete the subject matter research.

9. Develop the required training material.

10. Develop lesson plans.

Take Action

1. Provide learner-centered training.

2. Consider the adult learner's needs in the training.

3. Conduct the training using the best format.

4. Ensure all participants are involved in the training.

5. Recognize contributions as they occur.

6. Evaluate the training success against the need.

7. Determine if the training program was correctly followed.

8. Determine what performance improvements, if any, resulted because of the training.

9. Evaluate whether additional training requirements exist.

10. Take corrective action.

Summary

1. There are almost a limitless number of factors that can be considered when making the training decision. Among the most important are

   a. the customer

   b. quality standards

   c. training quality requirements

   d. the quality vision

   e. organizational plans

   f. the goal

   g. the bottom line

   h. assets

   i. needs

   j. conditions for learning

2. An improved training process promotes solid training and prevents hit-or-miss processes. The structured approach discussed here consists of:

   a. a thorough training need assessment or audit

   b. careful analysis of the data accumulated

c. the training decision based on who needs to know what and who should provide the training

d. developing solutions by defining the process, determine the real needs, and developing the program

e. taking action by conducting the training and evaluating the results

Bibliography

Abella, K. T. *Building Successful Training Programs*, Reading, MA: Addison-Wesley, 1986.

Brinkerhoff, R. O. *Achieving Results from Training*, San Francisco: Jossey-Bass, 1987.

Broadwell, M. M. *The Supervisor and On-the-Job Training*, Reading, MA: Addison-Wesley, 1986.

Cassner-Lotto, J. and Associates. *Successful Training Strategies: Twenty-six Innovative Corporate Models*, San Francisco: Jossey-Bass, 1988.

Craig, R. L. (Ed.) *American Society for Training and Development, Training & Development Handbook*, New York: McGraw-Hill, 1976.

————. *Training and Development Handbook*, New York: McGraw-Hill, 1976.

Davis, L. N. and McCallon, E. *Planning, Conducting and Evaluating Workshops*, Austin, TX: Learning Concepts, 1975.

Friedman, P. G. and Yarbrough, E. A. *Training Strategies from Start to Finish*, Englewood Cliffs, NJ: Prentice-Hall, 1985.

London, M. *Managing the Training Enterprise*, San Francisco: Jossey-Bass, 1989.

Mager, R. F. *Preparing Instructional Objectives*, 2nd ed., Belmont, CA: Fearon, 1975.

Mitchell, G. *The Trainer's Handbook*, New York: American Management Association, 1987.

Rogoff, R. L. *The Training Wheel*, New York: John Wiley and Sons, 1987.

Wedel, K. R. and Brown, G. *Assessing Training Needs*, Washington, D.C.: National Training and Development Service, 1974.

_____ CHAPTER 7 _____

Needs Assessment

The awareness that some sort of training is required follows the realization that continuous performance improvement is a necessity in any effort designed to become or remain competitive. It would be difficult to consider any sort of quality management program without training; every article stresses the training and leadership requirements.

Those embarking on a quality journey want to get started. They read the surveys and understand customers demand quality; they see companies gaining market share and increasing profit through quality; and they hear success stories relating how employee turnover is reduced, personnel costs cut, and employee satisfaction is going off scale—all because of quality. Who wouldn't be anxious to get started when these results are possible?

An immediate problem often arises in the rush to get moving, training assessment is forgotten. Various surveys relate that assessment is forgotten or ignored at least 50 percent of the time. This statistic is shocking enough by itself, but it is compounded when it is discovered what kind of organizations neglect assessment. Marginally successful organizations exhibit a marked tendency to adopt training programs without a needs assessment and without consideration of other alternatives. Those organizations noted for being goal oriented and innovative generally conduct assessments and carefully plan training as one of their options.

The first step in any training program must be a needs assessment. This audit provides the background information for the entire training program that must follow. A multitude of expensive and program-defeating ills are waiting to deter the organization that attempts to begin a program without an understanding of where it is in relation to need.

There are a number of untold factors that can unhinge any training program. Most of them result from poor assessment of need. Some of these are covered as trainer related problems in Chapter 15. The list begins with poor assessment procedures and covers other situations that evolve out of the problem either partially or completely. The following list of problems often occur when a proper assessment is neglected.

1. Training without consideration of the goal.
2. Training without application.
3. Training without near-term application.
4. Training to the wrong problem.
5. Single-level training, such as the tendency to train managers at the exclusion of other organizational levels.
6. Poorly prepared training, trainers, or participants.
7. The wrong training or trainers.
8. Inadequate background knowledge of participants.
9. An expensive packaged training plan that doesn't fit.
10. The tendency to quickly begin training and abandon it just as quickly when it isn't the miracle cure that was desired.

There is one last consideration that is important prior to a discussion of the assessment process. There must be a clear understanding of what the final data is expected to look like before the assessment begins. Generating statistics requires one process, lists of themes and problems require something else, and groups of participant comments demand yet another approach. The goals and objectives for the quality plan play a major part in the way data is collected. Organizational expectations also play an important role in the assessment design. Each of these factors must be known and planned for at the beginning of the process.

The Internal Assessment Process

This initial assessment is a task-by-task audit to determine what the organization actually is doing in comparison with what it should be doing. To this end, three separate areas will be examined as a workable process is developed. These areas include process, knowledge and skills, and attitudes.

Process

Process is the area that looks at how things are actually done against how they are supposed to be completed. It is extremely important to review every operation in an organization carefully under these terms. It matters little if the best equipment is on board if it isn't used correctly to its maximum capacity. The potential of a high-quality work force is negated by poor equipment and personnel utilization.

The first step is to determine how the process is supposed to operate by design. This step often is ignored at the beginning of an assessment. The result is predictable when incorrect assessment data becomes the basis of training. Training solutions to nonproblems and incorrectly analyzed situations lead to substantial waste of assets, training failures, and disillusioned trainees. Examples abound of processes that are out of control, and without understanding the process and its control limits, changes are made that place the process even further out of control. This can happen everywhere from the manufacturing floor to departments such as finance and human resource management.

The determination of the correct process generally is completed by a review of documentation for correct operations in each area, complete with checks of specifications, quality requirements, and so forth. Several basic questions must be asked and answered to determine process operation.

1. Who is supposed to do this process?
2. What equipment are they supposed to use?
3. Why is it done this way?
4. How are they supposed to do it?
5. Under what circumstances should it be done?
6. Are processes adequately outlined for the people who must complete them?
7. What results should be obtained?
8. Are workers knowledgeable of the expected results?
9. Do they attain those results?
10. If not, what is being done about it?

The second step of process assessment determines what is actually happening. This step is completed by observing the process in operation coupled with work force interviews with the people working the process. This provides answers to the following questions.

1. Who actually does what?
2. Why do they do it?
3. When do they do it?
4. How do they do it?

5. Are there deviations from the designated process?

6. Were deviations from the process approved?

7. Who approved the deviations and why?

8. Do deviations result in process improvement?

9. What results do they achieve?

10. Is the supervisor aware of the deviations?

11. Are these results the expected results?

12. Are deviations and changes documented?

Knowledge and Skills

Once the questions of process are understood, asked, and answered, the questions of knowledge and skills are addressed. These are areas well served by the three assessment techniques mentioned earlier. The assessment must be constructed to determine if employees know how to do things correctly and if they do, are they doing them that way. It determines if they are empowered to change and improve their processes, how important production and quality are to the operation, and so forth. The basic questions that must be answered follow.

1. Do the people involved have the knowledge and skills to correctly complete their assignments?

2. Do they operate as a smooth functioning team or as individuals?

3. Do they take part in ongoing training for improvement?

4. Have they received training in problem-solving methods?

5. Do they understand quality tools and how to use them?

6. Are quality tools used to improve processes?

7. Do they understand the importance of their operation and performance?

8. Do they have incentives in place to ensure performance in production and quality are at the best of their ability?

9. Do they understand the importance of production and quality initiatives in terms of their long-term job security?

10. Do they understand the importance of customer service and who their customers are?

Assessment questionnaires must be designed to answer these questions and other questions of importance that pertain to the operation. Supervisors and their managers should be aware of the correct questions to ask to ascertain the degree of knowledge and skills.

Some important revelations usually appear during the process, knowledge, and skills portions of assessment development. These revelations concern the knowledge and leadership skills of the people who are in these management positions. Another set of questions evolves for these people.

1. Do they know what the goal is?

2. Do they know how their operation impacts on the bottom line?

3. Do they understand the processes involved?

4. Do they know their people in terms of needs, strengths, and weaknesses?

5. Do they have the knowledge and skills to coach their subordinates and provide on-the-job training when it is required?

6. Do they routinely provide this coaching and training?

7. Do they recognize areas where they need personal assistance?

8. Do they seek this assistance so they can better support their people?

9. Do they use available incentives to enhance performance?

10. Do they support upper management in their quest for performance improvement?

11. Do they understand their importance in the organization's quest for production and quality improvements?

12. Do they understand who their customers are and how to best support and serve them?

Attitudes

Like processes, the questions of attitude often are ignored during in-house assessments. This area has the potential to provide substantial embarrassment for leaders. After all, they have a great deal to do with the attitudes of their people. Performance improvement and superb customer service will not occur when a poor attitude is prevalent in an organization. Employees treat customers in much the same manner they believe they are treated.

Knowledge and skills are of little value if the prevailing attitude is "Oh yeah, so what?" For a multitude of reasons, this type of attitude is evident in many operations within organizations we have visited. Sometimes entire operations are affected by it. Attitude has significant positive and negative impact, on performance. Assessment should be developed to measure attitudes at the CEO, management, supervisory, and work force levels. Areas that must be included are:

1. CEO preparation of and attention to the goal.

2. CEO preparation and promulgation of the vision.

3. CEO leadership styles and how they impact on performance.

4. CEO support for performance (production and quality).

5. CEO knowledge and service to her customers—all of them.

6. Management support for performance.

7. Work force support for performance.

8. Knowledge for and support of change.

9. Performance standards.

10. Understanding of performance standards.

11. Process ownership.

12. Compliance with the process requirements.

13 Training for performance improvements.

14. Efforts to improve performance.

15. Adequacy of resources and tools.

16. Results.

17. Customer concern.

Methods of Assessment

Assessment can originate in several ways. Success depends on such factors as organizational needs level, expertise of the assessment team, assets committed to the process, and so forth. For our purposes the choice is narrowed down to three. Any of these methods can work. The one which is employed becomes a judgment call that must be made by the people who will own the training program. The three discussed here are as follows:

1. An assessment conducted by an outside training/consulting team.

2. An assessment conducted by a specialized auditing organization.

3. An assessment completed by an internal audit team.

One important thought must precede any discussion of assessment. Regardless of who completes the audit, the goal must be known and specific questions developed to ascertain the following:

1. Does everyone in the organization know what the goal is?

2. Does each person know what her part is in reaching the goal?

3. Is everyone working to achieve the goal?

Assessment by an Outside Training/Consulting Team

In this first scenario an organization decides it wants some level of help to begin its program. Organizations within the federal government often begin this way because they need the audit information before they can issue a request for proposal (RFP) or grant a contract. For whatever reason, they often are hesitant to take on the total program as an internal self-help operation.

Some training/consulting organizations offer a mini audit as a prelude to in-depth discussions of any kind. This provides all concerned parties with factual information to deal with when discussing actual program content. In other situations it may be necessary to contact several potential consulting/training teams for estimates in order to get the program rolling. These are organizational decisions that must be made to best meet specific requirements.

General operating procedures in this situation may vary some, but a general outline assists with the understanding of the process. The outside team generally begins with a determination of what the organization's managers see as goals for the program. These goals often are outlined in terms of performance (production and quality) goals, asset or resource goals, profit goals, marketing goals, and customer service goals. Certainly the return on investment (ROI) will be a prime consideration at this level as well it should be.

Once management objectives are clarified, the assessment team endeavors to determine what this upper-management group believes the training needs are, the commitment level of the various levels to be trained, and if there are any hidden agendas. This attempt to clarify the sponsor's true objectives is necessary because at times outsiders are called in on one pretext (such as training for quality) when the underlying driving forces are reorganization plans, downsizing or terminations, or some other situation that could be detrimental to any training program.

This knowledge is useful for many other reasons. The assessment team must know what management-determined need is so they can handle the situation if the assessed need is different from the stated need. Perhaps training is not the problem, leadership is. The data gathered must substantiate the true situation.

The assessment team then solicits information from various levels of the organizations. Material is gathered in an attempt to see how well the various levels are prepared to understand and meet the needs and goals as they were developed. The perception of these various levels will be a major part of the assessment at this point.

The actual assessment outline that would be utilized by an external team will be much the same as that outlined for use by the organization in an in-house assessment later in the chapter.

There are strengths associated with using outsiders for assessment. The assessment team is well-versed on the subject of quality. The team is independent so it should not have to slant its assessment to appease the organization. These factors lend credibility to the results that are obtained.

There also may be drawbacks. Most training/consulting teams slant their effort one way or another. For example, some quality training programs slant their programs toward the human relations aspects whereas others lean toward the technical applications required for the program. In all probability, their assessments will be biased in the same directions. Some organizations have been accused of proving a need for their training by slanting their assessment evaluation. All of these could impact on assessment results. The questions that are asked or not asked, and the way they are asked impact greatly on the results obtained from any assessment/auditing procedure.

Assessment by an Independent Organization

Some universities provide organizational assessment services. In some cases they are a part of an assessment/training package as previously described. In other cases they are a stand-alone service providing assessment and evaluation of a situation. These universities offer certain strengths, such as the academicians on their staff available to prepare and evaluate the assessment. They tailor their assessment to their perceptions of organizational need. Although this may take considerable time, it is an assessment designed for the particular organization.

Independent assessment services also are available. Many of these services are tailoring their programs to the needs of the TQM program. Some of these offer both standard and tailored programs that fill most organizational needs. Standard programs offer many advantages. They audit needs that are applicable to all organizations. Since the assessments are ready for use they provide a fast turnaround of information. They are considerably less expensive than tailored programs, and, since they use a standard program, the results can be compared against the results of other organizations.

Many organizations offer extremely broad-based assessment services. They cover most quality subjects, customer service, company culture and climate, supervisory style, sales needs, communications pattern profile, and much more.

Reports are available complete with interpretation, graphics, and consulting services. Many have a 24-hour turnaround of assessment results from the time they have them until the reports are in transit back to the organization.

Some services provide materials so the organization can complete the assessment, or they will complete the assessment themselves. Services are provided for independent trainers, consulting services, and organizations.

This can be an excellent foundation for beginning a quality program if no one in your organization has assessment experience.

Assessment by an In-House Team

The third method discussed is assessment by an in-house team. This concept has many advantages that were touched on previously. No one should know more about the organization, its people, and its goals than the people who belong to that organization. Neither should anyone have more at stake for a successful outcome than those same team members. For these reasons and many others, we support an initial assessment from within.

Care must be exercised. Occasionally, in-house people cannot see the forest for the trees. They may have been part of the situation for so long that they assume it to be normal when it isn't. Hidden agendas often are involved. Many individuals won't want to change and may slant the assessment results toward a favored way of doing business. Occasionally, the people chosen to perform the assessment don't have the knowledge or skills to complete it correctly. Questions must be meaningful and valid or the answers will be worthless.

This discussion was not meant to frighten anyone off. Most of these problems can be avoided quite easily when they are anticipated.

Several methods, or combinations of methods, can be used to determine competency at this point. Questionnaires may be developed in several formats (Figure 7.1). Some provide a series of questions and ask that respondents rate the organization in these areas. Generally there are five steps such as Strongly Agree, Agree, Neutral, Disagree, Strongly Disagree; or Outstanding, Excellent, Good, Fair, Needs Work. The advantage of these questionnaires is that they are computer-ready for immediate data usage. The drawback is that they only contain information in predetermined areas.

This survey is presented so that we may evaluate attitudes, knowledge, and skills in areas that are deemed vital to our quality training program. Please answer all questions by circling the level you feel best describes that particular comment. Strongly Agree = SA, Agree = A, Neutral = N, Disagree = D, and Strongly Disagree = SD. Do not place your name on this survey.

1. I have been properly trained in the correct procedures for completing my job.
   SA A N D SD

2. My job performance requires that I use correct procedures on the job at all times.
   SA A N D SD

3. Production and quality are equally important within our work group.
   SA A N D SD

(Figure 7.1 continued on next page)

4. Our team was trained on team participation efforts.   SA A N D SD

5. Our team received sufficient training on problem-solving techniques.
                                                            SA A N D SD

6. Our team received training on the use of quality tools to solve performance problems.
                                                            SA A N D SD

7. Our team has the power to initiate performance improvements without significant red tape.   SA A N D SD

8. Our management team is extremely pro-quality in all areas of performance.
                                                            SA A N D SD

9. Quality customer service is important and the concern is evident in all areas of our organization.   SA A N D SD

10. Our organizational goals and vision are known by all workers.   SA A N D SD

11. The production and quality goals of this organization are clearly defined.
                                                            SA A N D SD

Figure 7.1   Sample Questionnaire Rating Organization

Although these are sample questions only, they would probably be a part of any survey concerning the organization's quality perceptions. It should be noted that each of these is written as a positive statement to which the respondent can agree or disagree. This is important because it makes it easier to complete and much more accurate, which adds to the document's validity.

The second type of questionnaire (Figure 7.2) outlines areas of interest as determined by the management and assessment team. Comments are requested in these areas which are then combined into an informational document for presentation to the management team. The strength comes from a much better command of what the levels of the organization know and perceive concerning the quality program. The obvious drawbacks are the time and assets required to complete and evaluate this type of questionnaire.

1. How would you describe your organization's vision?

2. How would you describe your organization's commitment to quality?

3. How would you describe your team's commitment to quality?

4. How would you describe your commitment to quality?

5. How would you describe your team's commitment to production improvements?

(Figure 7.2 continued on next page)

6. How would you describe your commitment to production improvement?

7. How would you describe the training you have received in terms of improving your on-the-job performance?

8. How would you describe your organization's goals for performance improvements?

9. How are your special talents used to improve your team's performance?

10. What have you personally contributed to performance improvement?

11. What have you personally contributed to increased customer satisfaction?

Figure 7.2   Sample Questionnaire Outlining Areas of Intent

Again, these are samples only, but they include valid questions for any survey. A last comment on the survey could request additional comments that were not previously covered in this document.

Combinations of these two types have the advantage of using the strengths of both of these forms while cutting down some of the time and asset investment. Another type of assessment is the open meeting forum where members of various levels are selected to attend meetings to discuss the various subject areas. This holds additional benefits for an organization. It exposes many ideas because responding is easier. It builds on other members' comments much the same way as other brainstorming efforts work. It also creates a sense of teamwork from the beginning. This often is used in conjunction with the previously outlined questionnaires .

Several recommendations deserve mention here. Whenever an open forum is used, the facilitator should use flip-chart paper to record ideas and comments as they are made. It is also a good idea to have some person with a penchant for details and knowledge of the subject taking notes. At the meeting's conclusion all attendees should be provided a format which they can use to submit additional comments. At times, things should be said, but an open forum is not the correct place for them. The results of the forum should be published as an official record while also being available for interested participants.

The task at this point is to develop an assessment procedure that accurately reflects the organization's needs. The three methods previously discussed serve as models for development, but the actual questions must be determined by the organization. The first three volumes of this program provide the subject matter from which questionnaires can be designed. This leads to the outline of a strong format for an internal audit.

Summary

1. A needs assessment is the first step in any training program. When handled correctly, assessments provide the basis for a solid, goal-oriented training program. This prevents a host of expensive and time-consuming sins that can adversely impact training.

2. The assessment process must consider three separate areas in the development of a workable program. These areas are the process, knowledge and skills, and attitude.

3. Three methods of assessment were covered in this section. These are assessment by a training/consulting group, a special audit team, or an in-house team. Each has advantages and disadvantages. The in-house team is recommended for this program. They understand the organization has a considerable stake on performance improvement. They also gain a considerable education in the process of conducting an assessment.

4. Three separate assessment methods were discussed which included two types of questionnaires and an open forum meeting. A combination of these types is most likely the means best suited to assess most organizations.

Bibliography

Abella, K. T. *Building Successful Training Programs*, Reading, MA: Addison-Wesley, 1986.

Brinkerhoff, R. O. *Achieving Results from Training*, San Francisco: Jossey-Bass, 1987.

Cassner-Lotto, J. and Associates. *Successful Training Strategies: Twenty-six Innovative Corporate Models*, San Francisco: Jossey-Bass, 1988.

Craig, R. L. (Ed.) *American Society for Training and Development, Training & Development Handbook*, New York: McGraw-Hill, 1976.

Davis, L. N. and McCallon, E. *Planning, Conducting and Evaluating Workshops*, Austin, TX: Learning Concepts, 1975.

Ellis, S. K. *How to Survive a Training Assignment*, Reading, MA: Addison-Wesley, 1988.

Friedman, P. G. and Yarbrough, E. A. *Training Strategies from Start to Finish*, Englewood Cliffs, NJ: Prentice-Hall, 1985.

Hamblin, A. C. *Evaluation and Control of Training*, New York: McGraw-Hill, 1974.

Kirkpatrick, D. L. *Evaluating Training Programs,* Madison, WI: American Society for Training and Development, 1975.

London, M. *Managing the Training Enterprise,* San Francisco: Jossey-Bass, 1989.

Mager, R. F. *Preparing Instructional Objectives,* 2nd ed., Belmont, CA: Fearon, 1975.

Mitchell, G. *The Trainer's Handbook,* New York: American Management Association, 1987.

Phillips, J. J. *Handbook of Training Evaluation and Methods,* Houston, TX: Gulf Publishing, 1982.

Rogoff, R. L. *The Training Wheel,* New York: John Wiley and Sons, 1987.

Wedel, K. R. and Brown, G. *Assessing Training Needs,* Washington, D.C.: National Training and Development Service, 1974.

CHAPTER 8

Analyzing Data

Information is of little value until it is properly analyzed, placed in a useful format, and used to present the needs that were discovered during the assessment. Up to that point it is work without a payoff.

This second step in the development of a quality training program determines what the collected information means. This process takes us from the goals and objectives of the quality program to the third step which involves the establishment of training goals and objectives that support the organization's quest for quality. The data collected in step 1 is compared with some known standard or standards so training can be designed to support the program correctly. In this case the goals and objectives of the TQM program provide the standard which will be used as a baseline.

Training objectives generally provide the means to move from where we are to ever-increasing levels of performance excellence. Thus, recovery to the norm from some problem area is not considered an objective. A target performance level is selected that is above the operating norm which requires process, attitude, skill, and knowledge improvements. This target level becomes the training objective near term. As this objective is reached, a new target is established which in turn produces the new training objective for that operation.

Remember ALP when establishing these performance targets. In some cases, acceptable levels of performance are based on cost and customer desires. This can be true in the carpet, textile, clothing, and automobile industries. The quality of the product can be continually improved, but cost must be a consideration and there often is a niche for various quality levels.

Worker performance improvements through training is another matter. It is difficult to conceive of an overtrained employee who cannot be utilized because he knows too much. The TQM process thrives on well-trained workers who can accept ever-greater improvement challenges.

A multitude of training needs will be uncovered during any assessment efforts. This is natural. Since training is a method to get from where we are to where we want to be as determined by the goal and objectives, priorities must be produced to first provide training which ultimately supports performance improvement and increased customer satisfaction goals. Some remedial or introductory training often is necessary and it must be considered as part of the training solution because it is necessary to support other quality-related training.

These goals and objectives provide a working framework that will be filled in as the program develops. The data that is being used must support the quality program, performance requirements, various organizational plans, and need.

Organizing Data

The way the data is analyzed is in large part determined by the way the data is gathered. If all data results from closed questionnaires that ask for statements to be graded, much of the initial analysis will be computer completed. Additional analysis will attempt to read between the lines and interpret the computer-generated results to establish greater meanings. From this information, projections can be made and certain conclusions established. These projections and conclusions then form the basis for the report which ultimately results in the establishment of training objectives.

Open-ended questionnaires add another dimension to the analysis. These require categorization of responses according to types of responses. Interpretation might include not only what the respondent meant to say, but the reasons behind her saying it. This can be a much more informative survey. However, the interpretation becomes more subjective and includes more of the biases of those completing the analysis.

The open forum contains even more potential for bias. The bias of the facilitator, note taker, participants, and those analyzing the results are all part of the subjective picture that results. However, when used to support the first two methods, additional data becomes available. Attitudes about performance surface that otherwise may not be evident.

The expected results determine how the data is organized. In some cases (such as numerical information from closed questionnaires) initial data can be grouped quite simply. After the data is read it can be divided into some form of groups. It is helpful to divide the data into categories as it is analyzed. The actual data that goes into each category is a judgment call of those preparing the assessment report. Three categories follow, along with samples of the information that might enter each category.

Fundamental data–This data is mandatory for the development of the quality training program. An example of this would be data concerning the correct processes and process control in comparison to the way operations actually are completed. Results compared against standards, variance, waste, and safety issues also are primary data. Anything that directly impacts on performance improvement efforts or customer satisfaction can be considered primary data.

Explanatory data–This data searches for the reasons why processes are handled the way they are, when they are, and why the particular equipment procedures, and systems are used. This data provides additional insight into the operation. Attitude may also be secondary data, although it could be primary data if the total quality situation is impacted by employee attitude.

Background data–This data includes information about employees, such as their backgrounds, education levels, perceptions of quality, knowledge of the goal, vision, and other things which have a bearing on the projected training. The audience's needs are vital; they are considered in the design phase and assist with the analysis of the data.

Nonnumerical data compounds the process. When open-ended questionnaires and open-forum formats are used, a content analysis is a valid starting point. The data is read for familiarization purposes and the information is placed in major categories (such as attitudes, skills, knowledge, and processes) or some other system that fits the situation and supports the use of the collected data.

A second reading is useful to place the ideas under the various major categories. This data is arranged and rearranged in different groups, additional categories, different categories, and so forth. Sometimes the information is categorized one way for one part of the analysis and differently for something else. The idea is to construct a format that best serves the established objectives.

After the data is organized, it is important to reread it for content. Has everything been covered that was predetermined as necessary? If not, more assessment may be required, different categories may be needed, and so forth. The data must satisfactorily relate to the quality goals and objectives.

Results of the Analysis

At this point it is important to understand how the assessment team functions in this process. It matters not who conducts the assessment (outsiders or an in-house team), they are acting as consultants. For the purposes of this book, the information generated during assessment is used to develop a successful training program. However, the information generated in the assessment process will also be used in a host of other ways.

It would be impossible to develop an effective quality program if the sole intent of the assessment was to simply change training. Such an idea would be totally unrealistic. The entire organization must change in ways that are inconceivable when the program begins. Change requirements continually emerge as the TQM process matures. The continuous training program supports these changes by providing the attitudes, knowledge, and skills to enable the work force to recognize and correct problems.

Other findings of the assessment team are equally valuable to the organization in its quest for excellence. These should be understood at the onset. A separate report should be generated by the assessment team with the assessment data. This report would review areas that lie outside of the training arena but are vital to the training program's success.

Organization

Often it is discovered during the assessment process that there is little rhyme or reason in the way the organization is structured. Sure, it made sense at one time, but that time has since passed. Since no outside force threatened the operation's stability, the organization remained unchanged as it grew. Positions were added here and there to handle new situations as they presented themselves. The organization got by that way or they would not have survived to undertake a quality program.

Is this organization's business plan adequate? Chances are, it is not. In fact, in almost all cases the energy required to initiate TQM originates from market pressure or strong leadership from outside what previously was the organization. Consider GE as a recent example of an organization going through massive change. Both market pressure and external leadership were involved in that company's changes. Market pressure is a continual force requiring constant attention on such a company. It is with any organization providing goods and services in a competitive market, especially the global market. The other factor in GE's case was Jack Welch, its CEO. He immediately recognized the need to change their organization, flatten out their chain of command, and simplify the way they did things. Change, quality, innovation—none of these could happen in the bureaucracy he inherited. So, he changed the organizational structure.

It is likely that the assessment team will discover areas that also should be reorganized within this operation. These become evident, especially if open-ended questionnaires and open-forum agendas are used to support their on-site visits and process studies. The assessment team must be aware of this potential and capture the thoughts and recommendations as they occur.

Personnel

A myriad of personnel situations that require attention will be uncovered during most assessment processes. Often individuals are ineffectively used on the job. They may be poorly led or organized. The wrong people may have been hired and retained. People may be placed in inappropriate jobs, jobs that do not match their skills, abilities, and interests. There may be no incentive or reason to perform to the best of their ability. Each of these factors impacts on performance improvement efforts and can seriously restrict the potential success of any training program.

Operation

"We do it this way because that is the way we have always done it. It works. We get by. Ain't that enough?"

It is never enough in a competitive organization and it is certainly not enough when TQM is being installed or you are fighting for survival.

Process assessments almost always turn up a number of operational process situations which require change. These may be the way operations are performed, the way equipment is located to perform the operations, the equipment that is being used to perform the operation, internal travel times between jobs, waste inherent in the process, and so forth. Correcting these situations will greatly improve performance, often at minimal cost.

Job Description

Many of the job descriptions in use do not describe the actual tasks people perform. Tasks evolve while the actual job description lags far behind. Experience has proven this can be an extremely inhibitive factor to change. "Hey Joe, check out my job description. It says that I do . . . . That's what I do and nothing more."

Considerable blame is thrown around when this situation crops up. The excuses for this situation are heard often, but the answer should be, "So what?" If we want to survive and thrive in an environment of excellence, these things must change. In most situations where there is a rational reason for change, all participants are treated fairly, and there is a potential benefit from the change, the changes are made easily. If there is no projected benefit from the change, why bother changing?

Equipment

The types of equipment-related problems discovered in an assessment tax the imagination. Some of these problems include equipment that cannot meet the specifications or performance requirements, poorly maintained and worn out equipment, operators who do not know how to use the equipment correctly, equipment that is not used correctly, equipment that is needed but not available, and more.

Leadership

Many managers still sit in an office somewhere removed from the people and operations for which they are responsible. They busy themselves with charts and graphs, reports, and the other management tools that surround them. The people actually performing the work of the organization are in the workplace going about their business as they see fit, with little guidance, support, or recognition. Why this happens is open to debate, but it is one of the greatest causes of performance problems. Leaders must be out where the rubber meets the road, learning what their people do and how they do it, assisting them in their efforts to provide quality goods and services. Nothing less will do in a TQM process. This may be one of the fears many managers have about TQM. They have not placed themselves in a leadership role and are not sure how to insert themselves now that the need has developed. Regardless of why they are not functioning in that role, it must be understood that the best training in the world will be less than effective if leadership does not provide the support to ensure the training is used and used correctly.

Open Resistance

There are contingents of resistance in most organizations that embark on the quality journey. Realization alone will help overcome some resistance. People fear change. They worry about job security, obsolescence, and all the other factors that they have experienced or know can happen, things that threaten their well-being. They wonder how well they will be able to function in a new and ever-changing, performance-oriented environment. They wonder what management's real objectives are. Many face changing to entirely new ways of dealing with people, especially customers, and the change can be frightening.

Solid leadership and caring management will alleviate some of these concerns. Training will overcome some of the attitudes that prevail. The establishment of an organizational track record that shows people they are important and will be cared for are other important parts of overcoming resistance. Attitudes, knowledge, skills, and culture can be positively addressed through solid training.

Developing a Report

When the data is organized and categorized, it becomes the basis for the sponsor(s) training report. This may well be the CEO in the case of a quality training program. Regardless of who it is, the information must be formatted to meet the sponsor's need.

This step makes sense out of the collected data, ordering it into a usable format through the development of a readily understandable document. This allows sponsors to read the document and ensure there is understanding in terms of report content and ability to meet the projected program need. The data must be clear and concise because it will generate questions the report should answer, or it should support the answers offered by the preparer. These questions and the degree to which they are successfully answered will ascertain the sponsor's level of acceptance. The report serves another purpose when it is properly prepared. It becomes a tool that promotes training development.

Established goals and objectives provide a ready guide for the report's preparation. The assessment should address each goal and objective as separate issues. The report must show the current level of support for the goals and objectives and the additional support required to achieve them successfully.

There are many ways to present the report. Remember, your professional reputation is on the line in every presentation. A strong written report is required, supported by an oral briefing with appropriate visual aids such as graphs and charts. The written report should be in a business format. Additional information is present in other volumes of this series. The following sections include the minimum recommended information.

Executive overview or summary–This section is placed at the beginning of the report and allows time-starved people to get a solid overview of the report. It generally follows the format of the rest of the report providing a capsulized version of the information deemed most important. When well-prepared, this section begs the reader to read the complete report. The opposite also is true. Poorly prepared overviews can doom a project.

Data collection–This section explains why the various data subjects were important enough to collect, what data was collected from whom, the methods used to collect the data, and by whom. The data must be tied to the performance goals and objectives of the quality program because these factors drive the training program.

Assessment strategies–This section outlines the assessment methods and strategies that were used, and how the data was manipulated to gather the insights and prepare the recommendations that follow. There should be a method to denote which data can be considered objective and which subjective. Assessment team perceptions should be denoted as such and not as facts. Samples of the information gathering materials usually are provided along with any collected numerical data.

Conclusions and recommendations–This section presents conclusions that can be drawn naturally from the assessment that was performed. From these conclusions, recommendations will be made concerning training that will support the quality program's goals and objectives. This section must focus the attention of the reader in the direction the assessment team understands to be best and for what reasons.

Alternatives–There may be reason to provide alternatives in some cases. If so, they generally follow the recommendations that have been presented.

Are You a Sales-Ready Trainer?

The assessment is complete and the training needs are real. The next step in the process is to acquaint the required people with this need with a proposal for meeting the requirements that were discovered.

Each person involved in an assessment must be ready to sell himself and his ideas to others. Other individuals could include the boss, subordinates, or others internal or external to the organization. The following checklist was developed from a sales program will help you prepare for this sales requirement.

Yes No

  ____ ____ 1. Was the organization's attitude concerning TQM and readiness for training determined before the proposal and presentation were developed?

  ____ ____ 2. Is the determined need based on the facts gathered during research and assessment?

  ____ ____ 3. Was assessment data discussed with concerned parties to alleviate misconceptions?

  ____ ____ 4. Does the proposal agree with the assessed needs?

  ____ ____ 5. Does the proposal consider current and future requirements?

  ____ ____ 6. Will the audience be able to agree with the proposal if it is presented correctly?

  ____ ____ 7. Are realistic alternatives included?

  ____ ____ 8. Are the potential risks realistically assessed?

  ____ ____ 9. Do the potential benefits and rewards of the proposal outweigh the risks involved?

Yes   No

_____ _____ 10. Does the proposal contain a method to measure performance against expectations?

_____ _____ 11. Was benchmark data used to compare this proposal against the efforts of other successful organizations?

_____ _____ 12. Was preparation made to answer the questions and objections that can be expected?

_____ _____ 13. Does the presentation contain research ideas, assessment data, and working examples to answer questions and overcome objections?

_____ _____ 14. Was audience expectations, knowledge, and experience considered during development of the presentation?

_____ _____ 15. Does the presentation require audience participation?

_____ _____ 16. Is the presentation developed in positive terms?

_____ _____ 17. Is the proposal presented in terms of " The real benefit to you is . . ."?

_____ _____ 18. Are handouts, graphics, and aids prepared to support the presentation with sufficient copies for all participants?

_____ _____ 19. Has the presentation team practiced the presentation for content, delivery, and time?

_____ _____ 20. Is the presentation team prepared for a resale in case the audience rejects the proposal?

Potential Problems

The assessment process can create a series of long-term problems if it is not handled accurately and completely. We know of numerous occasions where the assessment sponsor had predetermined ideas of what the outcome would and should be. Sponsors may be vocal about these expectations. This presents a problem for the assessment team.

When the assessment team is from outside the organization, providing a report contrary to the sponsor's desires may preclude a training contract. However, it is best that this difference be handled up front regardless of the end outcome. The problems and frustrations that arise from training that will not work detract from the organization's need.

In-house assessment teams face the same problems. Although it may not mean a loss of a job, it can still lead to frustrations and wasted training efforts. The best instructors, with the best program design, presented in the best way, will solve little when they are not training to need.

Because problems are sometimes generated that create internal conflict, there often is a temptation to bypass the assessment process. However, it is a temptation that must be resisted. Even though the potential for great differences exist, the assessment must be accurately developed and completely covered in the report stage. Shortcuts will only reap later problems.

Summary

1. The assessment step provides the basis for goals and objectives of the quality program to become training goals and objectives.

2. The training objectives of the quality training program must provide the means to move from where you are to ever-increasing levels of excellence.

3. Data must be organized to be useful. The data-gathering stage determines, to a large part, how the material is organized and analyzed. The way data is organized determines the ease with which the data can be utilized and the results that are obtained.

4. Although the assessment is discussed primarily to audit training requirements, other equally important factors that impact on the quality process will be discovered. Some of these situations concern organization, personnel, operation, job descriptions, equipment, and leadership. These factors also should be assessed and a report separate from the training report should be developed and presented as a part of the assessment.

5. The report generated from the data assessment must be accurate, complete, and meet the needs outlined by the sponsor. However, it must not be biased to support opinions of the sponsor if the data does not support these premises.

6. The person presenting the report must be prepared to sell the ideas and the proposal. People will only buy into ideas that are brought forward convincingly.

Bibliography

Abella, K. T. *Building Successful Training Programs*, Reading, MA: Addison-Wesley, 1986.

Brinkerhoff, R. O. *Achieving Results from Training*, San Francisco: Jossey-Bass, 1987.

Cassner-Lotto, J. and Associates. *Successful Training Strategies: Twenty-six Innovative Corporate Models*, San Francisco: Jossey-Bass, 1988.

Craig, R. L. (Ed.) *American Society for Training and Development, Training & Development Handbook,* New York: McGraw-Hill, 1976.

Davis, L. N. and McCallon, E. *Planning, Conducting, and Evaluating Workshops,* Austin, TX: Learning Concepts, 1975.

Ellis, S. K. *How to Survive a Training Assignment,* Reading, MA: Addison-Wesley, 1988.

Friedman, P. G. and Yarbrough, E. A. *Training Strategies from Start to Finish,* Englewood Cliffs, NJ: Prentice-Hall, 1985.

Hamblin, A. C. *Evaluation and Control of Training,* New York: McGraw-Hill, 1974.

Kirkpatrick, D. L. *Evaluating Training Programs,* Madison, WI: American Society for Training and Development, 1975.

London, M. *Managing the Training Enterprise,* San Francisco: Jossey-Bass, 1989.

Mager, R. F. *Preparing Instructional Objectives,* 2nd ed., Belmont, CA: Fearon, 1975.

Mitchell, G. *The Trainer's Handbook,* New York: American Management Association, 1987.

Phillips, J. J. *Handbook of Training Evaluation and Methods,* Houston, TX: Gulf Publishing, 1982.

Rogoff, R. L. *The Training Wheel,* New York: John Wiley and Sons, 1987.

Wedel, K. R. and Brown, G. *Assessing Training Needs.* Washington, D.C.: National Training and Development Service, 1974.

CHAPTER 9

The Training Decision

In all too many cases, training decisions are made based on the sales job that wraps up the analysis stage of the training cycle. Those presenting the report, who strongly believe training is a partial or complete answer, owe it to the people who commissioned the assessment to present the results in an unbiased yet forceful manner so that training will be a consideration.

Those who commissioned this process must then determine in their own minds if they agree that training is the answer. Perhaps it is only a partial answer (as it usually is)—just one part of the performance improvement effort. A correct decision must be made; it is owed to those involved with the assessment and everyone in their organization. Ultimate success rides on the decisions made at this point.

Six Important Questions

The questions asked to determine whether training is the correct decision are relatively simple. Although the answers are not complicated, they are important. They determine the shape and breadth of the entire training program that ensues.

Is This a Training Problem?

You just presented your report, creating a strong cause for a training program. Your sales strategy was perfect. It convinced Mr. Big, the sponsor, that the assessment group was on the right track to carry out the objectives of the new quality program. Then Mr. Big asks the question, *"Are we sure this is a training problem?"*

Without thinking you answer, "It sure is. Without training there will be little hope of success. A quality training program is mandatory."

"Then a training program will do it?" Mr. Big asks.

You start to answer and then remember the boss' reputation for holding people to the promises they make. You pause and he senses it. "Is there more?" he asks.

At this point it is extremely wise to pause and reflect. This seemingly simple question could have quite involved answers. Certainly, it is a training situation, but it is much more. Visionary leadership from the top over the long term, solid communications, solid management skills, rewards and recognition programs, and more also are part of the equation. It is important that everyone involved realize from the beginning that solid training is mandated, but the greatest training by the best trainers will not ensure quality, performance improvement, or increased customer satisfaction. It requires all of these and more. Should this not be understood at the very beginning, the training is doomed to mediocre results at best.

Will Training Be Supported?

Once the decision is made that training is indeed the problem or is necessary to solve the problem, a second question must be asked. *"Will the approved training program receive the strong support that is required from the top down?"* This all-important question must be asked and correctly answered with a resounding "yes" at the beginning of any training program. If the answer is "no," everything else becomes a mute point. Trained workers will not fix a situation caused by poor leadership at the management level. It just doesn't happen that way. Additionally, training in-house personnel may not always be the best solution to some problems. Before kicking off the training program, let's consider occasions when training may not be the answer.

At times it may be better to hire people who are already trained. There may be little time allowed for start up, or reaction time for the current situation may be extremely limited. Costs for training on-board personnel may also be prohibitive, although it usually is more cost-effective to train your solid employees than search the marketplace for others with requisite training.

It may be a solid decision to hire at least a cadre of trained personnel from outside when the process, service, or function is completely new to the organization. The new personnel can than be utilized to train people who already are in the organization.

In most cases, however, it is more productive to train people within the organization than it is to hire from outside. The people on board are a known quantity. Successful training programs generate positive morale because it shows the organization takes care of its own. Plus, when an organization conducts its own training it is tailored to need, designed to meet all requirements without a lot of unnecessary frills, and stresses organizational quality at every step.

Who Needs the Training?

"OK," Mr. Big continues, "I can agree that training is required and I'll strongly support it. In fact we all will, won't we?" he asks looking around the table at his management team. Everyone nods in agreement and Mr. Big continues, "We have a limited budget for training this year." At this point the all-knowing director of finance vigorously shakes his head in agreement.

Mr. Big smiles and continues, "Training isn't my only problem. I have customers complaining about quality, our production must improve or we won't make a profit, and our employee turnover rate is horrendous. How do we know *who needs the training?*"

Everybody needs training in a quality program and they all need some amount of training from the initial stages of development. Everyone must be made aware of the quality initiatives and how they fit into the vision, the goal, and the ensuing objectives.

Awareness alone won't do it. The total work force must become involved in transforming the workplace and that requires training. If training weren't a major portion of the problem, the people already would have created a quality workplace. Their desire to create quality is every bit as strong as Mr. Big's.

It must be understood that getting everybody started is important. However, everyone does not need each training topic to the same level. Therefore, it is important to answer the third question simultaneously in order to satisfactorily make sound training decisions.

What Do They Need to Know?

Mr. Big continues by answering his own question with a question, "I guess that question was answered by your presentation and report—everybody needs some kind of training. That's a pretty tall order given the production schedules that must be met and all the other problems, not the least of which is the budget. How do I know *what they need to know?*"

You explain to Mr. Big that the assessment discovered considerable need throughout the organization. They have been listed by department, structural level which includes the executive level, and priority as an appendix to the assessment report.

Mr. Big listens carefully while you explain, "This training will take time, a considerable amount of time. However, that fits right in with the TQM process because it also is a forever thing. We believe that the successes achieved from first-year training will increase profit and allow training a larger share of the budget in succeeding years. These will have continuing payoffs in improved performance which will continually improve profit. Besides, some people already have some understanding of the fundamentals.

"Program goals and objectives provided the first clues needed to answer this question. In the case of our quality program, a great deal of training in an ongoing program is required. Training objectives will be required for each different topic area and employee level in the organization. These objectives will be formed from the top down first considering your vision for our organization and the budget. We have . . . ."

What Do They Already Know?

At this point Mr. Big again interrupts, "OK, so we know what everybody needs to know. I found this appendix you mentioned and it looks like you really did a thorough job up to this point. I guess my next question is *how do we know what they already know?*"

Pausing, you quickly think this question through before answering. "Mr. Big, the assessment answered that for us. The questions used were based on the objectives you outlined for us. The survey sheets asked for employee opinions on the areas in which they believed they needed training and to what level. We also selected employees from each work area and held an open forum discussion. This validated the information to a degree. This was followed up with specific questions to supervisors and managers which paints a fairly accurate picture of what people already know.

"Appendix Two in your report outlines the average skill and knowledge level in the various departments. We went over these assumptions with the managers in charge of those departments to clear up any misconceptions before we printed them. In one case we had misunderstood a few things which changed the skill level assumptions.

"We call them assumptions because until performance is tested against a standard they must remain assumptions. However, the supervisors continually observe their individual operations so the assumptions appear to be valid.

"The next logical step was to subtract what they know from what they need to know to determine what the training objectives should be. Rough training objectives are outlined in Appendix Three."

Who Provides the Training?

Mr. Big smiles, quite proud of his assessment team and the results he achieved through it. He knew he was doing the right thing when he commissioned the team to act on his behalf.

"Well, you folks seem to have all the answers today. I'm proud of what we achieved here. I guess one last question remains, *who is going to provide all this training?*"

After thinking this question through, you begin, "Well Mr. Big, we're glad you appreciate this effort. These people did an outstanding job as a team. We don't have all the answers as to the specific names of people who will provide the training, but we believe we can do a large part of it through our own staff. That requires cooperation from all our managers because their people will be required to train outside their operation in some cases."

Mr. Big holds up his hand signaling a pause. "There won't be any problem getting this cooperation, will there?" He looks around the table intently, pausing to meet each manager's eyes, waiting for each one to signal there would be no problems before moving to the next individual.

"Done!" Mr. Big announces. "It is a done deal. I expect you all to make it happen. I'm willing to do my part, but that will require that each one of you keep me posted. Let me know how to help. I need a proposed training schedule by the end of next week so I can approve it. Is that a fair deal? Are we all in agreement on this thing?"

When everyone finished shaking their heads in agreement and making their verbal replies, Mr. Big raised both hands over his head signaling the end to the meeting.

Additional Observations

Answering the aforementioned questions may make the team hesitant to proceed because of the magnitude of the job that seems to be facing it. This is especially true when one considers the enormity of any training program that will deal with the range of subjects that must be covered in a quality program.

Before you pause long enough to become discouraged, let's look at the rest of the story. Certainly, it is a large program, but it wasn't meant to be completed today. TQM is a way of life and not a short-term project that is once and done. The training program is an ongoing one that will support quality starting at this point. There are many subject areas, but there should be numerous people available preparing the different sessions. In fact, the more people who become involved in the training efforts, the greater the total organizational commitment to the program.

A Decision Model

Many models are available for use in coming to the training decision. The one that follows compares employee knowledge and attitude. The two-dimensional grid displays knowledge/skills and employee attitude. The knowledge/skill line is understood to include all aspects of the job including operations, production, quality, safety, process control, problem solving, and quality tools.

Attitude toward both training and performance improvement is extremely important. Employee attitudes concerning the organization, production, quality, safety, process control, training, fellow employees, supervisors, and many more factors all impact heavily on training success and therefore must be a consideration in all training decisions.

Attitude and job knowledge interact to form a training decision grid that exhibits where training efforts will be most and least effective. This knowledge should assist greatly in the training decision that must be made. The grid is presented as Figure 9.1.

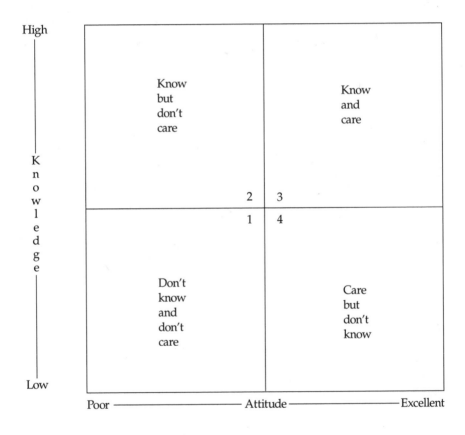

Figure 9.1 The Decision Model

It's Your Decision

Training is not the answer to every problem, nor will it help improve the performance of all individuals. This knowledge conserves time and saves assets which can be better used to train where there will be a payoff.

1. *Poor attitude and low knowledge*–It is highly unlikely that training will have any positive effect on people in this sector. They don't know their job and don't care to learn. It isn't important to them. Often they are disruptive forces in the training environment. Unfortunately, in real-world situations these people command a major share of supervisory time and training assets when there is little hope for a payoff from the effort expended. Most likely, "a change of As" is the best guidance to provide these individuals—change your attitude or your work address.

2. *Poor attitude but knowledgeable*–Training may help those individuals in this area, but only if they view the training as a usable, positive force indicative of organizational change. In that case, the training and the attention received during training will be motivational. Where the trainee perceives a personal benefit, the attitude often undergoes a positive change. Usually the individual's "go button" can be discovered during training, setting the stage for considerable attitude improvement.

3. *Excellent attitude and knowledgeable*–This situation supports high performance. These individuals already know their job and are doing it well. However, it does not signify a high payoff from training efforts. These people must receive continuous training to continue performance improvement. It is unfortunate that supervisors spend less time with these stellar individuals than they do the malcontents who don't know and don't care.

4. *Excellent attitude but low knowledge*–Training often is the basis for dramatic employee improvement. They want to learn and will when provided the opportunity. Because their attitude is good, they tend to use the training they receive to improve their performance. The greatest training payoff is achieved when assets and time are expended in this area.

Outlining the Program

The first step is to list the quality subjects in the order they will be presented. The next item is to assign the topics to the people or team who will develop and present them. A list of topics can easily be constructed using the chapter titles from the first three volumes of this program. Dates should be selected for presentation. One session per week works out just about right. There also can be a column at the end for comments. A sample is provided in Figure 9.2.

FIRST QUARTER TRAINING SCHEDULE

Subject	Trainer	Date	Length	Comments
The Quality Vision	Green	1/2	60 min.	Overview by CEO
TQM Overview	Green	1/9	60 min.	Program Intro
TQM as a Process	Smith	1/16	60 min.	
Getting Started	Jones	1/23	60 min.	
Planning Quality-1	Johnson	3/20	60 min.	
Planning Quality-2	Johnson	3/27	60 min.	

Figure 9.2   Outline of Quality Program

Some notes are important at this point. The vision and program overview were both presented by the senior person on site, in this case the CEO. This commitment from the top is essential to the success of the quality process. Training was scheduled each week with each session scheduled for one hour. In practice this turns out to be a workable schedule for both frequency of training and length of sessions. Originally this schedule was chosen to maximize training with minimum effect on production. Both production and quality increased measurably as time went on and both knowledge/skills and attitude improved. This training proved to be a significant motivational force over the long term. The schedule was maintained because it was one with which the participants were in step. It wasn't too frequent to bore them or too far apart so that they lost interest. Most sessions were an hour in length which is good for maintaining concentration with little or no impact on production.

Quality training requires another consideration. There is some level of employee turnover in virtually all organizations. It has been demonstrated that an active TQM program can drastically reduce this turnover. Even with minimal turnover, the training program must provide for bringing new employees into the quality program. Many scenarios are possible, but that isn't this chapter's purpose. The important thing is to realize ahead of time that this situation will arise and training can reduce both turnover and the impact such turnover has on the organization.

A master training schedule is developed for a rolling year at a time and updated at the end of each quarter. This provides a long lead time for the people who develop the presentations and coordinate the various aspects of the program. Each person on the training team was given a copy of the long-range and quarterly schedules and they also were posted on appropriate bulletin boards.

Earlier discussion mentioned the importance of identifying SMEs for the various training areas. It is now time to bring them up to speed so they begin preparation of the training material.

Objectives

Objectives provide the means of measuring to what degree training supports the effort to attain the established goals, how it works to transform the vision into reality, and how the organization is progressing toward a quality environment.

Design of each objective depends on such variables as what the objective covers, the level of people covered by the objective, and so forth. There may be as many as four parts to the training objective: a description of the trainee or learner, a behavior or performance statement, the way performance will be measured, and the measurement criteria which determines acceptable performance.

The overall organizational quality goal objectives will be the driving force behind the training program. From these the training goals and objectives are developed which, in turn, become the framework for individual course objectives. These objectives provide a certain standard against which the training can be evaluated to determine its level of success.

Five more or less standard objectives should be considered during the development of any training program. These objectives are often used with various scenarios.

- "Bottom-line" objectives
- Organizational objectives
- Performance objectives
- Learning objectives
- Action objectives

These objectives are listed in descending order in terms of which come first with the organization's bottom-line goals listed first. There is no way organizational objectives can be prepared until the goal objectives are prepared and understood. In the same manner, performance objectives are prepared after the organizational objectives are prepared and understood.

Bottom-Line Objectives

The goal or bottom-line objective is based on the reason the organization exists. In business this is profit, in schools it is properly educated students, and so forth. The profit objective demands organizational objectives pertaining to requirements to improved performance, customer quality service, and human resource management through a TQM program.

In a total quality environment the bottom-line objectives are never reached in actual practice because they are based on a moving target that is continually moving forward following the vision of "what can be in the future if we . . . ."

The ultimate objective remains the same while the other four objectives change to support organizational requirements and the various topics within this training process. The discussion of objectives begins with the first action objective, that being the quality vision.

In reality, there are two bottom-line objectives: the goal and survival. This objective fits every organization from government entities and school systems to business and industry. Quality organizations will survive and nonquality organizations that do not meet designated needs will be forcibly changed by outside forces or become extinct. The bottom-line objective is pursued through strong leadership, performance improvements, improved customer quality service, and a general dedication to organizational excellence by everyone in the organization.

Organizational Objectives

Organizational objectives apply to all operations within an organization. Quality vision training usually moves members of each operation to look at the way they function and then spurs them to suggest specific realignment steps or take realignment actions. Behavior patterns and organization changes after such training become an indicator to measure application of the training. For most of the quality training sessions, specific organizational steps may be outlined. Success toward meeting these objectives may be determined by performance success, organizational charts and graphs, written reports from management, and so forth.

Performance Objectives

This objective applies to all training discussed in this volume because quality training is training to need. It is especially applicable to on-the-job training since it focuses on specific actions that must be taken. Participants apply the attitudes, skills, and knowledge acquired in the performance of their job, their efforts on team evolutions, and their overall contributions to the quality program. Observation, appraisal by the supervisor, self-appraisal, performance improvement graphs, and bottom-line improvements will be among the standard techniques used to measure compliance in this objective.

Learning Objectives

Learning or training objectives are considered in more detail later. For now, this objective requires all organizational members to acquire certain attitudes, skills, and knowledge concerning the TQM program. Understanding and commitment to this objective is measured, in part, by response during the discussion period held at the end of each training session. Other indicators are listed under reaction objectives.

Note: Understanding and knowledge of the objectives will be tested often with written tests for classroom training, performance and operational tests for on-the-job training, and as progress tests during self-paced training.

Action Objectives

The action objective begins by building an awareness of the TQM program. Involvement, commitment, and ownership will follow as time passes and the payoffs from quality benefit the work force. Indications of success vary with the type of operation and the length of time they have been active with TQM initiatives. Employee attitude often is the first indicator that action objectives are being met. Other actions that follow (such as quality suggestions, program volunteers, performance improvements, and improved customer quality service) can be considered indicators of reaching this objective.

The Remainder of the Training Outline

Goals and objectives are only the first part of the training process. Let's examine the remaining parts that make up the training scenario.

Training Subjects

The first list of training subjects is developed from the list of quality subjects. To this, add training for operators, on-the-job training, task training, training for procedures and policies, and various human resource management training. Once the complete list of subjects is generated, their relative importance must be determined and priorities assigned. This determines the training schedule.

Prerequisites

Prerequisites or entry-level requirements (such as a certain level of reading or math literacy, some level of computer knowledge, manual dexterity, or system knowledge) can all be considered as requirements to begin the training. The list of prerequisites could be as long as that of the training to be held. It is in the best interests of the program to keep it as simple as possible.

Few people have in-depth knowledge of TQM during the initial implementation stages. Organizational performance improvement requires everyone to have knowledge of performance and customer satisfaction improvement subjects and skills to use them to some degree, with the level depending on the position the person fills. In this case, the training must be developed so that it can be tailored to the level of the people who attend the classes. Some may require a certain amount of remedial work before they can be a part of the regular training cycle.

Training Objectives

The development of training objectives using job descriptions, task and skill analysis, and the material covered thus far will be further explored in Chapter 11 where sample formats are presented and described. For now, the process of developing objectives has already been covered thoroughly. There are a few additional comments that pertain specifically to training objectives. They are developed prior to designing the training package which maintains a focus on both the customer or trainee need and the end result that is necessary for success. Simultaneously, they provide the means for both management and potential trainees to ascertain if the program and instructional level is appropriate for those who would be attending classes. Objectives also help the team that designs and instructs the program in their determination of what instructional method or combination of methods best suits this material. Along with this, objectives provide guidance on the types of aids which might best support the information. As with all objectives, training objectives provide a means to measure the level of learning that has occurred.

Objectives should be tailored to the level of competency required for successful performance of the task, understanding of the material, or the necessary attitude to successfully handle the project. Training or learning objectives should be constructed so that they are easy to measure and written in specific terms using verbs such as operate, change, identify, or list, rather than nonspecific terms such as know and understand.

Sample

Objective: As a result of this session, participants will be able to correctly change dies in 15 minutes.

Methods of Evaluation

Training success is determined by measuring what has been learned against some predetermined standard. The evaluation method for the sample objective could well be having the trainee change the die in a shop floor environment according to some prepared checklist that would be used during die changes. This provides the most accurate evaluation for this type of learning objective—the person either can or cannot do it.

Another evaluation method might be to have the trainee change the die in some type of simulated exercise. A third technique may be to have the person write down die-changing procedures. A fourth method could be to have the person identify the correct procedures from a group of such operations.

In Chapter 16 a soldering operation is discussed where many separate training mistakes occurred before a proper solution evolved. In any type of operation where classroom training is held to correct shop floor problems, several types of evaluation methods might be used. The person could be tested under actual production conditions or in a simulated exercise. Some sort of written test might also be used. Another one would check actual production over some amount of time to see that specified performance levels are met. This is an outstanding way to measure results for this kind of situation.

Written tests, performance tests under various conditions, or appraisal of long-term results are all valuable evaluation methods. Each method has advantages and disadvantages that must be evaluated by those preparing and holding the actual training sessions. The task becomes to select the method or combination of methods that best measures the learning objectives and performance that are desired.

The main purpose of evaluation rests within its ability to produce quality training that enhances performance. Were it not for this need, evaluation would lose much of its importance.

Training Methods

Training methods are another area with a multitude of possibilities, each of which are valid under the proper circumstances. Process and performance improvement training might be best suited to on-the-job training backed by computer-based training or classroom lectures. Quality training may involve classroom training of some sort with outside or on-the-job exercises. Computer-based training satisfies a host of needs from such areas as introductory material to advanced repair processes. Self-paced instruction supports a wide variety of different training situations, including learning activities associated with theories and basic skills development.

Another training situation is effective in certain cases. Field trips to organizations that have effectively corrected some situation, developed a new process, or designed a new operation offer an opportunity to witness training solutions that would not otherwise be available. This is especially true in the TQM arena where it serves both learning and benchmarking exercises. Companies travel to each other's sites to witness how quality and performance problems were corrected, and the training programs that are in place to promote these solutions. The 1990 Malcolm Baldrige Award winners gave much of the credit for their quality success to earlier winners who helped them develop their programs. Many major companies send members of their management team abroad to the Far East and to Europe, in order that they may study the latest performance techniques. The results achieved by these companies are self-evident.

Simulators make excellent training tools when conditions such as cost or equipment availability prohibits actual use. The military makes increasing use of simulators. Simulators are used to train complete Navy ship crews while they remain tied up to the pier. Weapon system simulators are used for training by all the services. Military and airline pilots spend a great deal of time on simulators, as do nuclear power plant operators. Although these complex simulators are expensive, the cost is minimal compared to the use of real equipment in actual circumstances.

Media Requirements

Media requirements are an important part of the process. Books, manuals, films, slides, videotapes, simulators, actual equipment, and more must be considered. Many of the needed materials will be available within the organization. The best part of using materials that are currently available is that the trainees probably have some familiarity with them.

Program Design

Program design receives much of its earliest structure from lesson plan outlines. Most lesson plans contain three sections that carry the main ideas. Although these may be broken out into additional sections, the main sections consist of the introduction or program overview, the discussion or presentation, and the summary section. The summary section often is divided into a program summary, testing, application, and critiques.

Several factors play important roles in program design:

Time availability–Production schedules, vacations, workloads, and time of the year are factors that impact on the time available for training.

Skill and knowledge level of trainees–This factor requires considerable attention. It may be that the workers require a combination of skill and knowledge training. Team training is especially useful in TQM and all participants could be from one operational group and have similar education and training backgrounds. These backgrounds must be considered, thus allowing a straightforward evaluation. In other cases in a TQM program, each level of the organization must be trained to some level to accomplish the job. These levels must be determined and the program designed to accommodate the range of skills and knowledge that will be present in each training session.

Current skill and knowledge levels can be obtained from background checks or supervisory interviews. In other cases pretests or questionnaires may be in order. The information produced in the data-gathering process can be of great value. You may intuitively determine levels by the types of positions the trainees hold.

Subject complexity–The more complex the material is, the longer it will take most people to grasp it correctly. More complex concepts may require substantial pretraining. The degree of previous trainee exposure to the material also impacts. Fairly complex operations where trainees already have a foundation knowledge often consume less training time than simpler concepts which are totally new.

Dependency on special equipment or facilities–Items such as simulators should have long-range schedules to make optimum use of them. Long-range planning becomes paramount so the equipment will be available at the planned time. Special rooms, such as training facilities, also must be planned for well in advance. When training uses the actual equipment in its work setting, a suitable plan must be developed that least impacts on production while it minimizes work area distractions at the same time.

Timing–Timing is crucial. Training must be held prior to the actual need. Yet, it also must be held as close to the time that the skills and knowledge will be used in actual work efforts because retention drops rapidly with time. This provides a narrow window of opportunity for training payoff.

Summary

1. This chapter begins with a discussion of six questions that must be answered before beginning any training program: Is this a training problem? Will training be supported? Who needs the training? What do they need to know? What do they already know? Who will provide the training?

2. A two-dimensional knowledge/skill–employee attitude grid provides insight into the interaction of two factors that impact on training.

3. A program outline is provided that presents a sample training schedule and discusses a master training plan.

4. A discussion of objectives covers five levels of objectives: bottom-line objectives, organizational objectives, performance objectives, learning objectives, and action objectives.

5. A training outline is presented that includes subject prerequisites, training objectives, methods of evaluation, training methods, media requirements, and program design.

Bibliography

Abella, K. T. *Building Successful Training Programs*, Reading, MA: Addison-Wesley, 1986.

Brinkerhoff, R. O. *Achieving Results from Training*, San Francisco: Jossey-Bass, 1987.

Carkhuff, R. R. and Pierce, R. M. *Training Delivery Skills, Part I*, Amherst, MA: Human Resource Development Press, 1984.

———. *Training Delivery Skills, Part II*, Amherst, MA: Human Resource Development Press, 1984.

Cassner-Lotto, J. and Associates. *Successful Training Strategies: Twenty-six Innovative Corporate Models*, San Francisco: Jossey-Bass, 1988.

Cooper, S. and Heenan, C. *A Humanistic Approach*, Boston: CB Publishing, 1980.

Craig, R. L. (Ed.) *American Society for Training and Development, Training & Development Handbook*, New York: McGraw-Hill, 1976.

———. *Training and Development Handbook*, New York: McGraw-Hill, 1976.

Davis, L. N. and McCallon, E. *Planning, Conducting and Evaluating Workshops*, Austin, TX: Learning Concepts, 1975.

Friedman, P. G. and Yarbrough, E. A. *Training Strategies from Start to Finish*, Englewood Cliffs, NJ: Prentice-Hall, 1985.

Hamblin, A. C. *Evaluation and Control of Training*, New York: McGraw-Hill, 1974.

Kirkpatrick, D. L. *Evaluating Training Programs*, Madison, WI: American Society for Training and Development, 1975.

London, M. *Managing the Training Enterprise*, San Francisco: Jossey-Bass, 1989.

Mager, R. F. *Preparing Instructional Objectives*, 2nd ed., Belmont, CA: Fearon, 1975.

Mitchell, G. *The Trainer's Handbook*, New York: American Management Association, 1987.

Odiorne, G. S. *Training by Objectives*, New York: The Macmillan Company, 1970.

Phillips, J. J. *Handbook of Training Evaluation and Methods*, Houston, TX: Gulf Publishing, 1982.

Rogoff, R. L. *The Training Wheel*, New York: John Wiley and Sons, 1987.

CHAPTER 10

Preparing Solutions

This chapter begins a study of the more mechanical aspects of training—developing the solutions. Every aspect of this process requires careful attention to detail. Lists, checklists, charts, and samples are provided to serve as a guide for the part-time trainer and a checklist for the professional during this critical evolution.

The format for this part of the book is changed slightly with less narrative and more chart-type examples. This approach aids comparisons and simplifies reviews. These last-minute checks before every presentation ensure nothing has been overlooked and everything that is supposed to be there is there. This often overlooked step can be critical.

Before you say "I don't have problems in this area," or "That won't ever happen to me," please read the following discussion of problems that recently occurred with seasoned trainers. This topic came up at an informal meeting discussing the agenda for a quality program and the necessity to lead it off with a train-the-trainer session.

One person was using the ASTD Train America's Workforce slide presentation. She had invested considerable time adding her personal slides to the program to match her presentation to the audience. She practiced and had it down pat. She arrived early for the meeting, set up her material, and made one last check of the slides. At that point she discovered she had picked up the wrong carousel. Luckily, she had a flipchart tablet and worked fervently to develop charts to present at the meeting.

Another trainer was using slides to sell a major training program to a group. He ended up with the wrong lens for his projector and couldn't enlarge the frames enough to see details.

A woman had an excellent lesson plan and handouts for a TQM presentation. It was a trial presentation and if it worked out she would be given a contract for ongoing training. She passed up overheads and a flipchart because the subject was simple; she planned on using the chalkboard which had been requested when she rented the room. Her plane was late arriving so she didn't have time to precheck the room. Arriving just when she was supposed to begin, she discovered there was no chalkboard—no contract followed her presentation.

One last situation is worth noting. A trainer had a contract for technical training and was trying to obtain a similar effort for TQM training. He was asked to give a sample presentation on leadership that was scheduled to last an hour and a half. He decided against making a new lesson plan and handouts, choosing instead to go with a prepared set that was designed for a full-day session. He ran out of time halfway through the presentation and was not invited back.

All of these experienced trainers made a slip-up because they took short-cuts or didn't make one last check. Although the chances might be slim, it could happen to you, too. Researching material and developing it into solid training material can be tedious work. Let's not take any chances that can negate a lot of hard work.

This chapter provides information to complete the research for training programs and develop corresponding aids to support presentation. Three separate types of material will be prepared to complete each training package: presentation, handout, and administration materials. The presentation material is used to present the training, the student handouts support the presentation, and the administration material supports the training program. Each of these will be discussed in this chapter and developed in later chapters.

The research that must be completed on the chosen subjects is our next project. In earlier chapters we discussed how to compile a list of the training subjects, complete a needs assessment, analyze the data, and answer the questions for a training decision. This information provides the formula for preparing a solution:

> Desired attitude, knowledge, and skill level − current attitude, knowledge, and skill level = training that must be completed.

This determines the research that must be completed in each subject area.

performance-based training
performance training

Skill-Type Training

Skill-type training poses a management challenge that must be met. Continuous performance improvement demands it. The value of this training in the quest for organizational excellence cannot be overstated. This importance requires the development of specific training systems to replace the haphazard methods that traditionally have been utilized for skill-type training.

The measurement of effectiveness for skill training also must change. Providing such training is just one part of the overall training process and there is no payoff for the organization, the trainers, or the people holding the training. Instead, payoff is achieved when the training leads to improved on-the-job performance.

Performance improvement is greatly enhanced when the results of such training are measured and recorded over time. Tracking such efforts to the bottom line adds additional impact for all those involved in the particular production process. Training thus tied to performance is called performance-based training. Figure 10.1 presents a flowchart representation of the process.

Performance-based training begins with a thorough review of position descriptions, job/skills analysis, and performance standards. This is combined with the input of the supervisor and perhaps an individual who is known for performance excellence.

Personal observation should be a priority for all trainers during the preparation for performance-based skill training. It is difficult, if not impossible, to successfully train to an area that is not personally observed even when the trainer is familiar with the process and was previously successful in completing this task. Often, things change rapidly in performance-improvement-oriented operations. Credibility is essential and it will be lacking to some degree when the trainer has not observed the operation. In fact, as previously mentioned, it is best when the trainer is from the operational group.

Specific steps guide the research and development of training material once the training that must be completed is known. The following guide can assist with the assembly of information for task-oriented training.

1. Collect information on the subject and/or locate a subject matter expert in addition to yourself. Remember, the person developing the course is selected in an in-house training program because he knows something about the subject.

2. Prepare a preliminary task list that outlines how the task should be performed. Job descriptions may be on file for many or all of the tasks.

3. When possible, observe an expert doing the task. You may even want to videotape the operation. It has application in the task analysis and probable later application in training.

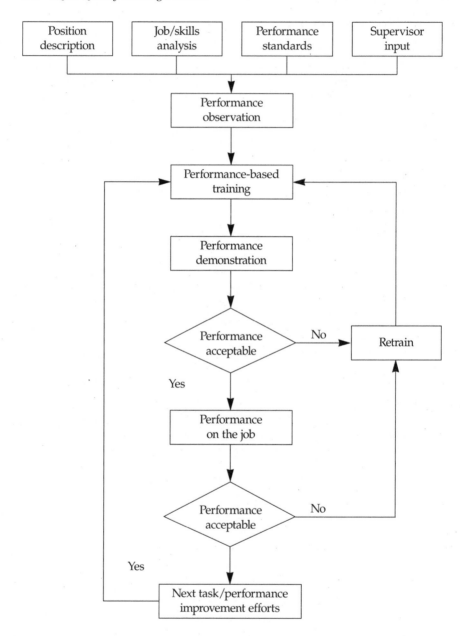

Figure 10.1   Performance-Based Training Flowchart

4. Evaluate and refine your original list. Flowcharts provide detailed look at the task breakdown. When another SME is available, ask that person to check the analysis.

5. Ask management to verify the analysis to ensure the task is completed the way it should be. There may be considerable difference between the way the task is being completed, previous job descriptions that may be available, and what management wants. These must be clarified before training.

6. Validation of the list with the people actually performing the task and their supervisors provides a check to determine if your observations are correct, process revisions have been made, and any performance levels outlined thus far are accurate.

7. Develop training criteria for the lesson. This involves grouping similar tasks together, placing them in a logical order, and planning a presentation sequence to cover the material the trainees need to learn at the correct level they must reach.

8. Compare the task analysis against established objectives, applicable specifications, and performance requirements.

Several potential training methods should be considered for performance-based training. The demonstration method is particularly well-suited for such efforts. Chapter 13 provides considerable guidance for these sessions.

Performance-based training should include a performance demonstration by each participant which includes those supervisors in attendance. Too often, supervisory personnel remain in the background so they won't be called on to demonstrate they have the know-how to do a certain job. This criteria should be discussed with supervisors before the training. In some cases they may want training apart from their workers. Supervisors, however, must be able to demonstrate a solid working knowledge of these skills. Those who cannot have a slim chance of being able to help workers improve their performance. Where possible, the supervisor should actually lead such training because nothing increases credibility more than successfully training others to perform tasks correctly.

Those individuals who cannot perform the task properly should receive additional training followed by another opportunity to demonstrate performance. At that time, those who cannot perform correctly may be in line for transfer to more appropriate duties. They cannot be allowed to negate the performance of their work team.

Demonstration does not complete the training cycle. On-the-job performance is what counts, and this must be observed over time to ensure the training actually increased job performance. Some individuals may be able to demonstrate performance during training situations and still experience difficulty in a production environment. This situation may force retraining efforts.

Many methods have been suggested in previous chapters to tie performance training to the bottom line. These provide guidance to measure payoff from the training which is the ultimate grading factor for training.

Knowledge-Type Training

Much of the initial training in any performance improvement program is knowledge based. Even topics such as problem solving and quality tools which are skills, when used, are handled in knowledge-type training sessions.

The first three volumes of this program provide detailed information, subject by subject, from which lesson plans can be developed. This knowledge-based material can be supplemented with in-house examples, works of other authors, and the trainers' personal experiences.

The remainder of this chapter is designed to assist trainers in their efforts to convert the information available into training programs utilizing formats which meet the training needs of each particular situation and organization. The sources of information listed will serve either knowledge- or skill-based training presentations.

Central Training Repository

At this time it is important for management to consider an aspect of training that is too often ignored. It is not enough to develop training materials. There must be a central repository for the training material that is controlled by some designated person for the storage of research material, aids, lesson plans, and so forth. Often the material and information gathered for one session will support others. Also, the lesson plans, student guides, and administrative material that support each session should be stored so they may be easily retrieved for future use. There is little time available for research and development that duplicates previously completed work.

Subject Matter Research

It is now time to begin researching the subject. This four-volume program provides the information needed to get most organizations started on the quality training program. At the end of all chapters there is a bibliography. These references provide additional useful information on each subject. Additionally, at the end of this volume there is a list that is divided into sections by subject matter. These books provide additional training tips, ideas, design sequences, and so forth. You may wish to purchase some of them for your organizational or personal library. Again, this series provides the information required to get the program off and rolling. Let's look at some additional places you can gather information for current topics and future lessons.

Libraries

Public libraries, state libraries, college libraries, and private libraries are all potential sources of information for the quality program. The 650 series contains information on every aspect of the quality equation including quality, leadership, management, training, and administrative subjects. It is important to browse through this section at the beginning of your research efforts in order to get acquainted with the types of works that are available. Later you can search for particular works in the computer or card system.

Certain private groups (such as trade organizations) also have libraries. If there is a quality organization in your area, someone in your organization might be a member. These groups may have books and other material that supports your program. Many of the members also have personal books they might lend. This contact provides an excellent avenue for contacting other professionals interested in quality programs.

Direct Mail

Training brochures and catalogs arrive in most organizations on a daily basis. Don't throw them away. A file of these should be maintained. Often they contain specific outlines that strongly support your efforts. They provide an insight on the way subject experts are handling the topic. They give indications of the directions the quality field is moving and provide potential for additional subject areas as your quality program progresses. You may need supplemental help as you progress and these organizations can provide it. There is the strong possibility that as your organization moves forward in the program, outside assistance will be required from professionals in particular subject areas.

There are many catalogs that contain training material in video or film format that can greatly assist your programs. More and more subjects are available on tape. The Juran Institute is an outstanding source of training and training supplies. Their catalog can be obtained by writing or calling The Juran Institute, Inc., 11 River Road, P.O. Box 811, Wilton, CT 06897-0811, (203) 834-1700.

ASQC
ASTD   yyn shoes

Bookstores and Book Clubs

Most large bookstores contain two sections that will be of value to you—the business and reference sections. Leadership and management books have long been a part of these sections. Lately some of the quality books are beginning to show up. An excellent source of reference books is the Executive Book Club. When added to bonus book possibilities, prices closely match bookstores that provide business discounts. At least someone, and preferably all those involved in the quality training efforts, will want to belong to the American Society for Quality Control (ASQC). ASQC has a large variety of offerings on the vast subject of quality in the form of courses, books, videos, and more.

Professional Organizations

Among the best of these is the aforementioned ASQC. This organization will support your program in invaluable ways. ASTD supports your training efforts and is thoroughly involved in many quality issues. The local chapter may have a subsection Technical Skills Training and Development (TSTD), which strongly supports quality training endeavors. Most of these organizations are listed in the local phone books. A call to them can pay great dividends.

Contacting Experts

Some organizations have quality staffs in place. Most of these have proven willing to provide assistance to organizations that are getting started in TQM. Organizations that have been actively pursuing the Malcolm Baldrige Award speak highly of other quality organizations that provided assistance.

If you are among the lucky ones, there may be an active Excellence Council or Quality Council in your area. Some of these groups provide cost-competitive training, volunteer consulting efforts, media libraries, and more. We worked for several years getting ours operational, and it has an excellent program for members.

The above three organizations, ASQC, ASTD, and TSTD, can provide various types of experts who may be contacted. Most people who are members of these professional organizations take pride in their networking ability and strongly desire to help others.

A few things should be considered when you call them. Plan your call or meeting in advance. Have written questions on specific interest areas. Keep calls or meetings short. Practice good listening techniques. Nothing will get you the bum's rush quicker than asking advice from someone and then refusing to let them answer you or contradicting what they say.

Developing Materials

Three types of materials were mentioned as being required to support a training program. These are discussed below.

Presentation Materials

Presentation materials are the materials used by the trainer or facilitator to present the subject. These include the lesson plan, required technical manuals, and media aids that will be used to support training. A good way to start is to take a lesson plan outline and begin filling in the sections with the material that has been gathered. An early step should be a decision of what kind of presentation best suits the material that must be presented. (There will be a section on this topic later.) Once all the possible holes have been filled, you have an excellent guide for gathering the remainder of the material.

Next, check the materials repository to see if any of the other material you need was previously researched by someone else. This may fill in more gaps. The appropriate manuals also should be secured at this time.

After internal sources are exhausted, a plan is developed to contact the appropriate sources from the list developed above. These should fill in the rest of your material needs.

Supporting Aids

Next, you must gather supporting aids. Aids are another area of training that are limited only by the imagination. Many of these may be actual equipment, simulators, and so forth. The chart that follows offers insight on some of the standard aids.

At this point it may appear that we are putting the cart ahead of the horse by discussing aids before lesson plan construction, and then lesson plan construction before methods of training. My formal indoctrination to training skills was an eight-week Navy instructor training school. We learned skills exactly opposite of the way this book covers them. Why was the order reversed?

Over the years I discovered that during the research for material, many potential aids also would be discovered. These later became integral parts of the training program. At other times the aids were the actual equipment that would be used. Knowing how to use the various aids and the relative advantages and disadvantages of each of them, helped build stronger sessions. It really doesn't make a lot of difference where they are placed in a book since aids are a stand-alone topic. Therefore, we decided to place them first to assist with the design of the actual training program. As aids become increasingly important in training decisions and programs, their relative importance will grow.

Media	Advantages	Disadvantages
Handouts	Provide reference material during and after training Excellent medium for lengthy or complex material Easy storage, reproduction, and revision Excellent support for other aids	Requires periodic review and update Requires revision of dated materials Reproduction quality is limited to the original
Chalkboard	Flexible and readily available Easily erased Good review device Pacing is controlled by instructor Great support for facilitator	Limited space available Easily erased by mistake Very predictable Messy Still media in a video world Small groups only
Easel/ easel tablets	Flexible and readily available Great review device Pacing controlled by instructor Pages can be saved as record	Predictable Penmanship problems Still media in a visual world Small groups only
Flipcharts and other displays	Prepared in advance Remain in order Reveal one point at a time Can display complicated items	Bulky to move Timely to construct Number of aids limited Small groups only
Overheads	Trainer faces group while in use Projector is in front of the room Room lights can remain on Varied techniques can be easily used	Bright stage may bother eyes Still media format Only transparent material be projected
Opaque projector	Projects color and form Projects originals directly Good for enlargements	Requires darkened room Bulky and noisy Heat may destroy the original Back may be to the room

Media	Advantages	Disadvantages
Slide projector	Can be used almost anywhere Rapidly display visual material Readily combined with other media Shows actual photographs	Slides can be expensive Requires development time Still media format
Films/videos	Films provide reality Creates motion and excitement Natural sound and color Material already is prepared Can compress or expand time	Usually expensive Films are quickly outdated Requires supplemental methods Sometimes difficult to adapt to current situation
Television and VCR	Easily records motion and sound in most environments Easily erased Instant playback Ideal for evaluation	Expensive to purchase Small screen unless expensive add-on equipment is purchased
Computer	Ready simulation of real-life situations Provides hands-on learning Immediate feedback	Expensive Not easily transportable Lengthy development time Generally not enough equipment to go around

Effective Use of Aids

There are advantages and disadvantages to each type of visual aid. Each adapts readily to certain situations and not so well to others. The knowledge of what works best, the time and assets available for training, the SMEs that will be available for additional assistance, and subject complexity all help plan effective use of aids.

A few general rules apply in all situations. Some are important enough that they are also included later under operating tips.

1. Focus on the audience, not the aid. Talk to the class, not to the aid.

2. Precheck all aids before the training session. Murphy's law states, "If something can go wrong, it will." Remove as many doubts as possible by prechecking.

3. Prepare an alternate plan of attack for all aids. This also assists in the explanation of difficult material should the aid not be enough.

4. Do not read visual aids to the audience. It is extremely frustrating to most participants. If your gut feeling says the material is too complex for some participants, it probably is the wrong aid to use. Allow participants time to read it to themselves and then discuss each item.

Media	Effective Operating Tips
Handout	1. Prepare handouts as a package that can be distributed before the training session begins. This minimizes confusion and allows the trainee to become familiar with the material before the session commences.
	2. Number all pages on handouts for easy reference. An index is recommended for all projects of any size. For quality projects, sessions should be given chapter numbers for easy reference.
	3. Three-hole punch or bind the material. This prevents the material from being lost and makes it easier to use.
Chalkboard	1. Remove information that is not relevant and clean the board before training sessions.
	2. Complex material and art work should be completed prior to training when possible.
	3. A lead pencil outline can be completed prior to class for material you wish to develop during class.
	4. Use a clean eraser and keep a damp towel handy to wipe your hands.
	5. Talk to the class, not to the chalkboard.
Flipchart	1. Develop complex material before sessions and number pages for easy reference during training.
	2. Place a blank sheet between each printed sheet to prevent distractions.
	3. Plan ahead and leave additional blank sheets in areas you plan to develop during training. Light pencil outlines assist in the development of complex diagrams.
	4. Position the easel for easy access and maximum student visibility.
	5. Use broad felt-tip markers and keep the caps on them when not in use.
	6. Talk to the class, not to the flipchart.

Media	Effective Operating Tips
Overhead projector	1. Save your lamp and prevent distraction by turning the lamp on when material is displayed and off when you are not using it.
	2. Transparencies are placed on the overhead as if you were reading them to the trainees.
	3. Have a small pointer and a few sizes of opaque material available. A pencil makes a good pointer to emphasize items on the transparency. Cardboard makes a good opaque to use for covering up portions of the transparency for effect.
	4. Use a print size that is large enough for the entire audience to read.
	5. Align the transparency and then face your audience. Talk to the class, not to the transparency.
Opaque projector	1. Use the lamp only during projection.
	2. Have someone ready to dim lights if you are not positioned to do so.
	3. Preposition the projector so that it correctly magnifies the material.
	4. Align the material and then face your audience. Talk to the class, not to the material.
Slide projector	1. Precheck for correct slide placement and order in the tray. Ensure proper operation and magnification.
	2. Remote controls are excellent when available.
	3. Have a spare projection lamp.
	4. Pretest for proper lighting.
Movies/ videos	1. Pretest for proper operation and when possible leave the equipment in a standby mode.
	2. In the case of movies, pretest for proper magnification.
	3. For videos, place the equipment for maximum effective viewing by the audience.
	4. If you plan to stop the equipment and discuss an idea, know the location ahead of time.
	5. Warn the audience about ideas and concepts alien to your organization before beginning.
	6. Have an alternate plan of attack should something go wrong.

Media	Effective Operating Tips
Computers	

Computers
1. Distribute prerequisite reading in sufficient time prior to the actual training meeting. Check to ensure understanding before commencing the training session.

2. Pretest for proper operation ahead of time.

3. Know who to call and where they are located should problems occur.

4. Have an alternate plan of attack should problems prevent using the equipment.

5. When required, have SMEs available to answer technical questions.

6. Plan for a maximum of three people per terminal, and one person is best.

Using Visuals

Visuals can add substantially to subject understanding. Remember, "a picture is worth a thousand words." Visuals also can be complicated and detract from the presentation. At times one gets the impression that visuals are used to show off or to display pretty colors. The following guide is intended as a checklist to determine if and when visuals are appropriate.

1. *Is it necessary?* Is a visual required to understand the presentation? Is the visual aimed at the particular audience? Do you have the time and facilities to use it? Is that portion of the presentation important enough for a visual? Is it planned to support or carry the presentation?

2. *Is it complementary?* Does the visual complement the presentation? Would words alone adequately describe the point you wish to make?

3. *Is it simple?* Does it make its point without excess symbols and words? Is it functional to explain a point rather than an ornate expression of art? Will one visual adequately explain the point or would overlays and multiple visuals work better? Is this visual suitable for this presentation?

4. *Is it readable?* Are the printing and graphics large enough? Is it clear enough for projection? Can it be seen from all areas of the room?

5. *Is it professional?* Is it neat? Are colors used effectively?

6. *Is it honest?* Are statistics correct? Have facts been distorted by the way they are presented? Is the picture presented correctly?

7. *Is it directed to the audience?* Does it benefit the audience? Is it used solely as support for the presenter? Is it an outline of the presentation or support for the presentation?

8. *Is it supportive of the objectives?* Is it needed to support improved skills? Does it support idea or behavior change? Can the audience understand the message?

Other Requirements

Support–It is mandatory to have organizational support from the top at the onset of the quality training effort. There must be some sort of support or there would have been no assessment effort. However, the support of all management personnel is required because their people will be called on as SMEs. They have to be willing to share the services of these people for some amount of time so they can meet both their job and training commitments. There is no sense in beginning the program without this support. Generally this does not become a problem once the need for quality training is established.

Budget–Training cannot be held without some assets, even though they may be limited at the onset. Therefore, a budget is a prerequisite for beginning the training evolution. Training personnel must ensure there is a proven training payoff that justifies their efforts so that training receives the emphasis required to continue performance improvement efforts.

Facilities–Some training will be held in the workplace, other sessions will take place in the classroom. Some type of training room must be made available for the training sessions if a special training facility is not available. Conference rooms are good choices provided they will seat the number of participants who are to be trained. Regardless of what the space is, there must be adequate seating. Attention also must be paid to the physical environmental factors such as heat, cold, noise, and interruptions. Any of these factors can negate training efforts and achievements.

Connections–The quality training program must be connected to the other programs within the organization. It won't do to have it at odds with other groups. For instance, if a training department is fighting the efforts of a quality team or management is fighting the efforts of either of these rather than supporting them, it spells disaster.

Summary

1. This chapter deals with the development of three kinds of training material: presentation material for use by the instructor, student material, and administrative material.

2. Much of the subject matter research is provided in this program's first three volumes. Other sources of information include libraries, direct-mail publications, bookstores, professional organizations, and SMEs.

3. The quality training program requires organizational support, a budget, training facilities, and a link to other programs.

4. Well-developed presentation materials must be prepared. These include lesson plans and training aids. Aids are used to support training and must be used correctly for maximum effect.

5. Visuals must support the presentation instead of being used in lieu of a presentation. They must be professional efforts and must support the objective.

Bibliography

Abella, K. T. *Building Successful Training Programs,* Reading, MA: Addison-Wesley, 1986.

Brinkerhoff, R. O. *Achieving Results from Training,* San Francisco: Jossey-Bass, 1987.

Carkhuff, R. R. and Pierce, R. M. *Training Delivery Skills, Part I,* Amherst, MA: Human Resource Development Press, 1984.

———. *Training Delivery Skills, Part II,* Amherst, MA: Human Resource Development Press, 1984.

Cassner-Lotto, J. and Associates. *Successful Training Strategies: Twenty-six Innovative Corporate Models,* San Francisco: Jossey-Bass, 1988.

Craig, R. L. (Ed.) *American Society for Training and Development, Training & Development Handbook,* New York: McGraw-Hill, 1976.

———. *Training and Development Handbook,* New York: McGraw-Hill, 1976.

Davis, L. N. and McCallon, E. *Planning, Conducting and Evaluating Workshops,* Austin, TX: Learning Concepts, 1975.

Eitenton, J. E. *The Winning Trainer,* Houston, TX: Gulf Publishing Company, 1984.

Engel, H. M. *Handbook of Creative Learning Exercises,* Houston, TX: Gulf Publishing, 1973.

Friedman, P. G. and Yarbrough, E. A. *Training Strategies from Start to Finish,* Englewood Cliffs, NJ: Prentice-Hall, 1985.

Kemp, J. E. *Planning and Producing Audiovisual Materials,* 3rd ed., New York: Thomas Y. Crowell, 1975.

London, M. *Managing the Training Enterprise,* San Francisco: Jossey-Bass, 1989.

Mitchell, G. *The Trainer's Handbook,* New York: American Management Association, 1987.

Proctor, J. H. and Thorton, W. M. *Training: A Handbook for Line Managers,* New York: American Management Association, 1961.

Note: Some of the chart material in this chapter is developed from material of various Navy instructor training programs.

CHAPTER 11

Constructing Training Materials

This chapter deals with the development of the materials for a training session. Three specific areas are covered: presentation material for use by the instructor, student material for use by the trainee, and administration material to properly administer the program. The road map of presentation material—the lesson plan—is presented first.

Developing Lesson Plans

Four separate types of lesson plans are discussed and developed. Each has relative advantages and disadvantages which will be compared on a chart. The four main choices are:

- Topical outline
- Manuscript
- Sentence
- Key word

The following important concepts apply to all lesson plans.

1. Lesson plans are crucial for training success.

2. Every subject must be adequately researched.

3. Develop twice as much material as you think you will need.

4. Ensure trainees know "what's in it for me" early on so they are motivated to learn.

5. Practice, practice, practice prior to presentation.

6. Use examples that pertain to the operation where possible.

7. Stimulate questions.

8. Use training aids.

9. Adopt the training to the groups level.

10. Never make excuses.

11. Remain positive.

12. Follow your lesson plan.

Each lesson plan should have an introduction, discussion, and summary. For brevity, the introduction and summary section examples are the same for each type of lesson plan. One similar to the one provided in the topical outline serves well for all of them.

The overall training time is established for participants in the introduction. For instructor purposes, time notes should be placed at the beginning of each section and at the beginning of each major point in the discussion. This reminder helps keep the presentation on track and provide the correct emphasis for each section. Actual discussion sections for each of these types follow.

Topical Outline Lesson Plan

The topical outline lesson plan is set up in a standard outline format. The major sections are identified by Roman numerals, topics by capital letters, with successive topics alternating between numbers and letters.

The following five-part topical outline lesson plan can be used for an in-house program for most training purposes. It corresponds to the lesson plans previously discussed with the summary section divided into three sections. The assignment section could be further divided into a testing section if desired. This sample contains a lesson on the construction of lesson plans.

"Title"

I. **INTRODUCTION**

    A. Greet class

        1. Give name/state lesson, and length of lesson.

        2. Pass out handouts.

        3. Present rules of class.

            a. No smoking (if that is the policy).

            b. Anyone can speak—one person at a time.

      c. No side conversations.

      d. Material presented in sequence.

      e. Questions welcome at any time.

      f. Due to time constraints and flow of lesson material, if the question:

         (1) Pertains to another lesson, it will be answered with that lesson or after class.

         (2) Is not applicable to the material, it will be answered on break or after class.

      g. No one has all the answers to any subject. All questions that cannot be answered in class will be researched. Present break schedule, if applicable.

    4. Encourage note-taking.

B. Overview/background–A standard lesson plan aids in material organization, prepares a presentation blueprint for the instructor, and provides for a proper review.

C. Need–Without a lesson plan, training tends to be haphazard and ineffective.

D. Reference material

    1.

    2.

    3.

E. Learning objectives–Upon completion of this session, you will have the ability to develop a lesson plan and a sample of a five-part lesson plan that will support your development of lesson plans.

F. Time: One 60-minute session

II. DISCUSSION

A. Basic types/uses

    1. Knowledge type–Academic material presented.

    2. Skill type–Craft material presented.

B. Construction.

    1. Recommend outline format.

    2. Five-part format presented here.

      a. Introduction

    b. Presentation

    c. Review or summary

    d. Application

    e. Assignment

3. Introduction

    a. Greet class.

        (1) Pass out handouts.

        (2) Provide class rules.

        (3) Encourage note-taking.

    b. Provide overview/background for training.

    c. Develop the need for this training.

    d. Present the reference material.

    e. Provide the learning objectives.

    f. Tell students time length of training session.

4. Presentation/discussion

    a. Introduce discussion.

    b. Provide overview.

    c. Explain the points.

    d. Present aids.

    e. During the lesson

        (1) Ask questions.

        (2) Seek participation.

        (3) Get students to answer other students' questions.

            (a) Can anyone answer John's question?

            (b) Sue, what do you think about Bill's comment?

        (4) Lesson plans should be personalized with notes, questions, and comments.

5. Review or summary

    a. Review objectives.

    b. Summarize main points.

    c. Question for understanding.

     d. An alternate form of review can be held by asking each participant to provide one idea picked up during the session. This provides ownership of the material.

    6. Application–This lesson will provide you with the knowledge and a usable outline to construct a basic lesson plan.

    7. Assignment (if any)

    8. Handouts (student handouts)

     a. Coincide with the lesson plan

     b. Level of detail depends on the topic and difficulty of material.

     c. Stresses the important points covered in the lesson.

III. REVIEW

  A. Types/uses of lesson plans

  B. Construction

    1. Introduction

    2. Discussion

    3. Review

    4. Application

    5. Assignment

  C. Personalizing

  D. Handouts

IV. APPLICATION–Use in developing your lesson plans.

V. ASSIGNMENT–None.

Manuscript Lesson Plan

The manuscript lesson plan provides a great deal of explicit data about the given topic. It is written to the depth the instructor believes necessary to answer most questions asked by trainees. This type is most often used when complex subjects will be taught and especially for the first time they will be instructed. It most readily adapts to the lecture–presentation method.

    This method is extremely useful when the instructor is unfamiliar with the material or the material is being prepared for use by many different instructors. Often main lesson plans developed by training groups are prepared in topical outline and then individual instructors personalize them in the form of topical outlines as they prepare to present the material.

Using the same information presented in the topical outline format, let's examine an abbreviated discussion section of a manuscript lesson plan.

II.   DISCUSSION

A. Basic types   This lesson considers two types of presentations that are classified according to use: the knowledge type and the skill type. The knowledge type of presentation is used whenever academic material is presented. Most quality subjects could be presented using this format. The skill type of presentation is used whenever craft material is presented. Most task-oriented presentations will use this format.

B. Construction   A five-part lesson plan format is recommended for the manuscript plan. These would include: (1) Introduction, (2) Discussion, (3) Review or Summary, (4) Application, and (5) Assignment.

      The introduction greets the class and introduces the instructor and the participants. Rules of the class are presented, an overview of the material is presented, the need and objectives are developed, reference material is discussed, and times are established.

      The discussion introduces the actual presentation through an overview of the material to be covered. The discussion then takes place with each point being explained in detail. Aids are presented which assist in the learning of these points. During the presentation the instructor asks questions and encourages participation. Students are encouraged to answer each other's questions where possible. Lesson plans are personalized ahead of time to add the instructor's experiences and knowledge that are not contained in the original plan.

      A review is conducted that summarizes the information that was presented. Questions can be answered to clarify points presented during the discussion.

      The application of this material to the actual work situation is covered next. Material with no immediate application should be avoided in training sessions.

      Any assignments should be provided after the application.

Sentence Lesson Plan

The sentence lesson plan provides a shortened method of the manuscript. It is used for less complex topics and to personalize manuscripts. Key points are determined and written out in sentence format.

II.   DISCUSSION

  A.
  • There are two basic types of presentations.

  • The knowledge type presents academic material.

  • The skill type presents craft material.

  B.
  • A five-part format is presented.

  • The five parts are the *introduction, discussion, review or summary, application,* and *assignment.*

  • The introduction greets the class, establishes rules, provides an overview, establishes needs and objectives, discusses reference material, and sets the time.

  • The presentation introduces the discussion, provides an overview, explains the separate points, presents aids, and seeks participation.

  • The review or summary reviews objectives, summarizes and clarifies main points, and answers questions.

  • The application tells how the material applies to the job.

  • The assignment presents any applicable assignment.

Key Word Lesson Plan

The key word lesson plan generally provides the key words the instructor needs to trigger his memory about the thoughts that need to be discussed. Knowledgeable instructors may use this plan for simpler subjects that they instruct often and about which they have a high degree of knowledge. Many topics that I instructed were presented in this manner. A few key points were outlined on a flipchart for two- or three-hour sessions. Many trainees like this format because it appears more informal. However, in each case, the material was well researched and longer plans were available if needed. Let's look at a sample.

II.   **DISCUSSION**

   A.

    • Two plan types

    • Knowledge

    • Skill

   B.   Five-part format

    • Introduction

    • Discussion

    • Review or summary

    • Application

    • Assignment

Comparing Lesson Plan Formats

Format	Advantages	Disadvantages
Topical outline	Easily constructed. Logically organized. Adapts to any size paper which allows movement in the training area. Can be made into flipcharts. Promotes trainee interaction.	Contains a brief sketch of the subject matter. Instructor must be well-versed on material. Requires more intense preparation prior to training.
Manuscript	Adapts to complex or lengthy presentations. Instructor has a great deal of readily available information The amount of information allows the instructor to have confidence she can answer questions that arise. Key words can be highlighted for easy reference.	Large volumes of information may make it difficult to locate a specific point. This format tempts instructors to read the material rather than present it. Development time is considerably longer. Trainees may be apprehensive when instructor shows up with a six-inch stack of papers.

Format	Advantages	Disadvantages
Sentence	Provides information at a glance during instruction. Key words can be high-lighted and easily referred to during training. Instructor can more easily read notes without giving herself away. Easy to construct. Compact.	More limited in amount of information available. Format does not lend itself to handling information in a sequence that was not preplanned.
Key word	Easy to develop. Flexible to use. No worry about getting out of sequence. Easy to follow. Provides for an informal presentation. Encourages participation.	The instructor must be very knowledgeable. Requires more advance preparation. Provides little information for follow-up training by instructors.

Personalizing Lesson Plans

Regardless of what type lesson plan is used, it must be personalized for the instructor who uses it. Without this effort, training sessions tend to be cold, dull, and boring. A small investment in time at this point pays big dividends during the actual sessions.

The session should match the people who will receive the training. Observations of the workplace and discussions with supervisors provide many of the best examples. Your personal experiences also are good sources. There often are parts of lessons you know will be challenged. Be prepared! Present testimonies and back-up opinions of experts, SMEs, and/or people the training group can identify with and respect. Such examples often preclude input from the argumentative individual who seems to go to training for one reason—to contradict whatever the trainer has to say.

Developing Student Materials

Student materials promote active student participation to some level which is in contrast to presentation materials that allow them to have a passive role. Workbooks, handouts, reference material, charts, questionnaires, and critique sheets are all student materials that promote activity. Self-paced and computer-based programs demand a great deal of student activity and less activity from the instructor, while simulators and actual equipment require an active participation by both instructor and trainee.

The student materials discussed here are of the handout variety because self-based and computer-based training generally is advanced past the material of a beginning quality program. In the case of a task such as building assemblies from breadboards, the material should be provided to the students complete with all the equipment necessary for the instruction. Large organizations like AMP, Inc., have electronics, electromechanical, hydraulic, and pneumatic simulator packages made up in kits so they can be easily transported to manufacturing sites for training. This prevents the expense and interruptions that occur when workers must travel to a central site.

Handouts are prepackaged in the order of need. They are then prepunched or bound. Participants should receive notebooks for prepunched materials. The materials should be numbered by page and chapter (where chapters are appropriate divisions).

Professional handouts set the stage for solid training sessions. Trainees are impressed when the material is well-done and a notebook is provided on the spot so they can keep their materials in order. The handouts Quality America, Inc., provides attendees (unless it is otherwise specified by the host) are completed outline lesson plans. This allows the students to return to their organizations and hold identical training without a huge investment in research time. During the training sessions they can personalize their lesson plans with the input from other students, the results of various class exercises, and the material presented by the instructor that would not normally be a part of the handouts.

This method works in an outstanding manner during practice. Students aren't forced to take copious notes and miss a good part of the presentation, and they still have the material they need.

A quiz or exam designed to test learning objectives should be prepared where it is appropriate. The test should cover the material presented to the degree that was decided by the objectives. Course critiques and evaluations are important parts of the program. These can be given at the end of a program or at the end of each section of training. Every training session should have some form of evaluation. The evaluation can be developed using the same grading criteria presented for the assessment. A simpler method also can be used such as the sample that follows.

1.   The level of information presented was:

   a. too difficult

   b. too easy

   c. just about right

2. This session covered:
   a. too much information
   b. too little information
   c. just about the right amount of information
3. The pace of this course was:
   a. too fast
   b. too slow
   c. just about right
4. The handouts were:
   a. excellent
   b. OK
   c. poor
5. These handouts will be:
   a. valuable
   b. useful
   c. worthless
6. The instructor was:
   a. well-prepared
   b. prepared
   c. poorly prepared
7. The training aids:
   a. greatly assisted learning
   b. assisted learning
   c. wasted time
8. More time should be spent on _____
9. Less time should be spent on _____
10. What do you recommend to improve this course?

Evaluations should be collected and reviewed by training personnel after each session. They also should be reviewed by the appropriate managers so they may assist in improving this quality program. They will ascertain ways to improve their vision of quality while they study perceptions of the program.

Administrative Material

Earlier a training schedule and a master training plan were discussed. Other materials also will be required for the correct administration of a quality program.

There should be a roster for every training session. This is easily handled by a form that is passed around for each trainee to sign. At the top of the form the title of the lesson and the date is entered by the instructor and then the employees sign it and add their employee number. This form is collected before the training is concluded and used to prepare an individual training record. Figure 11.1 serves as an example.

Title _____ Date _____

Instructor _____ Length _____

Name	Emp. #	Name	Emp. #

Figure 11.1 Training Attendance Record

Participants should be encouraged to maintain a personal record of their training. This assists in the routine update of their resumés while it serves as an ongoing reminder of the training received. The organization also should keep an individual record of training. We recommend that a simple computer program be used that has each individual entered by name and employee number. Following each session, some designated person enters the title of the presentation, date training was held, and length of the training.

These records assist both the organization and its employees. The organization can use it as a record for apprenticeship programs. Many industries now require subcontractors to carry out quality training. The federal government plans to require documented proof of quality training as a grading factor for bids. It also provides a certain measure of accountability. Employees can be held accountable to use training they have received. It was previously discussed how it helps the employees so everyone comes out a winner.

There also should be a form attached to each master lesson plan that shows the date it was used, by whom, and for what group. It should have a place for initials and comments concerning updating or revising the material. Figure 11.2 serves as an example of this form.

Subject _____
Developed by _____
Date _____ Suggested audience _____
Related material located under other titles or different documents _____
_____
_____
_____

Other recommended reference material _____
_____
_____
_____

Other recommended training aids _____
_____
_____

Presented by (Note: each person who presents this training is requested to log their
name, the date presented, to whom, and any comment) _____

Trainer _____ Date _____
Audience_____
Comments _____
_____
_____
_____

Trainer _____ Date _____
Audience_____
Comments _____
_____
_____

Trainer _____ Date _____
Audience_____
Comments _____
_____
_____

Trainer _____ Date _____
Audience_____
Comments _____
_____
_____

Figure 11.2   Lesson Plan Tracking Sheet

Material Validation

All training materials should be validated before they are used. This may be a simple process in which SMEs study the material for content and proper development. They would evaluate the material to ensure it met the established objectives, was clear and concise, technically correct, and appropriate for the trainee levels that would attend. They would recommend any changes required to clear up confusing issues, additions, and deletions.

Seasoned instructors should evaluate the material to ensure that instructor and trainee material have the same contents, and that consistency is maintained throughout. They should also check for relevance to the overall program and the needs of the designated employees.

Summary

1. Four types of lesson plans were discussed and samples developed: topical outline, manuscript, sentence, and key word. The relative advantages and disadvantages of each were compared on a chart.

2. Student materials also must be developed to encourage student participation. These may include workbooks, handouts, reference material, charts, questionnaires, tests, and evaluation forms.

3. Administrative material is developed to administer the program and record results. These records are valuable for both the organization and the employee.

4. Material should be validated before it is used. SMEs and seasoned trainers can conduct this validation.

Bibliography

Abella, K. T. *Building Successful Training Programs*, Reading, MA: Addison-Wesley, 1986.

Brinkerhoff, R. O. *Achieving Results from Training*, San Francisco: Jossey-Bass, 1987.

Carkhuff, R. R. and Pierce, R. M. *Training Delivery Skills, Part I*, Amherst, MA: Human Resource Development Press, 1984.

―――. *Training Delivery Skills, Part II*, Amherst, MA: Human Resource Development Press, 1984.

Cassner-Lotto, J. and Associates. *Successful Training Strategies: Twenty-six Innovative Corporate Models*, San Francisco: Jossey-Bass, 1988.

Craig, R. L. (Ed.) *American Society for Training and Development, Training & Development Handbook*, New York: McGraw-Hill, 1976.

———. *Training and Development Handbook*, New York: McGraw-Hill, 1976.

Davis, L. N. and McCallon, E. *Planning, Conducting and Evaluating Workshops*, Austin, TX: Learning Concepts, 1975.

Eitenton, J. E. *The Winning Trainer*, Houston, TX: Gulf Publishing Company, 1984.

Friedman, P. G. and Yarbrough, E. A. *Training Strategies from Start to Finish*, Englewood Cliffs, NJ: Prentice-Hall, 1985.

Kemp, J. E. *Planning and Producing Audiovisual Materials*, 3rd ed., New York: Thomas Y. Crowell, 1975.

London, M. *Managing the Training Enterprise*, San Francisco: Jossey-Bass, 1989.

Mitchell, G. *The Trainer's Handbook*, New York: American Management Association, 1987.

Proctor, J. H. and Thorton, W. M. *Training: A Handbook for Line Managers*, New York: American Management Association, 1961.

CHAPTER 12

Training in Action

Training methods must match training needs. This chapter provides several different training methods, each of which has a time and place where it excels. The major training methods are discussed after a brief introduction to instructional control. This topic will be picked up again in subsequent chapters.

Three approaches have been identified for instructional control: learner centered, instructor centered, and material centered. In all of them, the person who develops and presents the material determines the level of material which will be available. The direction and pace of instruction can vary in all of them. The instructor varies the pace in the first two and the trainee varies it in self-paced instruction. Until recently, most material was instructor-centered. The correct method to use under which circumstances remains open to debate.

1. *Learner-centered instruction*–Learner-centered instruction or training has gained a great deal of popularity in recent years. Many believe this came out of the demand college students made on institutions about the things they wanted to learn and how they wanted to learn them. Regardless of how it has come about, it is not a new concept. The Greeks studying under Socrates used this method to some degree.

   This concept is developed to a greater degree later. Contrary to the opinions of many, we believe this method supports most types of instruction with the possible exception of computer-based and self-paced training. You may make up your mind after covering the section on adult learning.

The hesitancy to accept this concept as king is largely based on a fear that class control will be lost. Each group of students arrives at training with different background experiences, attitudes, knowledge, and skills. These differences could present control or time-pacing problems under some conditions. It is believed, however, that these become nonproblems when the instructor is aware of them ahead of time and then prepares properly. The choice is whether we want to control the tempo of training (the one size fits all concept), or do we want to ensure that each group of students takes away those things most needed to meet the established objectives. If the latter is desired, learner-centered instruction should be the first method considered.

2. *Instructor-centered instruction*–The instructor determines the direction and pace in instructor-level training. Good instructors soon pick up the proper pace through student interaction and then provide the level of detail the instructor believes is important.

    SMEs may become instructor centered whether they plan to or not. They have a tremendous amount of knowledge about the subject and get caught up in the act of dumping it all on participants instead of providing them with the required amount.

    Most computer-based training is instructor centered. The program attempts to simulate certain conditions just as an instructor would. Only the most advanced simulators approach material-centered instruction.

3. *Material-centered instruction*–Usually self-paced instruction is material centered. The materials control the direction, pacing, and detail. Material-centered training is an excellent choice under some circumstances. There can be problems when it is pushed past its limits.

    For a period of time, the Navy chose self-paced training backed up by a live trainer in some of their programs. Economics played a major role in this decision. The technicians reporting to the fleet were found lacking in critical technical areas. It was the opinion of the experts that this problem stemmed from the absence of classroom interaction inherent in the self-paced programs.

Training Methods

Training methodology is an extremely important consideration in the training process. Several methods are discussed, and all of these can be effective in a quality training program when they are matched to training need. They are presented as stand-alone methods but in actuality, few are. They are combined to cover each topic most effectively. This discussion provides the understanding of methodology that promotes development of training sessions that meet established objectives.

Lecture

The lecture method is one of the best ways to convey pure information. Organizational directives, procedures, and so forth, fit the lecture method. A sermon is basically a lecture. It is probably the most often used, yet least effective, method of instruction after OJT. Much of the problem stems from lecture length and lack of supporting aids.

The audience's attention span limits the effective time in the lecture method. Lectures for high school students probably have an effective length of 15 minutes. Adults may add 5 minutes or so to the total, and college grads may have an attention span of up to 30 minutes. The effective range of lectures and the attention span are similar.

Considerations

1. Plan for maximum time utilization.
2. Consider covering one point only for greatest effectiveness with two points being the maximum.
3. Get directly to the point you wish to make.
4. Leave out all material that does not directly support the point you are making. Don't wander around the point.
5. Plan for examples, stories, cause-and-effect relationships, and other ways to hammer home the message.
6. Formulate questions to maintain focus on the point.
7. Provide practical application immediately after you make the point.

Presentation

The presentation method is an informal lecture. The difference is that effective presentations plan for considerable student interaction, while in the lecture method interaction is more incidental. Lectures are supported with other instructional methods and various aids, which make them an effective tool. When the presentation is developed to be learner centered, it becomes even more effective.

Because of the interaction and supporting materials, the presentation method has a much longer effective time. When accompanied by breaks and solid aids supported by other instructional methods such as case studies, multiday presentations are powerful. Many quality seminars are three days to a week in length and feature the presentation method of instruction.

Certain pitfalls must be avoided. A major concern must be pacing. One of the biggest problems that occurs in presentations is spending too much time in some areas, leaving little time for others. When this happens, the instructor's tendency is to dump the information at the end which negates much of the earlier success that might have been enjoyed. Another problem is inattention to learner needs. People learn by what they do, not what the instructor does. Keep them involved. Strive for continuous feedback throughout the presentation. This can come through trainee eye contact and attitudes, questions and comments from trainees, and response to your questions. Failure to stay tuned to the audience ruins the best planned presentations. Spontaneous reaction to participant observations and questions becomes a strong part of the seasoned trainer's presentation.

Considerations

1. The considerations under the lecture method apply to some degree. Items 5 through 7 are especially applicable.

2. Understand what the learning objectives are and how best to present the material to meet them. Remain focused to need.

3. Develop an effective lesson plan that meets the need and objectives. Plan for a direct route to the objectives.

4. Plan to act as a facilitator during parts of the session. Ensure that the material is learner centered. Maintain lecture portions of the presentation to 10 or 15 minutes.

5. Make use of appropriate aids to support the presentation. Handouts are extremely important in most presentations.

6. Use other instructional methods such as discussions and case studies where they support the presentation.

7. Prepare a solid introduction and summary to open and close the session. The first few minutes in the introduction often set the stage for presentation success or failure. The summary period will cement the material together and provide any information required for the next session.

8. Practice ahead of time. Remain tuned to your appearance and presentation skills, such as tone of voice and modulation, pace, and gestures. These skills are more important in lectures and presentations than in other methods.

Discussion

The discussion or question-and-answer method serves many purposes. Questions are posed which stimulate thinking to reach the training objectives. Excellent use is made of the trainee's attitudes, experiences, and knowledge because it maximizes participant interaction.

This method allows old ground to be covered rapidly when it is desired. New material can be interjected and tested for understanding. Closed-ended questions that can be answered with a "yes" or "no" should be avoided, replaced by the open-ended questions that promote participation. Open-ended questions begin with and answer the who, what, why, when, and how questions.

Another variation of the discussion method is the panel discussion that allows debate between subject matter experts. Often these provide for interaction with the audience at some point in the program.

Small group discussion is another way to utilize the discussion method. This process greatly supports presentations. The audience can be divided into smaller groups to discuss issues, ideas, case studies, processes, operations, and so forth. This is extremely important as a learning process because the trainee is interacting, which is the main way people learn.

At some predetermined time, the small teams regroup to present their findings. This is another learning experience.

Problems can arise if the attempt is made to use the discussion method purely for the presentation of new material or facts. This quickly dampens interactions, voiding the benefits of this method. Problems also can arise when a vocal minority are allowed to dominate the discussion. Few other people care to participate when this occurs. A major problem is that it sets precedence for more of the same and discourages others from attending followup sessions. Taking this a step further, promoting one-on-one discussions between the leader and another person is even worse than domination by a few. Issues must be developed that preclude this situation.

Considerations

1. Develop sound questions ahead of time that meet learning objectives. Questions for questions' sake accomplishes little.

2. Anticipate the answers and be prepared to provide new insights, examples, and additional information.

3. Practice until you are skilled in this method. It is extremely important in the quality program, especially in fixing problems and developing processes. The "what if . . . ?" becomes essential.

4. Provide for participation by all trainees. Never dominate the discussion and prevent domination by others because it deters success. Strive to remain impartial in the discussion, remembering you cannot jeopardize organizational needs by remaining silent on incorrect statements or judgments.

5. Control off-track discussions that do not lead toward the objectives. There is a thin line between this control need and intimidating the discussion.

6. This method can easily get out of hand. It is important to protect the rights of all participants and the organization while maintaining order at all times.

7. Recognize when the discussion has run its useful course. Summarize the discussion and switch to other methods or close the session.

Team Training

Team training is an important concept for quality training. It provides for the integration of SMEs in the training process in other than the lead role. There is the possibility of the synergistic process increasing training effectiveness, plus the potential for delivery of a great deal more information than one trainer could present.

There also is the possibility of the opposite taking place. Disagreement between the instructors can destroy the session. Time may be wasted as they determine what to do and how to do it. Or they can carry on discussions that have little relevance to the subject at hand.

Considerations

1. Select instructors carefully so their styles are mutually supportive.

2. Develop ground rules ahead of time and secure agreement on them from all trainers.

3. Divide the assignments prior to the training session to ensure that each person realizes what role he plays in the session.

4. Thoroughly discuss the subject prior to the session. This brings out areas of possible contention so that some sort of agreement can be reached prior to the session.

5. After the discussion, allow the trainers to decide if they are still in agreement on training as a team.

Case Studies

Case studies may be used as self-supporting training sessions or to support other methods of training. Case studies provide a situation with certain facts. The participants are then encouraged to discuss the facts using their knowledge of the subject so they can come to an agreement on the case.

This method is used to support other training methods. The final outcome or decision may not be as important as the process used to reach the outcome.

Problems can arise if the material is not carefully selected or is missing important bits of information required for sound conclusions. A proper introduction is mandatory and the problem must be well defined, as well as the situation in which the problem resides. Another requirement is a summary that outlines the conclusion through the process used to arrive at that decision.

Considerations

1. Ensure that the cases support the learning objectives, which should also govern the level of difficulty.

2. Make sure all the important details are included in the case.

3. Predetermine possible solutions or outcomes to the case. This requires that you also have the reasons why this solution is correct. Quality subjects should support or provide the logic for the decision.

4. Discuss basic problem-solving techniques with the trainees before beginning the cases. Too often participants are sidetracked with nonproblems.

5. Serve as a resource person who can answer questions that arise. This means the instructor must remain in the area during the case study.

6. Help the participants consider alternate solutions in terms of performance, customer service, and other quality issues.

7. Provide a proper introduction and summary.

Role-Playing

Role-playing is another effective training method, most often used in a supportive role for other methods. It allows participants to work together in real-world situations akin to those they may face in the workplace.

Similar to case studies, role-playing must be preplanned. Both the situations and the roles must be realistic. Fantasy situations quickly lead to participant dissatisfaction.

Considerations

1. Ensure the role situation supports the training objectives.

2. Establish characters to prove a point that is important to the training. Perhaps they must use a skill that is being taught.

3. Illustrate a single problem with each situation. The use of multiple problems may confuse the issue.

4. Endeavor to keep the players on track toward a proper solution. The audience can become lost when they get off track or lag.

5. Always ensure the situation is properly introduced. At the conclusion, summarize the results that have been obtained and discuss how they meet the established objectives.

Games

Games are utilized as supportive training. They can be used as icebreakers or to demonstrate a situation. When used correctly, participants appreciate them.

In fact, unless reminded, participants often get so involved they forget the purpose of the game.

Games can be used in all types of situations. They can test skills and retention, apply pressure situations to test for understanding of the material, or stimulate behavior that tests understanding of material. Each of these applications are valid uses of games.

One warning concerning games: Games carry the potential for problems when they are used as gimmicks or games are played for games sake. Games may grow old rapidly for many participants. Once is more than enough for some people.

Considerations

1. Ensure that the games support the established objectives.

2. Schedule games for periods when attention may suffer. Right after lunch and toward the end of the day are two times to consider.

3. Many training books outline games that can be played in various situations. Use these to provide ideas for creating your own games. There is a good chance that games published in books already have been used by some participants.

4. Don't overdo games. One game a day is more than enough. There are plenty of other training techniques to support your material.

5. Provide a proper introduction and summary. Make sure participants understand how the game relates to training objectives and the conclusions that can be drawn because of the game's outcome.

Other Training Methods

The demonstration method will be considered in Chapter 13 in conjunction with on-the-job training. Computer-aided training and programmed instruction also will be discussed to a more limited degree. Programmed instruction is simple in concept and will not be developed as a part of initial quality training.

Method	Advantages	Disadvantages
Lecture	Saves time. Special facilities not required. Readily adaptable to convey various information.	Limited attention span of participants. Limited to one or two points. Requires careful planning. No room for extraneous information. Usually quite formal.

Method	Advantages	Disadvantages
Presentation	Adaptable to most time constraints. Can be used to provide new information or clarification of standing information. Readily adaptable to support other training methods. Excellent method to convey factual material. Provides for easy transition to other training methods. Readily adaptable to large audiences.	Instructor carries the major burden of training. Easily becomes trainer centered, rather than learner centered. Trainees are easily bored. Students can become saturated with information. Information may need to be supplemented by aides and other training methods. Instructors may not allow for interaction.
Discussion	Encourages participation, involvement, and interaction. Stimulates peer learning. Provides a forum to use the knowledge and experience of all participants. Provides for a quick review of previous information. Excellent forum for discussion of issues. Provides a means to determine attitudes and feelings about the subject. Fosters team relationships.	Some participants may attempt to dominate. Sometimes difficult to steer and control. All members may not get to participate. Instructor may end up as a peacekeeper, rather than a guide. Easy to lose sight of the learning objectives. May showcase opinions more than facts or knowledge. High potential for interpersonal conflicts.
Team training	Presence of varied styles, ideas, and experiences. Synergistic effect can greatly enhance the level and quality of training. Trainers support each other. Great way to break in trainers.	More expensive. May foster open disagreement between instructors. Requires a good deal of preplanning to ensure agreement on key issues, and correct roles for each instructor.
Case studies	Excellent method to demonstrate performance.	Requires considerable development time and effort.

Method	Advantages	Disadvantages
	Versatile in that it can be used in all size groups or as homework. Creates a real-world situation without real-world penalties. Promotes teamwork. Build problem-solving skills.	Trainees may lose sight of the training object. May encourage unreal solutions because there is no penalty for incorrect solutions. The real problem may be overlooked or the problem may be oversimplified.
Role-playing	Promotes trainee interaction. Provides a method to use concepts taught in class. Allows participants to handle situations in their own way. Encourages participant creativity.	Requires considerable development time and effort. Easy to lose sight of training objectives. Can handle only one key point at a time. Easy for participants to get off the subject.
Games	Promotes participation and interaction. Makes learning fun. Provides a ready forum to test retention, recall, skills, and efforts under pressure. Promotes learning at difficult times such as after lunch. Provide a common learning experience.	Easy to lose sight of objectives. Games are easily overdone. Preparing games requires a certain amount of creativity. Requires considerable preplanning. Sometimes used under conditions that do not support game playing.

Team Training Exercises

The considerable turn toward TQM puts significant emphasis on training work groups as teams. It proves extremely effective, but then why wouldn't it? Professional sports teams don't practice all week as individuals and then try to get it together during the game—they practice and play as a unit.

Team training exercises using simulators prove to be quite like the actual operation with the addition of an instructional team present to monitor the exercises. When they are held in the actual workplace they are handled in the same manner. In practice, the more real the training situation turns out to be, the better the results will be when measured against the bottom line.

Team training is beneficial as an exercise when individuals must function together as a work team because of certain team dynamics that occur. These are important to recognize and build on in training situations.

1. The team members' shared purpose is to meet their operation's goals.

2. The have a known membership which is defined as the members of "our team."

3. They share a common team identification because they are members of this particular team. There is a great payoff in monogrammed team jackets as recognition of their excellence.

4. They share a feeling of interdependence because they are all in it together. The team can only achieve to the level of the weakest link. This factor often spurs all members to try harder during team training exercises—they don't want to let the team down.

5. They share a team relationship which increases the ability to communicate, provides support for team members, and influences the actions of individuals.

6. They carry a sense of self-discipline based on the needs of the team.

7. They share a feeling of unity based on interdependence and trust. This allows them to react as a single unit rather than a group of individuals.

8. They thrive on team recognition because each individual willingly gives up a share of his or her personal identity to become a team member.

Program Evaluation

Program evaluation is a continuous part of the quality training program. For accurate measurement, the evaluation system must be broad based and ongoing, with sampling conducted in all parts of the organization. Let's consider some of the ways to ascertain results.

Tests

Many different kinds of testing scenarios are possible. Narrative, essay, multiple choice, and true or false tests are all considerations for evaluating individual sessions of the training program. Performance on case studies could be another test for participants. Attitudes and knowledge can be discovered through the resulting discussion of solutions. Performance tests measure production and quality improvements on the work floor whether that work floor be manufacturing or the administrative offices. These can include everything from machinery operations to typing tests.

Critiques and Course Evaluations

These documents contain considerable insight into and information about participant perceptions of the training program. These must be carefully critiqued by the person responsible for the quality program. Observations that result from evaluating these sheets should be shared with trainers and others involved in the program.

Observations

In many cases, training cannot simulate actual work activities, nor can training solve all performance problems. This is especially true in the short run. Attitudes are not easily changed. Many of the situations that exist in the workplace in all organizations are multiple-cause problems which take time to correct. This brings us to observations.

Impromptu observations provide a sound method to study the workplace as things actually are happening. The way people perform their work activities, their preparation for tasks, the way they interact with other workers, and their attitudes are more readily apparent in this type of observation. These are important in program evaluations.

Scheduled observations provide a different look at the workplace. Employees have the benefit of knowing the observation will take place, which allows them to prepare. Most of them perform their work the way they *believe* it should be performed. Their ability to prepare for and carry out the task, their interpersonal skills, and the attitude they *believe* is desired will be evident in their work efforts.

There may be little difference between these observations. In this case the people or team being observed could be considered as true professionals who take a great deal of pride in what they do. In most cases there will be some difference between the way tasks are generally performed and the way they are completed when people know ahead of time that they will be observed. At least you will know if they understand how to do things correctly and what is expected of them in terms of performance. In this case the difference could be considered one of attitude. (In other sections of this program ways have been discussed to improve attitudes.)

At times the differences may be startling. Training will not solve this problem. Personal interviews may be desired to see if a determination can be made as to why this difference between actual and desired performance exists. As much as it may hurt, there are times when a change of work address is the only way these problems can be addressed.

Performance

No area has more potential to measure success than that of performance. After all, performance improvements and improved quality customer service are the main driving forces of the quality program. Therefore, these areas should be continuously monitored to determine what effect the training program is playing in performance improvement efforts.

Normal organizational statistics can be monitored to ascertain if these measures show performance increases. From these indicators, an intuitive decision must be made concerning what part training held in the success.

In the case of training for specific systems or operations, training payoff is easier to measure. Did training do the job or didn't it?

There are numerous other factors involved in improved performance. Is leadership providing the correct model for improvement? Are management practices supportive of the training program? Is there a reward system that encourages performance improvements. All of these factors must be continually monitored since training seldom is a stand-alone force in the quality program.

Corrective Action

Few programs run without the requirement for corrective action. Certainly the training program is no different. Continuous monitoring practices provide a number of areas that can be improved. At this point, the entire process begins again to sustain continuous performance improvement efforts.

One or more of the organizational objectives may require change. Some level of reassessment might take place to either confirm original finds or pave the way for additional change requirements. Operational audits may examine process changes, restructuring certain operations, or personnel changes.

Training changes might be in order. Additional training or training in other areas may be posed. Training for the trainers is another possibility. Program design is a never-ending possibility as the program matures. Outside training help might be requested. Creative ways must be developed to hold people accountable for the training they receive. Simultaneously, the work environment must be prepared to accept the positive changes which can only occur through training.

These possibilities are just a few that might turn up as the quality program evolves. Continuous monitoring, training, assessment, improvement, and change cycle are the guts of the quality evolution, and so the cycle continues. The best part of it all is that each roll of the quality cycle produces additional improvements for organizations that are truly tuned to quality.

Summary

1. Instructional control can be considered in three ways: learner-centered, instructor-centered, or material-centered training.

2. There are many different methods of conducting training. Some of them are stand-alone methods, and others are more suited to supportive roles. Those methods discussed in this chapter are: lecture, presentation, discussion, team, case studies, role-playing, and games.

3. A comparison chart presented the relative advantages and disadvantages of each training type that was discussed.

4. Program evaluation is an important ongoing process in the quality training program. Tests, critiques, evaluations, observations, and performance are all methods of evaluating success.

5. Continuous corrective action supports an ever-improving training program. Training, objectives, operations, processes, and perhaps even personnel, may need to be changed in the never-ending quest to improve performance and customer quality service.

Bibliography

Abella, K. T. *Building Successful Training Programs,* Reading, MA: Addison-Wesley, 1986.

Brinkerhoff, R. O. *Achieving Results from Training,* San Francisco: Jossey-Bass, 1987.

Carkhuff, R. R. and Pierce, R. M. *Training Delivery Skills, Part I,* Amherst, MA: Human Resource Development Press, 1984.

———. *Training Delivery Skills, Part II,* Amherst, MA: Human Resource Development Press, 1984.

Cooper, S. and Heenan, C. *A Humanistic Approach,* Boston, MA: CB Publishing, 1980.

Craig, R. L. (Ed.) *American Society for Training and Development, Training & Development Handbook,* New York: McGraw-Hill, 1976.

———. *Training and Development Handbook,* New York: McGraw-Hill, 1976.

Davis, L. N. and McCallon, E. *Planning, Conducting and Evaluating Workshops,* Austin, TX: Learning Concepts, 1975.

Eitenton, J. E. *The Winning Trainer,* Houston, TX: Gulf Publishing Company, 1984.

Ellis, S. K. *How to Survive a Training Assignment*, Reading, MA: Addison-Wesley, 1988.

Engel, H. M. *Handbook of Creative Learning Exercises*, Houston, TX: Gulf Publishing, 1973.

Hamblin, A. C. *Evaluation and Control of Training*, New York: McGraw-Hill, 1974.

Kearsley, G. *Computer-based Training, A Guide to Selection and Implementation*, Reading, MA: Addison-Wesley, 1983.

Kemp, J. E. *Planning and Producing Audiovisual Materials*, 3rd ed., New York: Thomas Y. Crowell, 1975.

King, D. *Training Within the Organization*, London: Tavistock Publications, 1964.

Kirkpatrick, D. L. *Evaluating Training Programs*, Madison, WI: American Society for Training and Development, 1975.

London, M. *Managing the Training Enterprise*, San Francisco: Jossey-Bass, 1989.

Mitchell, G. *The Trainer's Handbook*, New York: American Management Association, 1987.

Pfeiffer, J. W. and Jones, J. E. *A Handbook of Structured Experiences for Human Relations Training* (Volumes I–VI), LaJolla, CA: University Associates, 1974–1979.

Phillips, J. J. *Handbook of Training Evaluation and Methods*, Houston, TX: Gulf Publishing, 1982.

Rogoff, R. L. *The Training Wheel*, New York: John Wiley and Sons, 1987.

CHAPTER 13

On-the-Job Training

OJT remains the most often used type of training in America. Estimates indicate upward of 75 percent of the total training attempted uses this method. There are many potential advantages of OJT because it takes place in the work environment. Some of the most obvious advantages include effectiveness, because the training generally takes place on the same equipment, operations, or processes used in the day's work. There is immediate application and feedback on training success, and it's practical because "it's the job."

None of these, however, guarantees success. In fact, when the potential of OJT is compared to its general success or the resulting performance improvements, the results are not encouraging. What could be the causes?

A Realistic Look at OJT

The first problem is that most OJT is conducted by a work supervisor or a designated employee who may or may not complete training to the accepted standard. Each of these developed a personal way of completing the task that incorporates that person's idiosyncrasies along with personal likes and dislikes. He does the task his own way, not some approved standard way with quality procedures. It may be completely different from the method all of the other people doing this or similar tasks perform the operation, but it works for him (or at least someone perceives that it does). Without working to the standard, however, who can actually determine if it is completed correctly?

Thus armed with "my personal way of doing it," an individual tackles the job of training another person on the task. There is no way this process can be under control when there are no standard processes or quality standards in place. Even worse, there is no way to improve performance in a process that is not standardized.

The second problem impacting OJT is that the training often is unplanned; it just happens to correct a problem that arises. Can you imagine taking a vacation like this. You get up one morning, look at your spouse and say, "Let's go on vacation."

Your spouse looks at you, thinks a moment, and says, "That sounds like a great idea. We're due to get away. I'll start packing our clothes." Without further adieu, one throws clothes together, the other collects camping, fishing, diving, and hiking gear that may be useful if you run into a place to use them. The two of you cram it all in and on the car and take off for an automatic teller machine where you each make withdrawals. Then you head out on the road to enjoy a successful vacation. You drive until half of your money is expended and then head home.

Few would disagree that this would be a ridiculous way to begin a vacation. Without plans you don't know where you are going, what you are going to do, how long it will take, or much of anything else. Why would anyone begin OJT in the same manner and then wonder why the training didn't take?

Lack of planning presents two other problems. First there are interruptions by other employees, distractions of all kinds, noise, and any number of other factors that distract participants and interfere with the training conducted in the actual workplace. Without planning, all of the adverse situations that take place in every work environment also occur during the training session. Noise, interruptions, incorrect material, and more. Murphy's law states that it could not be any other way.

Time is the second problem. The supervisor already had a full day planned, so there isn't much time remaining for the training. The attitude becomes, "C'mere and let me show you how to do that so we can get on with what has to be done today." The supervisor then quickly does it once, turns and asks, "Got it?" The trainee nods agreement, and the supervisor goes off to tackle the day's work while the employee returns to what she was doing before she was so rudely interrupted.

There also may be some amount of resistance to the boss showing an employee how to do anything, especially if the boss isn't good at the task or has less than a stellar performance record. People may resent training from the boss for a number of other reasons. This is a difficult attitude to overcome under any circumstances and it becomes even more difficult when there are no plans that set the stage for the training. There is little difference when the trainer is another employee. She also has her own job to complete, and this is just another interference, more work with little personal reward.

Another problem exists when the would-be trainer has little or no training experience, knowledge, or skills. Completing a task yourself is one thing;

showing someone else how to do it correctly is quite another. Training success under these circumstances compares to a person who had played one year of high school football walking on the field with the Steelers and becoming an overnight success. It could happen, but the odds are overwhelmingly against it.

One final potential problem must be understood. Often training begins with OJT as a stand-alone exercise. There are instances where this is possible, but more often than not, OJT supported by other types of training and education are a better way of ensuring training success with performance payoffs.

This introduction would make it appear as if OJT is a lost cause, but that isn't the case at all. It can be an extremely effective way of training, especially when it is supported by the training methods previously covered.

Beginnings of a System

There must be a systemic process for every operation that includes standards and specific steps that are taken to ensure the process is completed the correct way each time. Without systematic ways of completing tasks, uncontrolled variability reigns king. Unfortunately, that is the shape many organizations are in today. Many grew out of one-person shops, expanded to small- and mid-size companies while they survived with almost no organization. At some point this system will not support the expanding operation and the company endeavors to produce a system that will.

In developing a system, overcomplication can becomes a major problem. People tend to develop elaborate systems that spell out every detail of every operation without considering if the job should be done at all. Perhaps it should be accomplished, but the current process is not the best that could be devised. *Keep It Simple, Sam* (KISS) is the rule of the day. Elaborate systems generally are doomed to failure because people don't have the time, energy, or desire to maintain them.

Job Descriptions

If your organization has good job descriptions, dig them out. They generally contain a suitable description of the job. Chances are that you may not have job descriptions or they may be out of date. At times they are overly general or so inflated that they are of little value, but they do represent a starting point. A good first step is to go to a library and select a book or two on job descriptions. (Most libraries have them.) It is not difficult to institute job descriptions. The process begins with the development of a training program for supervisors which contains sample job descriptions that pertain to your organization. Production, quality, and customer service requirements are addressed as needed. After the appropriate training, supervisors help their people draft their own job descriptions. These are collected by the supervisor, checked for accuracy and format, then submitted to the appropriate person.

This evolution requires less time than imagined when it is tackled as a team project. It affords everyone the opportunity to lay out their job the way they think it can best be performed, gets people involved in their jobs, and serves as a beginning for your training program. It also serves as a basis from which you can evaluate and improve the way you do business.

A job description is required to serve as an example for this part of the OJT process. The job description used in Volume II is presented again here as Figure 13.1.

Job title: Computer operator

Organizational unit: Computer center

Reports to: Computer center supervisor

Liaisons with: Assist personnel within the computer center and customers from other departments to accomplish the mission of the center and ACME Company.

Job function: Provide computer-centered services for all departments within the company.

Responsibilities:
Operate computer hardware and software utilized within the computer center.

Ensure all assigned projects are completed on time and completion information is entered in the daily log.

Assist customers in their efforts to define projects and determine completion schedules.

Maintain equipment in a clean and safe condition.

Maintain accurate logs of equipment malfunctions and report malfunctions to the appropriate person.

Maintain an inventory of computer processing supplies and reorder as required.

Performance criteria:
Correctly operate all designated hardware and software.

Ensure agreed upon customer requirements are fully met.

Produce work to the agreed upon standard achieved during performance goaling sessions.

Responsibilities: Qualifications
High school degree or general equivalency degree with two years of related experience. Experience may be substituted by appropriate education above the high school level.

Prepared by: A. Searfoss

Approved by: T. Quinn

Effective date: November 1991

Figure 13.1   Job Description Sample

Task Lists

The job description provides the basis for a task list to support the OJT effort. Operating and maintenance manuals, observations of the task in process, videos, questionnaires, and interviews with employees are other useful sources of information for development of a task list.

The task list is then prepared defining the individual tasks that are required for satisfactory job performance. In the case of the computer operator, these tasks include operating computer hardware and software, completing computer assignments, maintaining a task and an equipment malfunction log, assisting customers, maintaining equipment, maintaining a supply inventory, and ordering supplies.

Each of these overall tasks are then subdivided into the basic tasks inherent in each of them. Operating computer hardware might include the actual computers, input equipment, modems, and printers. One or more of these could be broken down again. Perhaps there are several types of computers and printers that must be used.

Once the task list is outlined it should be checked with an SME, perhaps the computer center operator in this case, and someone already performing well on the task. After any changes are made in this process, the task list should be verified as correct with the responsible manager.

The task list can then be used to develop objectives and criteria for training. Performance standards must be determined, how performance will be measured is listed, any particular conditions that might impact on either training or performance outlined, and if any margin for error is acceptable. Various methods of training should be outlined when the task analysis sheet is developed. The same format can be used for skill analysis. The example provided in Figure 13.2 serves as an exhibit for the first few tasks discussed in this task analysis.

Each different learning requirement is listed in order by tasks and subtasks with the training requirements listed after them. Abbreviations such as D = Day and W = Week can be used. There is no apprenticeship for this person, but often there is for other jobs. The apprenticeship program spells out training in terms of so many hours for each subject. Classroom is organizational training whereas education is off-site from a college, university, tech school, learning center, and so forth. OJT could include operations under instruction. Other programs can be used for simulator training, CBT, self-paced training, and so forth.

Training Objectives

Job descriptions and task and skill analyses outline what the training objectives should be. For those who have been involved in developing an

Task Analysis

Department: Computer Center   **Position:** Computer operator
Prepared by: A. Searfoss   **Date:** November 1991

Task	Attitude/Skills Knowledge	Apprenticeship	Classroom	On-the-job	Education	Other
General						
Supply inventory	Inventory computer supplies and reorder			1d		
Customer service	Assist in task-defining schedule completion date		2d	1d		
Computers						
Operate mainframe	Load tapes, run programs		1w	2w		
Operate printers	Operate printers and switching equipment Forward projects to correct customer		1d	2w		
Personal computers	DOS Word Perfect Lotus		2d	2w 2w	3d 3d	
Maintenance						
Clean equipment			.5d			
Administration						
Project log			.5d			
Equipment malfunction log			.5d			

Figure 13.2   Task Analysis

apprenticeship program, official approval by federal and state councils requires this evolution with the amount of time and the type training required outlined for each separate task area.

Too often it is not the way courses are developed for many organizations. A great many programs begin by someone sitting down and saying, "I think two days of hardware training, one day on printers, one week on software packages . . . will about do it." The correct mix may be reached over time but it does not represent the ideal way to produce learning objectives.

A training objectives form provides a standard format for developing learning objectives. A separate form is completed for each training objective that requires training. Figure 13.3 develops a training objectives form that is usable for virtually any type of training. These are more or less standard forms that are quite widely used. The sample form can be used for tasks from administrative efforts to the shop floor.

The *task section* describes the assigned task in specific terms. Action verbs such as "construct" are used; the description must be clear, concise, and correct.

The *attitudes/skills/knowledge section* is the same as the task and skills analysis form.

The *job environment section* describes the environment in which the task will be performed. It is a realistic description of the conditions that impact on the job performance.

The *job standards section* provides the standard against which task performance will be measured. The standard must be realistic and presented in terms that can be accurately measured. The training standards must relate to the on-the-job standards the trainee will encounter.

The *training objectives section* states the performance that is expected of the trainee when training is completed and reflects the job's task requirements. These objectives reflect the true requirements under which the employee's performance will be judged.

This example is more administrative than those tasks that would be found on the shop floor. It is presented because administrative tasks tend to be more difficult to develop than more mechanical functions. Proper procedures for a task such as overhauling a pump are outlined in the maintenance sections of the manuals provided when the pump is purchased. Should these not be available, the process just outlined provides the means to develop them.

Additional Training Methods

Most of our efforts to this point were spent building a training program outline, creating objectives, discussing lesson plans, and outlining training methods. Three additional training methods will be covered here as the beginning of an OJT training process is outlined.

Training Objectives

Department: Computer Center   **Position:** Computer operator
Prepared by: A. Searfoss   **Date:** November 1991

Task:

Attitude/Skills/ Knowledge	Training Method					
	Appren- ticeship	Class- room	On-the- job	Shop	Educa- tion	Other

Job environment

Job standards

Training objective

Figure 13.3   Training Objective Form

The Demonstration Method

Successful on-the-job training requires a method to convert concepts and theory to practical application in the workplace. The demonstration method of training is an extremely effective way of accomplishing this transfer.

With the demonstration method, people learn by imitating the instructor's actions. By watching the instructor, students form mental pictures of the process that they later try to copy in practice sessions. Specific details and actions come to life in real-world situations. The demonstration method has an advantage over other training, which too often presents general theories and the actual application may be fuzzy.

The practice sessions allow the student to perform the task under supervision. This permits immediate feedback concerning the level of success in copying the process, ways to further improve performance, and additional information that can be helpful.

Practice sessions get people involved. As they practice, their self-confidence improves. Continued practice removes the resistance to change and reluctance to begin new procedures that most trainees have at the start of a program.

There are some potential problems of which to be aware. We all tend to form different mental pictures of what we see during the instructor's demonstration. A way to overcome this is to make the demonstration as simple as possible, keeping the detail at the level required for performance. Structure the format around key steps or operations that must be performed. These steps should be outlined in the objectives.

The demonstration must exhibit the actual procedures. For intricate operations, the process may be repeated a second and even third time to cover special skills that are involved. A recommendation is that in these operations the trainer demonstrates the operation and then allows the student time to practice. The trainer can then repeat the process demonstrating the skills that apply and let the trainee practice. The skills should be divided into simple steps which applicants can readily perform.

A word of caution is appropriate here. The trainer should practice the session ahead of time using the actual equipment that will be used during the training session. A clumsy presentation will make the operation appear more difficult than it is. The trainer must be skillful at the process that is to be demonstrated or the confidence of trainees can be shattered. There are all kinds of problems that can result when the instructor holds presession practice on one piece of equipment or system and the training demonstration is held on another.

Of equal importance is trainer monitoring of students. Some people do not learn as well as others using this method. They can easily grasp the theory, but have trouble during the application phase. For these individuals, additional discussion on the application, followed by more demonstration and practice may be required.

There are many ways to assist this transfer of information. Films, slides, and video presentations can demonstrate the concepts. The same concepts can be demonstrated on simulators. Computer-based training provides yet another way to demonstrate how to correctly complete the procedure. Where possible, the procedure is demonstrated using the actual equipment doing the actual operations required to perform the process in the workplace. Other training methods can be used to support this effort.

Computer-Based Training

CBT offers possibilities almost beyond belief as technology rapidly pushes forward the development of the equipment that is used. The current use of laser disc technology has expanded this method greatly in recent years.

CBT provides hands-on training using video presentations of actual equipment. The trainees' activities control the training process. Instant feedback is provided for both answering the questions successfully and for failing to answer them correctly. It is a highly effective method of training. Because of the interaction, learning takes place readily without an instructor's presence.

Last year I was auditing a major corporation's training program for a training article. They allowed me to go through a CBT program for a fluid pump maintenance process. As I write this lesson, I can picture the tools and follow the procedures for tearing down the pump, replacing the packing and bearings, and reassembling it. For those who learn well by pictures, this process offers almost immeasurable opportunities for performance improvement training.

Another benefit is that the systems can be developed with log-on identification sequences so the programs are available at all times of the day. Companies that provide these opportunities are discovering that many employees train on their own time. The incorporation of monitoring programs allows the completion of successful training sessions to be automatically recorded in student training records. This data can be used to certify that requirements are met for the purposes of documentation for apprenticeship programs, promotions, recognition, and so forth.

These programs also are being offered to supplement off-duty literacy training. The advantages of this training should be explored by all companies. The costs probably are less than most would think possible and markedly less when you equate it to the cost of full-time trainers who are being used in ways that are no longer required.

Programmed Instruction

Programmed instruction is self-paced training based on a series of information blocks, followed by questions that are immediately verifiable by the trainee. Instructors or trainers are not required except as resource persons. It can be used for partial or for complete courses on all sorts of subjects. However, this instruction may be better suited as remedial training developed to bring trainees up to some specific level of performance prior to the presentation of more difficult concepts.

I find several drawbacks to this type of instruction. The first problem concerns the illiteracy rates in the United States. Seventy-five million Americans are functionally illiterate or read at the most basic reading levels. This makes the use of programmed instruction impossible or ineffective in many cases.

Programmed instruction also is dull and boring for many people. The mechanical way material is presented can be demotivational. The learner must be highly motivated to complete these programmed instruction sessions.

A Sample OJT Program

The sample method of a successful OJT program that is presented herein results from a visit I made to a Fortune 500 company last year for a training article I was writing. The multinational corporation is actively involved in training, much of which is OJT oriented. They have a great diversity in the equipment they use. State-of-the-art machines are accompanied by considerably older equipment that still performs satisfactorily. Training to such a situation could be a nightmare. However, it is not true for this company.

Consultants vs. Trainers

The previously described company has a well-organized and well-led training team. Team members do not consider themselves as routine trainers, but as training consultants on call to assess and help solve training problems.

When a potential training situation is discovered through worker reports, supervisory requests, assessments or whatever method, the training team becomes involved. A team is quickly developed which (at a minimum) consists of a training consultant, supervisor of the operation, and a worker/SME. A quick assessment is performed to determine if the problem is training-based or somewhere else (such as maintenance, equipment shortcomings, or leadership).

Once the decision is made that it is a training problem, the previously covered assessment procedures are completed. The assessment's depth revolves around the problem's complexity. When training objectives are reached, an SME from the work group interacts with the training group to develop training. The training program could be developed utilizing all kinds of combinations of classroom, demonstration, CBT, and so forth. The SME also is trained on training development, and presentation skills.

After the training is developed, the SME returns to his work group to conduct training or assist with training. This allows for training by a known performer, who also functions as a coach. The process begins with a brief overview that presents the program's background material. The training is then conducted along the lines of a standard coaching process.

1. The coach explains the training to be held.

   a. The goal of the training.

   b. The reason it is being presented.

   c. How it will benefit the participants.

2. The coach verbally discusses the process.

3. The coach completes the process.

4. The coach asks and answers questions.

5. The participants then complete the process individually.

6. This action is discussed and questions are answered. All unclear areas or rough spots are repeated until understanding is reached.

7. Correct application is immediately recognized and praised.

Participant response tends to be excellent because the training is conducted by one of their own. The SME/trainer/coach benefits because of the training and knowledge received during development of the training package. The organization benefits because the trainer returns as an improved member of the production team in the workplace who tends to be more supportive of the organization and its training programs.

Everyone who was involved in this training, in any fashion, was highly supportive of it. Performance improvements are well documented and based on proven success. Currently, they are expanding the program.

While I was at this company, all of the CBT equipment was in use by trainees who were in for training on their own time, improving their skills and increasing their promotional opportunities. They were working all types of programs ranging from administrative to mechanical. I cannot picture running into a group of trainees who were more enthusiastic about training. Like a majority of employees in all organizations, these people want to improve their performance to produce quality.

Field Training

Field training is yet another application of OJT. This evolution is especially applicable in training for topics such as sales. A certain amount of classroom time generally is held to provide the attitude and knowledge training that provides the background material. In too many cases, training is considered complete after the classroom session when it should be just beginning.

Phase two of field training is the application of the attitudes and knowledge to develop the actual sales skills. This is the part of the process where payoff is achieved. It could be considered a derivative of the demonstration process covered previously covered in this chapter.

The training sequence presented herein is one we have used for many years. I am not aware of where the idea originated, but it was used in a sales training program over 15 years ago. Each one of these steps can occur during the same day or days apart. It all depends on the subject and time allotted for training. The outline follows.

1. *Step one*–The trainer does all the work with the student observing. The trainer runs through the process several times ensuring that each detail is correct. The steps are thoroughly discussed between each application.

2. *Step two*–The trainer and student alternate. The trainer helps the student out when difficulties are experienced. The trainer continually observes student performance and critiques both positive and negative aspects of it.

3. *Step three*–The student is on her own and does all the work while the trainer watches and critiques her actions, efforts, and techniques.

4. *Step four*–The trainer creates a problem using one of the mistakes the student made or a mistake previous students committed. The trainer then allows the student to correct the problem while he watches. The trainer assists the student if it is required.

5. *Step five*–Training continues with the effort concentrated on the areas where the student has the greatest difficulty.

6. *Step six*–Performance is critiqued on an ongoing basis. The continuing evaluation process serves to continually upgrade performance.

An OJT Recap

This chapter developed an OJT program and presented several different methods of training that support OJT. It also covered sample OJT and field training sessions. The following is a quick recap of the principles of OJT:

1. Usually used for skills training.

2. Useful for individuals or small groups.

3. Without a solid OJT program, there is a strong possibility that people are learning incorrect techniques from trial and error or their teammates.

4. TQM requires OJT in the workplace, whether it be shop floor, computer, or a sales call.

5. OJT must have a plan even though it may not be as formal as those used in the lecture method.

6. Teaching process:

   a. Tell them

   b. Show them

   c. Have them show you

   d. Repeat until performance is satisfactory

Summary

1. OJT is not without its problems. Most of these are caused because the training does not follow the guidelines of standard training programs.

2. An OJT program (like all training) begins with job descriptions, task lists, task and skill analysis, and training objectives. Examples of each are presented.

3. Three additional training methods are presented because they support OJT. These are the demonstration method, CBT, and programmed instruction.

4. A sample OJT program is presented from an organization that is showing substantial results. This discusses trainers as internal consultants, coaching techniques, and field training procedures.

Bibliography

Abella, K. T. *Building Successful Training Programs*, Reading, MA: Addison-Wesley, 1986.

Brinkerhoff, R. O. *Achieving Results from Training*, San Francisco: Jossey-Bass, 1987.

Broadwell, M. M. *The Supervisor and On-the-Job Training*, Reading, MA: Addison-Wesley, 1970.

―――. *The Supervisor as an Instructor*, Reading, MA: Addison-Wesley, 1970.

Carkhuff, R. R. and Pierce, R. M. *Training Delivery Skills, Part I,* Amherst, MA: Human Resource Development Press, 1984.

————. *Training Delivery Skills, Part II,* Amherst, MA: Human Resource Development Press, 1984.

Cassner-Lotto, J. and Associates. *Successful Training Strategies: Twenty-six Innovative Corporate Models,* San Francisco: Jossey-Bass, 1988.

Connor, J. J. *On-the-Job Training,* Boston, MA: International Human Resource Development Corporation, 1983.

Craig, R. L. (Ed.) *American Society for Training and Development, Training & Development Handbook,* New York: McGraw-Hill, 1976.

————. *Training and Development Handbook,* New York: McGraw-Hill, 1976.

Davis, L. N. and McCallon, E. *Planning, Conducting and Evaluating Workshops,* Austin, TX: Learning Concepts, 1975.

King, D. *Training Within the Organization,* London: Tavistock Publications, 1964.

London, M. *Managing the Training Enterprise,* San Francisco: Jossey-Bass, 1989.

Mitchell, G. *The Trainer's Handbook,* New York: American Management Association, 1987.

Proctor, J. H. and Thorton, W. M. *Training: A Handbook for Line Managers,* New York: American Management Association, 1961.

CHAPTER 14

Learner-Centered Training

This chapter is directed toward the adult learner who receives training in the quality program. Many of my thoughts and beliefs on this subject were developed during and after attending a program called How to Teach Grownups developed by Practical Management Associates. The focus is on adult learners, endeavoring to understand how and why they learn. Isn't that what is important, the actual learning that takes place and supports performance improvement?

The session ahead provides ideas to assist you in your training endeavors so that learning can be maximized. That is this book's focus—developing a system that has the potential to gain the most benefit from training assets as measured against the goal.

Most instructors preparing for training sessions start by asking themselves a few basic questions. Over the years, these or similar questions are asked to start train-the-trainer type sessions: "What are your immediate considerations when you are about to begin a training session?" The following are typical answers received.

- Why me? Why was I chosen for this subject?
- What do I know about the subject?
- What information should I include?
- What aids should I use?
- How should I instruct this?
- Where should I hold training?

All of these statements are natural reactions. Perhaps the first one is one of shock for being chosen to handle the particular assignment. The others are natural follow-up questions and reflect a natural human tendency—the concern for *me*.

Humans tend to think of themselves first when considering any situation. Individuals look at their reunion picture and search out their photo as the first order of business. It would be unnatural to do anything else. Therein lies the problem. In training the orientation switches from the me- or trainer-centered thinking to learner-centered training where the greatest payoff is achieved.

The six questions previously asked change when the learner is considered. The first question remains valid because it focuses thinking on what someone saw in us, the things we know or have the capability of teaching others. The remaining questions become learner focused.

- What should the learners know?
- What do the learners know?
- What information is needed most?
- What method of training best supports their learning need?
- What aids would best suit their learning need?
- Where is the best place to hold training to meet their need?

Many train-the-trainer type courses focus on those things the trainer does. Although they are important, appearance, stage presence, voice, mannerisms, aids, and class control are not learner centered. I am not sure who originated the following statement but it is most applicable. *"Learning takes place from what the learner does and not from what the trainer does."* Based on this premise, please check that the following statements that are true.

____ 1. A trainer's platform skills and interesting anecdotes are not as important for training payoff as those things the learner does during the training sessions.

____ 2. Trainer enthusiasm is helpful, but it will not guarantee a learning experience will take place.

____ 3. Solid learner-centered instruction can take place even though the trainer is not an excellent speaker.

____ 4. A trainer can cover learning objectives without causing a learning situation to take place.

____ 5. A trainer must realize that providing the required knowledge and demonstrating the correct skills is only the first part of the learning experience.

____ 6.   The trainer must ensure students correctly do those things necessary to accomplish the desired learning.

____ 7.   Trainer-centered instruction focuses on the trainer and that trainer's skills.

____ 8.   Learner-centered instruction focuses on the involvement and interaction required by students to learn.

____ 9.   All training material can be developed with a learner-centered focus.

____ 10.   Training aids readily support learner-centered training.

Of course, all of these items should be checked true. There probably were no great revelations in this exercise, but it does serve to hammer home the idea of learner-centered training. However, would you have marked them all true prior to beginning this program? If you would have, would you know exactly why you were doing so?

Discovering the Adult Learner

Many sessions on adult training now begin with a discussion of andragogy and pedagogy. Because of this, the terms are defined and commented on here, also. The definitions presented are more or less standard and serve to define the terms as they are commonly used:

Andragogy–Providing instruction based on the way adults learn; or self-directed, student-interest-oriented instruction.

Pedagogy–Providing instruction based on the way children learn; or teacher-directed, subject-matter-oriented instruction.

Although these definitions are suitable for educational efforts, they do not meet the real-life situation of most adult learners. Virtually all adult learning sessions outside the college classroom are trainer directed because the goal and the organization, profession, law, or safety and operating procedures mandate what will be taught. Therefore, organizational training almost always will be trainer directed. Hopefully, it also will be learner centered.

What Is Different About the Adult Learner?

The adult learner is wiser and becomes more so with time. Although peak I.Q.-based intelligence and peak physical being are supposed to occur during the early twenties, human vocabulary, knowledge, and skills continue to grow throughout life. As we grow older we become more realistic with our expected achievements and happier with who we are becoming. For the average person who remains active, the brain never peaks and continues to create quality work over the lifetime.

Adults tend to underestimate their potential learning ability, often because they base their current and future potential on what they achieved during secondary school years. Virtually every adult can learn any subject given time and the attention of people competent to help them learn it. They have a wealth of disconnected experiences to draw upon, and the skilled trainer assists their learning process by connecting this background to make learning new processes easier.

The varied experiences the adult learner brings to the training session generally support the trainer and the training effort. The individual needs and desires that will be fulfilled by training may differ somewhat, but their overall needs and the training objectives should be in line. When they aren't, visionary leadership should be questioned immediately.

The adult wants training that meets the requirements of her organization and profession, helps to improve her performance, and keeps her operating within the law. To best satisfy these needs, the trainer should be aware of differences that exist between the more mature and experienced adult and the inexperienced youth in learning situations. These differences were taken from notes gathered from a radio broadcast.

Adults have longer attention spans and can sit longer without creating disturbances if they have comfortable seating. Their attention span, however, is less than most trainers believe. Various estimates are between 8 and 10 minutes in length.

Adults come to training with needs based on real-life experience. They have the bigger picture and want to know how the training objectives match their personal and work goals. They expect to learn how to do the things that are important for success, which causes them to look for the pertinent facts that apply directly to their needs. Nice-to-know information is often ignored.

Children have shorter attention spans and little real-world experience in most areas. They want to be entertained while they are learning. The teacher must bring the real world to them in a manner that captivates their attention, provides them with a need, and carries examples that they can understand. The teacher provides most of the information for the child and all the rewards in the form of praise and evaluations such as grades.

Adults often learn as much from other participants as they do from the instructor. Their shared experiences and examples provide a rich learning experience for everyone. Adults know the value of their time and want to maximize the effectiveness of training while children seem to have little concept of time other than too much of it is spent in school. The adult's reward comes when the training received supports their needs and goals.

Adults often are taken advantage of in training sessions. This is especially true in higher education and training sessions with adults. It occurs because they have the ability to pay attention longer without fidgeting, the desire and need to learn, and the willpower to go back on their own time and pick up those subjects they didn't learn during training sessions. They are given trainer or professor centered lectures with little emphasis on their needs as a learner. This forces participants to burn the midnight oil outside of class to learn what they could have learned in class.

Effective trainers develop and instruct their sessions tuned to the learner. Every step of their plan is developed with the idea of keeping the student learner involved in some way. Self-questioning sessions (like those covered throughout this book) are one way to achieve this. Games, role-playing, case studies, and so forth, are additional techniques that allow learner involvement in every phase of training. OJT with demonstration and coaching techniques follow this same game plan.

Training effectiveness also requires trainers to instruct at the student's knowledge and skill level. Trainers always must stay tuned to the class and each individual as they progress through their sessions. Feedback such as facial expressions, fidgeting, inattentiveness, and daydreaming warn the trainers it is time to shift gears because they are losing their audience.

Trainers must continually remember adults want learning experiences that provide long-term payoff on the job, improve their personal life, and assist them with career plans. The degree to which they see all of these needs being met often determines how much they invest in the training sessions.

Adults want their training to support their organization and, in turn, have their organization support the training they receive. Nothing is more detrimental to a training program than students returning to a workplace to hear their supervisor remark, "That's great stuff for the classroom, but we operate in the real world here." Supervisors must have an input on quality training through the establishment of objectives and the determination of who needs what. When they have that input, they usually support the program.

One last concept greatly improves training sessions. The training should be presented in terms of "the real benefit to you." When people understand how quality training benefits them, they are eager to participate.

Establishing a Learning Climate

Similar to a sales call or hiring interview, the first few minutes of a training session are crucial. They should be as pleasant and interesting as is humanly possible. Many trainers begin every training session with an icebreaker. These are especially effective if they pertain directly to the training session instead of being stand-alone games. To be sure, those sessions that begin on a negative tone will be difficult to turn around as time passes.

A few minutes devoted to small detail prior to the arrival of trainees can be most valuable when training is held apart from the workplace. Important items include ensuring that seats are available for all participants, the temperature is correct, and the aids are ready.

The lesson plans presented earlier provided for student greetings. When participants don't know each other, short introductions are in order. This can be handled quite easily by having each person introduce himself, the operation or organization he is from, and something about himself.

People should be made comfortable. Allowing them to remove ties and so forth helps ease the situation. At the same time, it is best to spell out the rules for the session and the importance of group participation. A brief discussion of the expectations each person has of the training serves as an excellent icebreaker. It also helps the instructor to learn why people came and where to place emphasis, use special examples, and so forth.

Steps to Learning

Learning is a process for transferring information from one mind to another so that the correct learning takes place. Somewhere along the line someone told me, "Too often the process is one where information is transferred from the lesson plan of the instructor to the paper of the student without going through the mind of either." This cannot be allowed to happen in a training session.

It is vital to success that every trainee absorbs the information in a manner that allows each person to correctly use this information on return to the workplace. In addition to learner-centered training, the correct learning process must be followed.

The process used in the program involves distinct steps. Just as a ladder must have all of its steps to be useful, learning must include all steps for maximum effectiveness.

1. *Attendance*–It goes without saying that people must attend training in order to receive its benefits. Too many hang their hat on almost any excuse to avoid training. A major problem is when the organization's executives are the first to be "too busy" to attend training today. It sets the stage for people at every level to be too busy for training and at that point the training program might as well be terminated. Those who attend have no power to put the training to work.

2. *Awake*–Those in attendance must be awake. It is surprising how many individuals show up for training and allow their brains to sleep. This is both a trainer and participant problem. Contrary to popular belief, little knowledge is gained through osmosis in the classroom.

3. *Attentive*–Everyone involved in training must be listening. This includes the trainer and each participant. This can be difficult and the trainer must help people through their listening deficiencies. The trainer also

must listen to gain knowledge of need and follow through by meeting that need.

4. *Interested*–Interest is a mutual trainer–student responsibility. The session must be well-prepared with solid material and participants must have a reason to be there. People are seldom attentive when they have no interest in the subject. Someone once said, "There are no dull subjects, only dull presenters," and that may be true to some degree. However, sending people to sessions they won't use and could care less about is a prescription for trainer problem and wasted assets.

5. *Interactive*–Interactive sessions maintain interest and foster true learning experiences. The more people do with the material during sessions, the more material will be retained for use on the job.

6. *Goal oriented*–Sessions that won't be used in some way to support efforts to reach the goal won't be effective. Participants must understand the purpose of the training.

Capacity to Learn

Earlier it was established that most adults are in classes to learn. Their lives and careers depend on it. Often trainees come to class prepared and perhaps even eager to learn until such things as the training, trainer, or environment turns them off to the learning process.

As a trainer, there are several important considerations that must be met. You must know what material has to be covered. You should have the knowledge they need and be prepared to assist them in learning it. They probably don't know it all or they wouldn't be there. However, in many or most sessions, there will be someone present who knows as much or more than the trainer about a particular area. Their involvement will assist the trainer in this learning experience.

Time is precious for adults, and their capacity to learn material during a given amount of time is limited. You know what the students must learn. The learning objectives established this. The assessments provide a great deal of information that helps establish what participants should already know. During class sessions, you must ensure they know what they are supposed to know. You can do this by requesting brief background descriptions, asking questions, watching reactions, and other feedback techniques. The difference between what they must know and what they know is what you must teach and they must learn. That is why the actual presentation of material may be different for each class.

Remembering the student's learning formula will help conserve valuable training time.

The student's formula:

MUST KNOW – ALREADY KNOW = WHAT MUST BE LEARNED.

The student does not come to class as an empty container ready to be filled. Her long-term memory is loaded with experiences and knowledge that will assist with assimilation of this material. However, let's hope the short-term memory is not working on something else and is standing by to receive and process information.

Initial icebreakers designed to get people out of their outside thoughts and into the training at hand can be most productive. One trainer passed out Post-it™ notes and had each person write down the outside things that were on their mind and discussed them for a short period within subgroups. It tended to focus considerable attention on the training at hand.

Four keys to learning are covered in some detail. These include:

1. Readiness

2. Proper presentation

3. Retention

4. Reward

The following material is presented in terms of the way it is presented in train-the-trainer classes. This method is a variant based on a lesson the instructor used in the Practical Management Associates program How to Teach Grownups (mentioned earlier). The session is presented in this manner because many embarking on a quality training program must prepare train-the-trainer programs for their organization and this one serves well in practice. Although I haven't seen this program advertised in 10 years, if you see it advertised it is well worth attending.

The illustration in Figure 14.1 serves as a model for four separate functions in the teaching, learning process: the ability to receive information, short-term storage of information, assimilation capacity, and the way long-term information supports the learning process:

1. There is a limited capacity to *receive* information. This is represented by the size of the funnel which allows only so much liquid to be received at a time.

2. There also is a limited capacity for *short-term storage* which is used for quick recall for classroom purposes, quizzes, and similar situations. This is demonstrated by the size of the container holding the funnel. In training situations the short-term memory could be processing all kinds of extraneous information and problems when participants arrive. It is important to provide immediate focus on the learning experience and then strive to maintain it during the entire session.

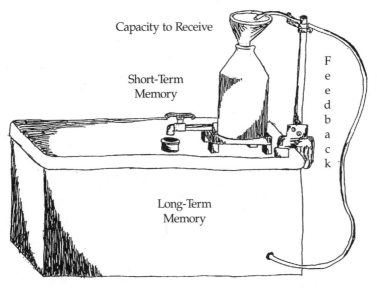

Capacity to Receive

Short-Term
Memory

F
e
e
d
b
a
c
k

Long-Term
Memory

Figure 14.1 Four Functions of the Teaching/Learning Process

(Courtesy of John A. Johnson)

3. There is an *assimilation* capacity with long-term storage which provides the ability to integrate, change, adapt, interrelate, and recall information for future use. However, the actual capacity of the brain's long-term storage capacity is almost beyond belief.

4. There also is a *siphon* that carries information from long-term storage to short-term storage in order to help process new information. The brain quickly performs this function with little conscious effort by the student.

Armed with this model, we are almost ready to start pouring information into our model. Let's check to see how we're doing.

- Is the exact subject clear?

- Is the material organized into teachable units?

- Is a solid program designed that starts with first things first and progresses in an orderly fashion?

- Are the necessary aids developed?

- Is the program learner centered?

- Its everything checked? Great! We're ready to pour in the knowledge.

Remember that there almost always is more than enough information available on any subject that requires our training services. Our job will be to sort out that information so that the learner receives the amount of information needed to produce the desired results. A big mistake trainers often make is to dump all their knowledge of a particular subject on the helpless folks in the session rather than providing them with the need to know information. The trainer also must get the information into a usable format that supports the subject. Since we are going to pour in the information in this demonstration, a liquid format will be used.

In classroom demonstrations this learning process begins with an opaque jug such as a bleach bottle with a funnel in it. There usually is some amount of liquid in the opaque jug but participants do not know how much. The funnel has a cover over it, and several containers of liquid are available to pour into the jug. The opaque jug is sitting in a large tray to catch the spills that will occur. If you plan to use this demonstration, be sure to practice it ahead of time. (Of course, it is best if all session material is practiced before classroom presentations.)

The First Learning Key–Readiness

With the class watching, the instructor pours the liquid toward the opaque jug, striking the cover that was placed on the funnel cap. As it spills, the instructor asks, "What happened?"

General answers include: "The lid was covered." "We weren't ready." "We must get ready." This leads to the first key to learning: *readiness*.

Readiness requires that people attend sessions, remain awake, and stay attentive. To do this, the trainer must create interest using all the methods previously discussed and all those things that are possible within her imagination.

Attention must be focused on the topic and the bridge created between that topic and the goal. These relations are much more important than many imagine. It answers the *why* in terms of potential benefit. The session should be sold in terms of, "The real benefit to you is . . . ."

The importance of readiness is stressed further by the bus story. It is read to the class with little introduction other than, "I have a story to read to you." The bus story follows.

The Story

You are a bus driver beginning a shift at the bus terminal. The bus is empty as it heads downtown to city hall. At the first bus stop 3 men and 5 women board the bus. At Maple Street, 7 men and 2 women get on while 2 men and 1 woman get off. At the next stop 5 men and 3 women board while 2 women and 1 man depart. At Pine Street, a man with a dog guide and 2 women get on and 1 woman leaves. At Oak Street, the man with the dog guide departs while 4 men and 1 woman get on. At the Fifth and Broad Street stop, 5 women and 4 men get on and 1 man and 1 woman depart. The bus arrives at city hall and everyone gets off.

After the story is read a transparency with questions is placed on the overhead (minus the answers). The class answers the questions and they are recorded. At that time, any number of scenarios can follow.

Questions

1. How many men got off at City Hall? *19.*
2. How many women got off at City Hall? *13.*
3. How many stops were made? *7.*
4. What was the bus driver's name? *you.*
5. What implications are in this example?

The number and range of answers for the first four questions are almost unbelievable. The implications are different. The participants generally come up with the implications quite readily. As a variant, participants divide into groups to come up with the answers to the final question which are then discussed. Some implications follow:

a. Start by telling people what to look for.
b. Provide them with the pertinent facts. Example: No one needed to know about the dog guide in this case.
c. Arrange it in a logical manner. In this case the problem is confused because the sequences are mixed up, men–women, then women–men. The boarding–departing order is not always the same either.
d. Get the learner involved rather than listening. Would it have made a difference if we had made a chart to keep track of things, assigned various statistics to different people, and paused for feedback as we went along?
e. Take the learners from where they are to where they must go.
f. Explain how this is accomplished.

Following this exercise, the trainer agrees with the people, and using the techniques called for in the implications exercise, the story is reread. This time it is no contest. They get the answers.

The Second Learning Key–Presentation

In everyday experiences, there is almost nothing that happens with which adults don't have some associated background experience. Computers serve as an example. The person may know little about computers, per se, but knows about MAC cards, computer billing and billing mistakes, modern checkout scanners, and a variety of different types of video games. Move from the known to the unknown.

The cover is removed from the funnel symbolizing the student is now ready to learn. The liquid is poured into the funnel using the following scenarios.

First–Pour sloppily and spill some. Ask *"How are we doing?"*–no focus.

Second–Pour too fast and let water overflow. Ask *"How are we doing?"*–too fast.

Example in training: Three hours of material left and 15 minutes of time. *"What usually happens?"* The big nonstop dump to throw out all the material. *"How effective is this?"*–not very!

Third–Pour slowly, pausing to let water drain out of funnel. *Now, how are we doing? Pretty good!*

Fourth–Overflow jug. Ask, *"What happened?"*–too much at one time.

The second learning key is a technical one. *Proper presentation.*

The keys to proper presentation follow.

1. Present the information at a proper rate. The key is the *class'* ability to *absorb* the information.

2. Check for assimilation *during* instruction. Do not wait until the end, it may be too late.

3. Use training aids to support the presentation and not as the key to the presentation. Aids can be used to:

   a. Multiply and magnify the training effort.

   b. Motivate the student by arousing interest.

   c. Introduce the subject.

   d. Organize the lesson.

   e. Promote understanding because they can appeal to all senses.

   f. Help with retention because they drive ideas home.

   g. Facilitate feedback.

The Third Learning Key–Retention

It is important to understand the way we learn so the presentation can further support retention. Our senses play an important part in the way we learn and how well we retain information over the long term. Some people have greater strengths in one of their senses than they do in others. The following model is developed from the way the average trainee learns:

1. *Visual*–Research shows that we learn most things through our eyes. Strong visuals allow students to watch the session over in the form of mind movies. It is estimated that 87 percent of our learning takes place through the eyes.

2. *Auditory*–This is the second most important sense for learning. Some people can process verbal information quite easily. However, those best equipped for auditory use still rely most heavily on the visual. Hearing provides another 11 percent of our capacity to learn.

3. *Kinesthetic*–Another important, although small by percentage, way we process information is by feeling. There are two ways we process feelings. Visceral is the internal feeling exhibited by such things as *gut feeling*. Tactile is the external feeling and sensations that affect us. The other senses provide the remaining 2 percent of our learning.

4. We learn more, with longer retention, when the learning is a combination of two or more different senses. This, however, does not say we should rely on movies and videos as a main sense of training. Students learn the most by doing.

The third key to learning success—*retention*—ensures the information and skills provided are available for use after training. Proper presentation of excellent material is of little value in itself. It must be retained and put to the use as it was intended and in the correct way.

Reinforcement for *retention* can happen in many ways.

1. Ask questions, provide and request examples, use problems and case studies.

2. Demonstrate and then have the students complete the task. People learn best by doing.

3. Vivid experiences reinforce the learning experience.

4. Strive to have demonstrations that require the learner to siphon information from their long-term memory to reinforce what they are learning. For example, equate the current process being learned to one you know they already understand.

5. *Repetition* is a key reinforcement for retention. Key points can be repeated throughout the course. Key process can be repeated over and over again similar to learning to type.

6. Realism is vital. The closer the training experience is to the real job, the more apt the learner is to apply the new attitudes, skills, or knowledge.

Three kinds of learning take place in the classroom and this section on the keys to learning support all of them. These kinds of learning can be remembered by the word ASK.

A ttitudes

S kills

K nowledge

Application also could be discussed at this time. However, unless the trainer is also the group's leader, application is out of the trainer's hands once the student departs the classroom. To a large extent the participant's work environment determines just how much of the training he uses.

The Fourth Learning Key–Reward

People and teams do those things that reward them. The most important information presented in the most effective way seldom leads to a payoff unless training holds a reward.

Recognition and reward is an important part of any training session. Trainers should search for ways to recognize participants. "That's a good answer Jane," "That worked well Jim," or "Good thought Jean," all encourage participation and contributions to the training effort.

The potential for posttraining reward resulting from contributions during training supports the learning climate. Awards like Honor Person for longer programs gives many employees a goal.

The ultimate reward that spurs people's performance includes those things that can improve their life because they improved their skills through training. The potential for promotion, bonuses, team rewards, and so forth, provide significant incentive for learning new knowledge and skills.

Motivation to Learn

The motivation to learn parallels the motivation for anything else. One cannot motivate another; you may influence them, but motivation comes from within. The trainer's job becomes one of providing an environment that encourages and allows trainees to become motivated for the learning process that must take place.

Many successful leaders believe the two greatest motivational factors are *success* and solid *training.* Training is what this book is all about, and, hopefully, it provides the skills necessary for success in the organization's quality endeavors.

There are two types of motivators. The first type, *intrinsic motivators,* are internal forces that make one want to become a better person. These include the desire to improve, create, and learn. Intrinsic motivators are the longest lasting. There are three basic forms of intrinsic motivators.

1. *Intellectual motivators*–focus on the need to learn and create.

2. *Psychological motivators*–relate to the need for self-respect, self-esteem, and self-pride.

3. *Social motivators*–involve the need for recognition, respect, and approval of superiors, coworkers, or team members.

The second type of motivator is *extrinsic*. These external incentives are offered by another to influence us to do something. Usually it involves perks such as money, raises, bonuses, or some additional benefit. Extrinsic benefits are short-term motivators. It is the trainer's responsibility to ensure the learning environment is such that the trainer is motivated to learn.

Question: What can the trainer do to promote a *learning* environment?

It is important to understand the factors that motivate adults to learn. Some important ones to remember for all phases of the training evolution follow:

1. They understand the need to know the material.

2. Their interest is maintained.

3. They have early successes in the learning processes.

4. They are given recognition and credit during the session.

5. Individuals and the class are praised and blame is avoided.

6. The trainer is professional and treats participants as professionals.

There are some things that provide a motivational learning environment while they support learning in other ways. Some of these include the following.

1. Learning is enhanced when new material adds to previously acquired knowledge. Learning totally new skills is considerably more difficult.

2. Individuals are motivated by different factors. A certificate may motivate some people while others would care less about it. Participant interest in developing increased job proficiency often is a sound motivator especially when improved job proficiency carries monetary reward.

3. When participants see positive results from training, motivation for additional training usually is greatly enhanced. This is another area where building small successes is vital to long-term success.

4. When a participant's work success is dependent on a group's success, it is generally best to train that group as a team.

5. Training periods should generally be kept to four hours or less because people get tired during longer sessions. Difficult concepts such as SPC may be taught better in several two hour sessions.

6. Training sessions immediately after lunch may be virtually useless in terms of a payoff.

7. People generally remember material that is necessary for high performance much longer than material incidental to their job. Material that is used soon after training is much more likely to be remembered. Large amounts of material are forgotten soon after training sessions.

It is equally important to understand the factors that motivate trainers. Some of these quickly stand out and support efforts to obtain volunteer SMEs for the in-house training program.

1. Opportunity to gain new experiences through the training situation.

2. Opportunity for self-expression through training.

3. Opportunity to assist others in the learning experience.

4. Opportunity for self-determination because training is an independent pursuit to varying degrees.

5. Knowledge that successful training builds self-esteem through the accomplishments of helping others learn.

6. Knowledge of the rewards and recognition that comes from successful training endeavors.

Summary

1. The focus of this chapter is the process by which adults learn. Crucial to this idea is the comment, "Learning takes place from what the learner does and not what the trainer does."

2. Many deep-rooted myths severely impact on training adults. Most of them have their basis in trainer-centered training and all of them inhibit learner-centered learning.

3. Adult students, their needs, and the way they differ from youth were covered in terms of ways to improve the adult learning process.

4. The keys to learning provide the stepladder for effective training.

5. This session discusses the capacity to learn and techniques to ensure adults are provided the opportunity to learn. Learning keys help the trainer understand how to develop and present training for effectiveness.

6. The motivation to learn is an important aspect of the learning process. Motivators are important for both the trainee and the trainer in the quest for solid training that pays off in performance improvements.

Bibliography

Asionian, C. B. and Brickell, H. M. *Americans in Transition: Life Changes as Reasons for Adult Learning*, New York: College Entrance Examination Board, 1980.

Broadwell, M. M. *The Supervisor as an Instructor*, Reading, MA: Addison-Wesley, 1970.

Campbell, D. D. *Adult Education as a Field of Study and Practice*, Vancouver: Center for Continuing Education, University of British Columbia, 1977.

Carkhuff, R. R. and Pierce, R. M. *Training Delivery Skills, Part I*, Amherst, MA: Human Resource Development Press, 1984.

———. *Training Delivery Skills, Part II*, Amherst, MA: Human Resource Development Press, 1984.

Cooper, S. and Heenan, C. *A Humanistic Approach*, Boston, MA: CB Publishing, 1980.

Craig, R. L. (Ed.) *American Society for Training and Development, Training & Development Handbook*, New York: McGraw-Hill, 1976.

Cross, P. K. *Adults as Learners*, San Francisco: Jossey-Bass, 1981.

Engel, H. M. *Handbook of Creative Learning Exercises*, Houston, TX: Gulf Publishing, 1973.

Knowles, M. *The Adult Learner: A Neglected Species*, Houston, TX: Gulf Publishing, 1973.

———. *The Modern Practice of Adult Education*, New York: Association Press, 1970.

McLagan, P. A. *Helping Others Learn*, Reading, MA: Addison-Wesley, 1978.

Pfeiffer, J. W. and Jones, J. E. *A Handbook of Structured Experiences for Human Relations Training* (Volumes I–VI), LaJolla, CA: University Associates, 1974–1979.

Rogoff, R. L. *The Training Wheel*, New York: John Wiley and Sons, 1987.

Tough, A. *A Fresh Approach to Theory and Practice in Adult Learning*, Toronto, Ontario: Ontario Institute for Studies in Education, 1971.

———. *How to Teach Grownups*, Canoga Park, CA: Practical Management Associates, 1979.

CHAPTER 15

Preventing Training Problems

Everything is not always smooth sailing in any kind of program. Given the human elements, interpersonal relations factors, the time elements, the glass house environment, and the program's importance, it is possible that no operation has more potential for problems than training. For that reason an entire chapter is devoted to that subject.

This is not to say that training is automatically a disaster waiting to happen. It is not. This chapter examines what can happen and provides an understanding of potential problems so that plans can be generated to prevent their occurrence. As with any other part of the TQM effort, prevention of poor quality is the rule in training.

Many situations impact on training effectiveness. This chapter contains discussions of some of the significant problems encountered over the years with typical training programs. Perhaps you have been a part of some of these and can relate to the problems encountered. The three areas that will be studied include trainer-related, assessment-related, and environmental problems.

Trainer-Related Problems

This chapter and Chapter 16 examine trainer-related problems, but in different ways. This discussion is geared toward training beliefs held by many that create organizational problems.

Trainers as Special People

Many individuals think of trainers as special people with unique skills that most people do not possess. That is probably true to a point because all people are special and each person has unique skills. However, given the opportunity along with proper training and encouragement, most people can be effectively utilized in training assignments of one kind or another.

Everyone who can stand in front of an auditorium and hold effective training won't become a polished speaker. Then again, everyone doesn't have to become a speaker. Many training assignments are on-the-job efforts where most people can become effective. Other small group sessions can be completed in an outstanding manner by people who would be ineffective in an auditorium-type situation.

The problem is that many organizations don't provide enough people the opportunity to train. They have the feeling that training should be left to training professionals. There never will be enough assets to allow such professionals to conduct all the training required in an organization dedicated to TQM, even if it were the most effective way of conducting the training, which it is not.

Trainers and Enthusiasm

Enthusiasm is helpful for anyone to have and is useful in most situations. Would-be leaders must make the effort to become enthusiastic if they hope to gain followers in the quest for excellence. Unenthusiastic leaders foster unenthusiastic followers—the prescription for a slow death of any quality initiative.

Individuals, however, should not be excluded from training assignments because they aren't bubbling over with enthusiasm. In fact, many readers have endured training sessions put on by enthusiastic individuals who appeared extremely phony and lost most of their audience. False, put-on enthusiasm is spotted immediately.

Sincere people who care for others, their job, and their organization adequately overcome any deficiency in enthusiasm with empathy, professionalism, and a sense of caring for the learner and that learner's needs.

Technical People Make Terrible Instructors!

Many technical personnel have heard the above comment applied to people in their particular profession. A one-word answer applies best—phooey. Technical people, on average, make no better or no worse instructors than any other group. How they acquired this reputation is difficult to understand.

The important concept is to marry the correct trainer to the right need. Some advanced technical personnel are deep thinkers with a broad understanding of their profession. They have difficulty getting down to the level of the rookie or the nontechnical person in that area, but they do well when they are training others with a similar background. They may also do well as a trainer of quality subjects outside their professional field.

The technical person who can remain learner-focused will succeed in most training situations. The first 14 chapters of this book were designed to prepare trainers for this learner-focused approach and will do just that when the plan is carried out.

She Just Doesn't Have the Platform Skills

Speech, gestures, and other platform skills are important and every trainer should work to improve them. However, these are not the most important part of training. The first focus is not on platform skills but on the learner's needs. What does the learner need, want, and desire? What is their current skill and knowledge level in comparison to the need generated by their job? These are the important initial questions that must be answered. The trainer who correctly answers them and prepares a plan to assist learners meet those needs is well on the way to training success, given the proper training situation.

Nothing supports quality training more than conscientious people with a strong desire to help others learn, but they must be given the opportunity to do so. Experience helps, but it takes opportunity to gain experience. The organization that doesn't actively cultivate the training skills of all who are capable is wasting its human assets. Training is one of the most important skills any leader can develop. Platform skills can be polished for those with the desire to train others.

Experienced instructors are not always excellent instructors. Some may have terrible habits and others lack the practical knowledge or don't understand the subject on which they are trying to train others. This problem can occur in both skill and knowledge type training areas. Fine actors can provide training, yet might not have a handle on their subject. This is the case in many video presentations, but it works well because no one can question a video presenter. However, these people know their lines and can get their message across to the viewers. The experienced SME who provides learner-centered information generally rates well by participants with an interest in the subject matter.

Poorly Prepared Training or Trainers

Poorly designed training is difficult to overcome. This adds emphasis to the importance placed on monitoring the developmental progress of training materials and lesson plans. It is essential to have material designed to fit the need, level of knowledge of trainees, and time frame for training. Equally important is the method for imparting this information. Which method or combination of methods best serves the trainees in their quest to learn the material: OJT, classroom, self-paced, or a combination of these and other training methods? This question must be carefully answered at the onset of training and continually asked throughout the process as training is provided and results are evaluated.

The best training design can be defeated by trainers who are ill-prepared. Who hasn't been in a learning situation where the leader of that meeting seemed to be viewing the material for the first time or was reading it because the information was unfamiliar? Given the choice, no training almost always is better than poorly prepared training or trainers.

The Wrong Trainer and/or Training

Trainers often are chosen because of such nebulous reasons as, "They have been around here long enough to know how to do things correctly," "They don't seem to need much help in their work," or "They always seem to get the job done." No audit was conducted to ascertain if they *complete the process correctly, using proper safety methods, in an expedient manner, that promotes solid performance.* When any one of these four critical items is eliminated or overlooked, the results can range anywhere from mediocre to disastrous. These trainers surely will be more expensive and may be potentially dangerous.

The following true story is an example that exhibits the wrong trainer providing the wrong training, plus a multitude of other training sins.

A machine shop machined pump castings. Each worker was expected to produce eight finished castings per shift. This had long been the performance standard and it almost always was met by all employees. There were no incentives or encouragement to produce more. In fact, there was a disincentive to do better which came in the form of the attitude and comments such as, "If we do any better than that we will work ourselves out of a job."

A new man was hired who had considerable previous experience in a high-performance, quality environment. A fellow worker was chosen to show him how the shop completed the machining operation. The new man was then given the go ahead to begin work on his own. This new employee turned the first one out using the process he had just been shown. He then sat on his tool chest for over an hour reviewing the process and the equipment he had available at his work station. He then went to work.

At the end of the evening he punched out as directed after writing the number of castings completed on the back of his time sheet. When he reported for his next shift, the supervisor approached him concerning the number of finished castings he had produced. "Did you complete seven or eight castings on your last shift?"

The new man replied, "Neither. I completed 78 of them." No one could believe him. Immediate visions of 78 ruined castings were conjured up, an expensive debut for sure. They sent the new man to the lounge until all of his castings could be completely quality checked. They discovered 78 castings, all well within tolerances in every aspect of the machining operation. The new man was then quizzed. It seems that over the years the company had replaced old equipment with newer machinery. Old employees learned to use this new machinery by applying the knowledge and skills that they learned on previous equipment. They routinely taught new employees the operation and no one learned to use the new equipment anywhere near design capacity. Had the new man not been experienced, chances are the other employees would have never learned how to use their equipment correctly.

This is not an uncommon situation and it does not rest solely in manufacturing. It is present in every type of organization. How many computer systems are used for word processing only? How many word processing programs are utilized anywhere near their capacity? Examples are present in many parts of every organization, some more than others. Copiers are another example of a machine that generally is not utilized anywhere near its potential. The greatest example, however, rests with the people who belong to the organization. These are the most valuable and often most underutilized of all assets.

Inadequate Knowledge of Trainees

Too often the students ability, skill, background knowledge, and ability to learn are not considered when the training is being developed. This can result in training that goes right over the student's head. In this case, not only is valuable training and production time lost, but the trainee is left confused and frustrated.

The other side of the coin also wastes time and money. The training is too basic, thus boring participants. Nothing new is learned and the value of followup training will be questioned because of the experience in this case.

Assessment-Related Problems

This problem was previously mentioned. Significant long-term training difficulties arise through shortcomings in this area.

Poor Assessment Procedures

Improper or lack of audit or need assessment encourages a multitude of training sins. There seems to be a problem and, without further adieu, training commences. In a few cases the training provided may solve the problem, but in most instances the results are poor, which may further result in a feeling that no training is worth the effort and assets expended.

Here is a case in point. New specifications required higher quality soldering connections. The people in the soldering operation were brought together where they were briefed on the new, more stringent requirements. They returned to work after this training session, and those in charge believed the problem was solved. This belief was shattered when QA/QC began rejecting over 50 percent of the boards that were coming off the line. The solderers were taken off the line for more training. Each person received a personal copy of the new specification and was warned that their performance had to improve to match these requirements. Nothing improved. If anything, performance slipped. Training was then provided on soldering techniques. Little changed.

Finally, an audit was held on the process. It was then discovered that the current equipment was incapable of consistently providing the required results to meet the new specifications. Engineering was called and worked with the day shift line supervisor on the problem. They came up with a design modification to the soldering machines which made the machines capable of consistently providing completed joints well within the specifications.

Unlike some organizations, this group learned a lesson on training procedures from its previous false start. Engineering and the day shift line supervisor got together and designed new procedures for the operators so they could correctly operate the modified machines. The line supervisor personally tried the procedures on one of the machines and discovered they worked even better than they had originally believed possible. The line supervisor then trained each operator on his shift and the other two shift supervisors individually on the process. The results were nothing short of amazing. Both production and quality improved greatly and worker attitude followed.

Training to the Wrong Problem

This situation generally is caused by poor assessment procedures. Perhaps you have been a part of a problem-solving process where the wrong problem was solved. One organization was hard at work trying to solve an employee attitude problem that it believed was adversely impacting on performance within a major department.

This was the initial situation. The process already had passed the problem determination stage and several possible solutions were being discussed. These included such typical considerations as pay-for-performance and earned-time-off for performance improvements. The organization had recently changed supervisors because of the situation. The change had produced no positive effect to date and actually may have fostered some negative consequences. This new supervisor was attending a one-week seminar on effective human relations. His manager wanted assistance with an incentive program to boost sagging performance, and they hoped to have it roughed out by the time the supervisor returned.

Early discussions centered around how the group had progressed to the solution part of the process. It seems that the department had recently installed a new process that was promoted as a guaranteed performance improver. It required new computer operations, some new equipment, and different documentation procedures in addition to the overall process changes. Some initial training had been held, which the manager believed would be adequate. The following conversation represents the initial brief.

"Everybody in the department should be up to speed. We spent three days running everyone through a training cycle. Their old supervisor was unable to meet the challenges presented by the new process so we removed him and replaced him with a guy we know can kick fanny. He's away at school right now rounding off some of his rough edges. We want to have an incentive program roughed out to support him in his efforts to turn this operation around when he returns. Time is precious."

Copies of the training audit or needs assessment that had served as the basis to establish the training were requested for informational purposes. Copies of the course critique sheets that were used after the training was held, plus any analysis they had completed also were requested. The answer received was typical of many training situations.

"We didn't conduct an audit as such. The people who set up the system told us what it would do before we bought it and they provided the old supervisor with operations training. We knew the results we needed so we had the training team and the old supervisor prepare a three day training session. We didn't solicit critiques even though training recommended it. They seldom seem worth the effort. Besides, our biggest problem was a supervisor with a negative attitude about the new system and the training so we replaced him with a team player."

A visit to the department was conducted to assist with the understanding of the new system. The three hours invested there proved most enlightening. Conversations occurred with many of the people in the department. There was an almost universal hesitancy to discuss the system in any detail along with a complete reluctance to talk about any problems they were encountering. That is, all were reluctant with the exception of one group leader. She jumped with both feet when asked about the training.

"Sure we received training, if you want to call it that. For three days a trainer explained what this new process would do for us in terms of how the new system would speed us up and how it would track our performance problems. The training was held while the new system was being installed. They didn't want any wasted time and that's a quote. During training we never saw the new equipment or the new records we would be required to keep. When they arrived we were told to go through the tutorial when we had time. At the same time we were expected to keep material flowing through this place. Right! Now people are keeping records by hand because they don't know how to operate the new system and don't have time to learn it either. What good is it? Joe wasn't too happy about the situation and went to his boss. It earned him a new work address."

She seemed to get that all out without pausing for breath. Two things were learned: The old supervisor was named Joe, and the action he probably took to get himself replaced was an unhappiness with the new system and the training. Armed with that information, the manager was approached about the possibility of conducting a quick, one-day audit to determine potential solutions that could help them. With some hesitancy, permission was granted.

The findings of that brief audit were indicative of the causes of many of the performance problems encountered in organizations. This is especially true when training is initiated as the solution without an audit or needs assessment. Some of the factors that adversely impacted in this case follow.

–The group that sold the new process to this organization did not understand the old process. The group manager that bought it was in the same boat. He had recently transferred in from another part of the operation.

–The work groups that were going to use this new system were never consulted at any point and, to a person, they did not believe that a new system was needed. Their opinion was based on the fact that the old system had never been fully utilized and several beneficial suggestions to make it perform better had been ignored.

–The work force resented the new manager. They believed Joe, their previous supervisor, had earned that promotion to the management position. When he didn't get it, they were upset.

–They were further disillusioned when Joe was replaced because he spoke up about the problem. It was believed he was removed solely because the new manager felt threatened by him.

The recommendations made to overcome the problems uncovered at the time of the audit were based largely on audit-discovered need and recommendations attributed to the work force in one way or another. This is not different than it is in many similar situations. The people who do the work often can provide a great deal of insight on the problems they encounter and how to correct them. Since they have a stake in the process and a strong desire for improvements, they heartily endorsed these initiatives. However, management could not believe cross-training and quality training initiatives with the recommended performance charts could overcome their original problems, so it was hesitant to introduce any of them. Nor was management anxious to implement later suggestions.

Several years have now passed since this situation was first uncovered. An additional supervisor has come and gone. The leased system that had been installed was never utilized anywhere near its potential because its potential far exceeded that needed for the type of effort in which it was placed. It was an expensive operation that seriously impacted on cash flow. A new supervisor is now in the process of returning to a system like the old one. He has reviewed many of the past recommendations that were made and is, in fact, putting them in place.

This situation involves many negative training examples and may seem a worst case scenario, but it is not all that uncommon. The reason for less than optimum results in many cases is not due to the lack of training, but the lack of a proper training system. The training process presented herein works. It may be replaced tomorrow by something better, but we are confident it will continue to produce excellent results with reasonable investments of time and assets. There are many factors that adversely affect any training program and these must be understood at the program's onset so they can be recognized and eliminated. This maximizes payoff in performance improvements. Let's look at these other negative factors.

Training Without Application

Training for training's sake wastes time and assets. It also gives participants the wrong attitude concerning training. Most people do not want to waste their time and when they are forced to, it upsets them. They often view follow-on training as more of the same. In this case, even valuable training that meets the need is not heeded fully, so it is rendered ineffective. Since there will be no performance improvement because there is no application, management may equate this situation to problems with all training and have no hesitancy in cutting training assets when cuts must be made. After all, "Training isn't producing any positive results."

Training Without Near-Term Application

Training that is not used in some fashion near term is comparable to training without application. Retention drops rapidly for training knowledge and skills

that are not utilized. When training has been held on a subject such as problem solving, the team should be put to work solving a problem immediately.
This should not be just a practice situation, either. Every operation has more
than enough real problems. It doesn't need to make up situations. The same is
true for most other training efforts. Either use it or lose it.

Environmental Problems

The major problem with environmental factors that impact on quality training
is that those who could change the situation are the ones who generally cause
the problem in the first place. This is one instance where recognition is a major
part of curing the problem.

Training Without Consideration of the Goal

The odds are against a positive bottom-line-oriented result occurring
from any training that does not consider the goal. Training that isn't tied
to the goal wastes considerable assets without providing much help to the
organization.

Packaged Training Program

There is the possibility that a packaged training program will exactly meet
organizational needs—then again the odds for such a fit are not good. This is
not to say that a packaged program will not support your organization. Many
can be tailored to the organization if so desired. The problem begins when the
organization looks for a cure-all quality program to be installed by outside
interests who will then ride off into the sunset leaving behind a well-honed
quality machine that will provide spectacular results.

This just doesn't happen. It takes ongoing training, and the organization
must become involved in the program to make it work. Outsiders would find
it difficult to have the level of commitment over the long term that is required
to make the quality process work and grow.

Poor Training Environment

The material facilities where training is held can adversely impact on training
results. Conference rooms with poor lighting, heating and air conditioning,
acoustics, or ventilation can detract from expected results. Constant interruptions from other personnel or the telephone are negative forces that must be
reduced or eliminated. Loud noises from nearby machines or other operations
are additional problems that negatively impact on training initiatives.
Although some of these may not be eliminated completely, the trainer must

strive to reduce these distractions to their lowest level. A familiar problem that can be almost completely avoided is improperly functioning training aids. All aids should be completely checked out prior to each session to ensure they are ready to roll. Spare projection bulbs should be on hand along with fuses where applicable. Fallback positions that don't require the aids save embarrassment when failures occur during presentations.

Poor Training Reinforcement

The tales are legend of employees who have been trained only to be told, "That's good information, but we do things differently here," or "We're doing all right without all that quality stuff." Almost as bad is the person who receives training, but is never evaluated to determine if the training is properly used and, if it is, to decide if the training meets the need. For any training to have positive effect for long-term performance improvements, the environment must not only support the actions initiated by the training, it must force the use of the training. Any environment that does not force the use of training is saying that the training wasn't valuable.

Nonutilized training is a hindrance to performance. Production time was lost and training costs were incurred while the frustration of the employees was increased because they wasted their time on training that would not be used. Even if the work environment changes at some later date through management change or new needs, there is little chance that the training will be of any value. Retention is poor for training that is not used near term.

Single-Level Training

Every organization is multilayered starting with the chief executive officer or similar position. One of the biggest problems encountered in motivating some organization to move in a quality training process is convincing people in charge of the need for the training at each level.

Statistics show that managers receive the lion's share of training money, even though they are one of the smallest groups in organizations. It would be a satisfactory situation if the managers would return to their workplace and train their charges, but that doesn't happen in most situations. There also is a need for executive training in the TQM process, which doesn't occur in enough cases, either.

A manufacturing facility recently was audited to determine what their training needs were for the institution of a TQM process. The initial meeting pointed to a wasted effort. The corporate president and a newly appointed director of quality were in attendance. The president wanted a TQM process but all of his actions demonstrated his being outside of the training for this process. He was dropping the complete process into the lap of the newly appointed director of quality while simultaneously giving this person a lot of direction, some of which seemed contrary to an effective program. It is difficult to achieve a TQM process in this type of environment. Every level in the organization must be cognizant of the need for the training and understand the attitudes, knowledge, and skills required for program success. Experience has proven there can be no other way.

An employee of a world-class manufacturer of connectors provided a positive example of how quality training should be conducted. When this manufacturer decided to put its commitment to excellence program in high gear, its CEO assisted by the president, VP quality, and VP sales and marketing personally provided the initial training to their top managers. This was followed by the members of this same team providing follow-up training to the top 120 managers. These training sessions paved the way for its quality training program. Would you think this company is serious about quality and quality training? Do you think its employees think the company is serious about quality and quality training?

Incorrect Training Methods

Incorrect training methods often compound the problems that first prompt the decision to train. One method of training is decided on when another method would be more appropriate. The decision often is based on expediency, rather than training effectiveness.

An earlier discussion covered training that was held while equipment was being installed. As a result, no one actually knew how to operate the system in the environment in which it was installed. As discussed, the results were detrimental to the operation. This example can be found in most organizations at one time or another.

Quickly In and Out

Many organizations rush into training programs, praying for a quick fix. When it doesn't occur (which in won't), they quickly jump back out of that training and go on to something else. Perhaps it will be another training program that will fix all the problems. It may be a switch to a new management system, different approaches to leadership, or TQM.

Regardless of what is tried, ultimate success elude those who practice this quick fix approach to anything. All of these tactics can provide significant improvements in any organization, but none will work as quick fixes. Performance improvement takes time and a combination of training, cultural, organizational, and process change working together over time to best serve the continuous improvement needs of any organization.

Insufficient Training

There are many causes of insufficient training. Many organizations suffer from this problem. The training need may not be fully recognized or funds may not be available to support training. An antitraining attitude often is the culprit. Here is a comment by a now-retired vice president of a technical company. "I don't bother training people. I buy trained people. When they can't do the work, I fire them and hire someone who can." He was deadly serious and his track record proved he meant it. Many organizations may not verbalize this thought, but they practice it.

Examples are legion where companies changed product lines or processes and made sweeping changes in work force personnel instead of a wholesale retraining evolution. This is not a practical solution if one desires low employee turnover and a high employee loyalty factor.

Over the years, this example was found representative of one discovered in all kinds of organizations. With few exceptions, it is almost always a better bet to go with the people you now have on board. They are known quantities who have been evaluated many times and deemed worth keeping. The current problems in our secondary educational systems make it an even better bet to go with the team already in place. The era of skilled employee shortages that was predicted a few years back, is now upon us.

A training plan based on the other organization plans (such as business, marketing, and quality plans) provides a more effective way of dealing with this type of situation. The attitudes, skills, and knowledge of current employees is a known factor and is certainly better known than those of new employees who would be hired in such a scenario. A long-range training plan would make allowances for the new skill and knowledge training required for a major changeover and such training could be implemented in steps. The attitude portion of the equation would take care of itself when employees determined the organization was taking care of its own.

Procrastination

Procrastination has been defined in various ways. One descriptive definition is that "procrastination is the greatest work saver ever invented by man." The procrastinator says, "We are going to begin training as soon as . . . ." You can fill anything in the "as soon as" spot, and it has probably been uttered. As time progresses, excuses that tax the imagination are inserted in this space. Each excuse prolongs the start of training and the work that accompanies it preventing a training or a solid TQM program effort from ever getting off the ground.

Some time ago, a site manager resigned from a company leaving behind ongoing technical, quality, and apprenticeship training programs that were producing excellent results. The new site manager had been a valuable member of the training team that had made this program effective. In the ensuing years, the training program became a nonexistent entity. It wasn't because this man didn't realize the benefits of the program or didn't want to bother. Quite the opposite is true.

This manager is a good man who must be involved in every aspect of the organization. He has difficulty letting go of anything, especially things he enjoys doing. With his day now crammed with other projects, he does not have time to maintain the same commitment to training, yet he will not delegate or simply oversee the training program. Instead he comes up with a continuous string of excuses as he procrastinates on resuming the project even though quality and production are negatively impacted, customer satisfaction suffers, and business is going through a downturn. "We intend to resume training when the new contracts are in place." "We are going to start training once more when we get the new people trained as instructors." "We intend to start training people as soon as we complete the move to a new location." "Training will resume as soon as . . . ." We have already covered the rest of the story.

Summary

1. There are many problems that can thwart the best-intentioned training efforts. Most of these can be prevented if they are considered as a part of each training development process.

2. The basic areas of training problems can be divided into three specific areas: trainer-related problems, assessment-related problems, and environmental problems.

3. Most of the problems that are trainer originated arise from basic misunderstandings concerning trainer qualifications. Factors such as enthusiasm and platform skills are given a greater degree of importance than they usually deserve.

4. Incorrect training assessment or the lack of assessment seriously hampers training evolutions. Successful training comes through knowledge of need and application of training to meet the discovered need. This will not occur without assessment.

5. Organizational environment can seriously dampen the effects of training. Training without consideration of the goal, packaged programs which don't apply, poor training environments, and poor training reinforcement are potential problem areas that must be foreseen. Preventing training problems is just as important as any other prevention exercise that relates to performance.

Bibliography

Brinkerhoff, R. O. *Achieving Results from Training,* San Francisco: Jossey-Bass, 1987.

Broadwell, M. M. *The Supervisor and On-the-Job Training,* Reading, MA: Addison-Wesley, 1970.

————. *The Supervisor as an Instructor,* Reading, MA: Addison-Wesley, 1970.

Craig, R. L. (Ed.) *American Society for Training and Development, Training & Development Handbook,* New York: McGraw-Hill, 1976.

————. *Training and Development Handbook,* New York: McGraw-Hill, 1976.

Davis, L. N. and McCallon, E. *Planning, Conducting and Evaluating Workshops,* Austin, TX: Learning Concepts, 1975.

Eitenton, J. E. *The Winning Trainer,* Houston, TX: Gulf Publishing Company, 1984.

Ellis, S. K. *How to Survive a Training Assignment,* Reading, MA: Addison-Wesley, 1988.

Engel, H. M. *Handbook of Creative Learning Exercises,* Houston, TX: Gulf Publishing, 1973.

London, M. *Managing the Training Enterprise,* San Francisco: Jossey-Bass, 1989.

Mitchell, G. *The Trainer's Handbook,* New York: American Management Association, 1987.

CHAPTER 16

Additional Training Concepts

This chapter is devoted to training concepts that can improve your total training program. In many ways it is a summary of the first 15 chapters because some of the topics were previously mentioned. However, each is important enough that a more structured discussion is in order.

After some deliberation, it was decided to present these concepts in a semi-outline format. This approach allows a rapid review of these ideas during program development and again prior to training sessions. The material is presented in no particular order since it is all supportive and equally important to the training effort.

Training Resistance

Trainers often are confronted with initial resistance in their sessions. This is not an unusual occurrence. In most cases the situation can be handled with a minimum of frustration and difficulty if a few simple concepts are understood and used.

Change of any kind tends to meet with some resistance and a solid training program stands for change. That's what training is all about—providing new knowledge and skills to improve performance continually. Such efforts can incur more than their share of grief because people usually are content with things the way they are, at least content enough that they are not actively seeking change. Many fear the unknown and wonder what sinister plot is behind the training initiatives. Others wonder if it is management's way to get more out of the work force at less cost, something most workers are not whole-heartedly behind unless they too will receive a benefit.

Seldom is resistance generated during the training session. People often rebel when they are sent to training against their wishes. They may feel they have immediate problems in their work center that demand their attention, and they resent not being there to handle things. This should be understood because their career depends on on-the-job performance, and they may not consider or recognize training as a productivity enhancer.

Many managers do not discuss the training need with their people before the person attends training sessions. This leaves them wondering why they were sent in the first place or how it is supposed to help them in terms of doing their job better. Many involuntary participants have had negative training experiences in the past which leaves them pessimistic about any kind of future sessions. There are other external concerns that may impact on training sessions, such as family problems and other personal situations that the trainer cannot control.

Causes of Resistance

The outlined process will help overcome program resistance. The first step is to understand the possible causes of resistance. Reasons for resistance might include the following:

No choice–People often are sent to training against their wishes. Adults want to have a say in their future and the things they do. Organizations that sell their workers on training in terms of, "The real benefit to you is . . ." face far less resistance than those who don't. Providing training as a reward also reduces resistance. Adults see what is right for them to do and most of them willingly cooperate with process and organizational improvements when they see a benefit. Providing workers with an input into the training decisions allows them to feel they have some control of their destiny.

More pressing matters–At times, trainees perceive there are more pressing needs than training that were left unattended because of the training session. For example, a report or proposal with a near-term deadline may be waiting for them and the training may force it to be late or rushed. It is incumbent for management to ensure there are long-term training schedules available so people can plan around them. Supervisors and managers must also plan workloads so they don't continually interfere with scheduled training. Occasionally training must be rescheduled, but if it happens often it signifies that the planning effort is not very effective.

Not relevant–Training that is not perceived as relative to their work or personal needs seldom succeeds. There are several ways this problem can be sidestepped. Training schedules with course descriptions assist trainees in their efforts to tie training to their need. Clearly stated course objectives also help. Supervisors should be briefed on all training well in advance so they can help sell people on the benefits. In many cases this problem stems from supervisory comments such as, "I don't know why you're going to training. The boss says you go, so you go. That's enough for me and it oughta be enough for you."

Negative experience–There are few people who haven't had some sort of negative training experience in the past. These experiences leave a bad taste in their mouth for future efforts. It is important to make all training experiences positive and work with people during initial stages so they don't relate negative past experiences to the potential benefit they will derive from quality training.

No explanation–No one bothers to explain the training need or the program. Individual employees have no input into the training decisions and no idea where it all is headed. There are few people who put much energy into any initiative that begins in this manner, yet so many efforts continue to foster this type of situation.

Signs of Resistance

Recognition of the signs of potential resistance is paramount to setting aside the problem. Some of the signs include:

Refusal to participate–The person who walks in, sits down, crosses his arms and legs, and scowls in your direction can be assumed to be discontent with his current address. When this posture continues, it signifies resistance will be encountered.

Sleeping–Some people have a difficult time staying awake when they aren't active. However, most people will attempt to remain awake during training exercises which they realize will benefit them. The person who lays her head down before class and begins sawing logs isn't all that anxious to be there. She's making a statement.

Disruptive behavior–Many classroom troublemakers do so because they are frustrated with some aspect of the training process, or they enjoy being noticed more than they enjoy learning.

Side conversations–Two types of people make side conversations during training: ignorant folks and those who are showing training resistance.

Smart answers–Smart answers often are used to show those in attendance that "I don't want to be here and I'm not going to contribute to the program."

Challenge to authority–The troublemaker asks barbed or trapping questions that are difficult or impossible to answer. Challenges are put forth concerning the material, the instructor, and the statements of other trainees who are trying to get something out of the program. The trainer's authority may be openly confronted when it is possible to do it without bringing too much wrath down on the culprit.

Overcoming Resistance

Regardless of the reason for resistance, it must be dealt with quickly before it detracts from the learning experience of other participants. No one has the right to interfere when others are trying to learn, and trainers have the responsibility to ensure that disruptions of any kind do not continue.

Don't be afraid to take action. Most situations will take care of themselves when the perpetrator understands the trainer will not allow the disruptive behavior to continue. Other participants generally assist the trainer with her efforts to produce a meaningful session.

A proper introduction often precludes most resistance. Explain the purpose of the training to the participants in terms of, "The real benefit to you is . . . ." Ask them why they are attending and what they expect to get out of the session that will assist them in their self-improvement efforts. Seek out areas where they feel a particular training need. Use a large easel to jot down areas that were not scheduled to be covered, but fit into the lesson should there be time to cover them. This paper can be posted as a reminder to cover the additional topics when it is appropriate.

Complete a self-check–A self-check is the first step once resistance is encountered. The question to ask is, "Could my manner be contributing to this resistance?" If the answer is "yes" or even "maybe," readjustments are required. The trainer cannot afford to lose the class for any reason. Several questions are in order. Do you:

1. Tend to pontificate or act in a condescending manner?

2. Come across as a know-it-all and act as though the things you may not know probably aren't all that important?

3. Stray from the subject to areas that have little relevancy?

4. Hog the available time leaving little room for input by others?

5. Cut others off without allowing them the courtesy of hearing what they have to say?

6. Treat participants with less respect than you expect in return?

7. Openly criticize participant ideas without hearing them through?

8. Place more importance on your own ideas or on the ideas of select people than you do the others?

9. Engage in other classroom partiality such as ignoring some who desire to input while continuously encouraging the input of others?

10. Endeavor to be a performer rather than a trainer?

Discover Why

Once it is determined that the resistance is not trainer generated, action must be taken to alleviate it. Proper questioning techniques often overcome the problem. Some appropriate questions might be:

- Can you explain why you are here?
- Can you explain why you feel that way?
- Can you see any way this training can support your career?
- Can you tell me if I'm doing something to make you dislike this session?
- Can you tell us why you believe this material is not valid? Relevant? Correct?
- Can you tell me how we can make this a beneficial session for you?

Be supportive–Support all participants and their ideas. When you cannot agree with an idea it is OK to say so. A good way to handle this is to say something like, "That could be a questionable way to do that, John. Let's see how some of the other people would handle it. Anybody else have any comments?" When the idea is questionable you can bet there will be comments forthcoming to contradict the input.

Provide a benefit–Ensure participants get their money's worth for the time they invest. Conduct learner-centered training and tie it to their needs

Don't be afraid–Most situations can be resolved. The important thing is to recognize and confront problems immediately. Often resistant participants undergo an attitude change once they understand that others don't see the session as a problem or they see the problem they are causing others who want to learn. At times, other participants will assist in getting the problem under control.

If all else fails—confront the individual. Speak to him on a break. It is important to wait until the break because confrontation in front of others spells trouble. You may want to arrange a break early in the session so that the problem can be discussed. Ask what the real problem is and try to understand him. Request his support because generally you can't help him with the problem. Most resistance is brought to the session and not generated within. If these steps don't work, ask him to leave. You cannot afford to continue without his cooperation, and one individual cannot be allowed to disrupt beneficial training that others need. Any trainee who must be asked to leave class should have his actions reported to the appropriate supervisor for action.

Personal experience has been that few people are ever required to leave a training session. Once they determine you are sincere in presenting a solid session and want their help to do it, the problem disappears. However, resistance won't go away unless it is addressed.

Training Pitfalls

There are all kinds of traps waiting for trainers. Some of them were mentioned in Chapter 15. Experience helps one to recognize them so they can be prevented.

No need–Excellent training that has no organizational need or requirement will be seen as providing little value simply because it doesn't. Training must meet the needs of the goal, strategic plan, business plan, market plan, quality plan, and training plan. It also must benefit the people who have a need to know. Training that helps the trainee maintain a quality resumé is especially valuable. If it would help another employer, it will certainly help her current one.

No learning–Covering the material does not mean learning took place, and without learning, training is just so much wasted time. It is the trainer's responsibility to assess the level of training taking place frequently in order to ensure payoff. This can be accomplished through a solid questioning procedure. Listen to the input of trainees and continually monitor the response level. Seek their input and wait until you get an answer when you ask questions.

The expert syndrome–"Hey, I'm the expert here." Those who act this way haven't heard the definition of expert. "Ex" is a has-been and "spurt" is a drip under pressure. No matter what level of knowledge you hold, don't act like an expert. Allow others to discover your knowledge level. Always ensure opinions and knowledge of participants are accorded the same value as your personal ideas.

I'm important–"I'm the trainer, therefore, I'm important." You are important and so is everyone else. You should be better organized with more focus on the material, but that doesn't make you more important than other participants. You cannot pontificate and hold the participants respect. The trainer's leadership role provides a measure of authority, but not superiority. Your importance is measured by your effectiveness. The real question becomes, "How much will their performance improve because of this training session?"

My performance–The "I knocked 'em dead" attitude has no place in training. The purpose of this session is to train the audience, not entertain them.

Have fun because it assists with the learning experience, but don't become a performer. The purpose of training is knowledge sharing rather than amusement. Remember that training sessions should be learner centered and that places the emphasis where it belongs. The same goes for the tendency to make a speech. Training and speeches are a world apart and once again, training is the purpose of the session.

Tips

These tips support the efforts of all trainers. Some such review is an important way to prepare for presentation because this list will prompt recall of other important areas on which you wish to place emphasis.

Never make excuses–Never apologize or make excuses for anything. Excuses place your knowledge and the potential value of training in question and you don't need that. Some of the common excuses heard include:

- "I never did this or taught this before."
- "You probably know this subject better than I do."
- "This is not my strong suit."

Remember, if the organization felt someone was more competent, they would have selected that individual for the training assignment. Since they didn't, you are their person and there is no reason to apologize for anything.

Watch your presentation–Be careful with jargon, technical terms, clichés, and acronyms with which all participants are not thoroughly familiar. Explain technical words that must be used and might not be understood by some in the audience. Aids require special attention. Avoid talking to them instead of the audience and check all training devices ahead of time. Number any note cards in case they become mixed, or dropped. Staple note sheets in sequence or put them in a notebook so they remain in order. Keep a good presentation sequence—TELL, TELL, TELL. Tell them what you plan to tell them, tell them, and then tell them what you told them. Follow up: "And in conclusion, as a result of this training, you will be expected to . . . ." Elaborate on the results you expect. At the next meeting or on visits, check for results. When you don't follow up, the training seldom is applied to its full potential.

Be aware of distractions–Avoid physical distractions such as pacing, rattling change, or playing with your keys. Hands in the pockets also can be a problem. Keep the pointer aimed toward the aid and not the people. Beware of "you know," "OK," and similar sayings.

Beware of jokes–Be careful with jokes. Some people can tell them while others cannot. Those who can't might easily bomb an entire training session through ill-advised attempts to joke. Jokes, stories, and anecdotes must support the points you are attempting to make, and you should be good at telling them. Be yourself—not an entertainer. Sessions should be fun, but that doesn't mean you have to be a clown to create that atmosphere. Retention always is higher when people enjoy the presentation.

Don't be a know-it-all–Admit it when you don't know something. Ask the class for help because there often is someone in attendance who does know. If it is important, ask the person who asked the question if they would look it up or volunteer to find out yourself. All questions should be answered correctly and concisely. Never overlook integrity.

Lead–Do not try to control—LEAD. Every training session will be a stern test of the trainer's leadership ability, organizational skills, and commitment to quality. Allow disagreement to a point but don't allow a few negative individuals to monopolize the sessions or provide a division in the class. Never allow disruptions. They seldom have any point other than someone trying to prove a point that doesn't need to be proved. Be careful of the *"windbag.* Ask him to discuss the matter during the break. If necessary, remind him of the time constraints, and cut him off gently. Beware of the *assumptive attitude.* Assume tends to mean makes an ASS of U and ME. Training must be worth the time and assets expended, and it is up to the trainer to ensure that happens.

Trainer attitude–The trainer's attitude is vital. Exhibit interest, dedication, knowledge, and enthusiasm while serving as a guide or facilitator to steer the learning experience. Be caring and supportive, show respect for participants and their ideas. Never embarrass others, instead search for ways to provide encouragement to increase learning effectiveness. The trainer searches for common ground for agreement so everyone can become a contributing member.

Research your material–Thoroughly research material before presentation. Quality presentation and material are mandatory. Material content is dictated by the type of training, desired results, and origin of material. Meet with supervisors ahead of time to obtain material and examples that apply directly to their process or operation. Monitor work processes to ensure you understand them before training. Aim all training material toward the results you expect to achieve.

Presentation skills–Maintain group contact through solid eye contact with each individual. Develop your own style and build on those things you do best. Work on voice projection while maintaining tone and pace awareness because it supports your presentation efforts. Be on guard against the tendency to read material because it greatly reduces effectiveness. Speak at the participants' level starting with their understanding. Be time conscious and adjust the emphasis to meet course objectives. Reinforce the information as you progress through the lesson and again during the summary as you review all key points.

Questions–Learn to handle questions because they can kill the session. Anticipate possible questions that might be asked and prepare answers before the session. A good time to do this is when you review the material prior to the session. Treat all questions as important and endeavor to answer them as they arise. Stay positive and don't become defensive. Clarify ambiguous questions by paraphrasing them until you and the other person are on the same wavelength, then answer them. Resist the urge to blurt out the answer immediately. Take some time to consider it. Break complex answers into parts before attempting to answer them and try to keep answers geared to the course objectives where possible.

Some trainees may be gunning for the instructor. Resist the urge to put them in their place because you may alienate the class. Watch for the participant who arrives with loaded questions and waits for the opportunity to use them as if there is a bounty for trapping the trainer. Experienced trainers have pat replies thought out and practiced ahead of time to help them out of these sticky spots.

1. "Sounds like you may have an answer for that. Would you share it with the rest of us?"

2. "That may not be an easy question to answer. Could we discuss it during the break after I have had some time to think about it?"

3. "I hadn't thought about that. Could we discuss it after class?"

4. "Perhaps somebody else has thought this through. Is there anybody with comments on this question?"

The answer to the last question may surprise you. One participant answered, "Yes, I have a comment. I'm wondering if John is trying to disrupt our training or just make himself look foolish."

Remember physical aspects–Rotate the training setting to different offices, restaurants, and so forth, where that would be appropriate. Vary the room's physical layout. Some workable layouts include the horseshoe, round table, and the normal classroom. Each choice has advantages.

Administration is necessary–Develop a system and maintain good records. Save lesson plans and outlines for future use. Maintain training records to provide accountability. Utilize training information in annual evaluations. If some people will be allowed to miss training sessions, designate who will be allowed, when, and why? Expect a lot from training—inspect to ensure you receive it.

Beware of the Negative

Taking care to ensure the negative doesn't occur is just as important as making sure the positive happens. Attention to this part of the process can be assisted by the following outline:

Unused training–Training that cannot or will not be used is so much wasted effort and assets. Training will not produce performance improvement unless the trainee's work environment actually forces the use of the training material. An environment that does not force the trainee to use the training signals that *"the training was not really that valuable."* If the environment changes at some later date, there is little chance the trainee will retain the information he had because of disuse over the time period. Unused training is a hindrance to production. Production time is lost, training costs reduce profits, and a certain level of frustration is encountered by all who are associated with such efforts.

Lack of supervisory enforcement–A supervisor's attitude toward training largely determines how her subordinates feel about training and how much effort they will expend. The supervisor is the only person outside of the individual who can ensure the training pays for itself in results. Without a payoff in performance, there is little reason for holding training in most cases.

Discouraging Atmosphere

- "Forget it, we don't do it that way here."
- "We're not ready for that yet."
- "We don't have time for that."
- "We're doing all right without it."
- "We tried that once before and it didn't work."
- "It costs too much."
- "That's not our responsibility."
- "It just won't work."

Frustration–Supervisors and/or policy prohibit change, which negates the effects of training. Any change, regardless of who initiates it, will meet with resistance at the outset. Management must be aware of this potential resistance and overcome it.

Creating Training Effectiveness

Training effectiveness is dependent on a system. Longer-term training programs (such as those attended in conjunction with quality training) require additional effort to ensure payoff is accomplished.

Planning–Planning is extremely important for effective training. The first step is picking the correct course—the one that best meets the need. All potential programs must be thoroughly analyzed. Several deciding factors should be considered.

1. *Fit*–Does this program readily meet our needs?

2. *Cost*–Can we afford it?

3. *Potential benefit*–Will it do what we need it to do to meet the goal?

Precourse preparation–This section is completed by the participants immediate supervisor. The training objective, background for training, and course outline is explained to participants. The explanation includes how training relates to the job requirements and how it will be used on the job. Follow-up assessments and training assignments are discussed.

During course work–The trainee takes notes and develops future lesson plans when assigned. He works to ensure that all course objectives are covered to the extent that meets his needs. For longer programs (those longer than one week), the supervisor may require a mid-program status report.

Post course followup–The supervisor and participant review and critique the course as it relates to meeting the established objectives. The supervisor solicits additional information from the participant and they decide how to use it. An implementation plan is developed to put the training into action. The supervisor also determines how the participant will use the training to teach subordinates.

The Training Sequence

This recap is presented in lieu of a summary since the material in this chapter tends to summarize many of the points presented throughout the book.

1. Consider the training objectives

2. Develop a training plan

   a. The training plan must dovetail with other company plans such as strategic quality, business, and market plans, and it must be supported by the budget.

   b. It must match the organization's training objectives.

   c. It must be planned around available assets.

   d. It must meet organizational quality goals.

   e. Individual lesson plans must be developed as required.

3. Select the training team. The trainer must:

   a. Be interested in training.

   b. Be committed to quality.

   c. Enjoy people.

   d. Have patience.

   e. Want the training assignment.

   f. Be empathetic.

   g. Be willing to train to the audience's level.

   h. Be respected by colleagues.

   i. Have time for training and training preparation.

4. Prepare the trainers

   a. Provide trainer training:

      (1) In-house

      (2) Outside sources—seminars, toastmasters

   b. Provide training methods:

      (1) Lecture or presentation

      (2) On-the-job

      (3) Demonstration

      (4) Self-study

      (5) Role playing

      (6) Case studies

      (7) Discussion

   c. Practice actual training exercises

   d. Critique trainer and training material

5. Prepare trainees

   a. Emphasize the benefit to the employee.

   b. Make clear how it will improve the organization and its quality.

   c. Make clear any requirements that will transpire as a result of the training.

6. Train

7. Evaluate the training

   a. Did training meet the objectives?

b. Trainees can be surveyed about training.

c. Work processes and quality can be reviewed for improvement.

d. Trainees can be tested on training.

e. Results can be tabulated to improve on future training.

Bibliography

Brinkerhoff, R. O. *Achieving Results from Training*, San Francisco: Jossey-Bass, 1987.

Broadbill, M. M. *Achieving Results from Training*, San Francisco: Jossey-Bass, 1987.

Craig, R. L. (Ed.) *American Society for Training and Development, Training & Development Handbook*, New York: McGraw-Hill, 1976.

―――. *Training and Development Handbook*, New York: McGraw-Hill, 1976.

Davis, L. N. and McCallon, E. *Planning, Conducting and Evaluating Workshops*, Austin, TX: Learning Concepts, 1975.

Eitenton, J. E. *The Winning Trainer*, Houston, TX: Gulf Publishing, 1984.

Ellis, S. K. *How to Survive a Training Assignment*, Reading, MA: Addison-Wesley, 1988.

Engel, H. M. *Handbook of Creative Learning Exercises*, Houston, TX: Gulf Publishing, 1973.

London, M. *Managing the Training Enterprise*, San Francisco: Jossey-Bass, 1989.

Mitchell, G. *The Trainer's Handbook*, New York: American Management Association, 1987.

CHAPTER 17

Customer Connections

Many ties exist or should exist between training and customers, both internal and external to the organization. Up to this point, each chapter was tied to the previous chapter, the goal, and trainee needs. Justifiably, the goal and participant needs are given considerable emphasis. After all, the participant is a customer and she is the only person who can ensure training efforts have an ultimate payoff, and training payoff is absolutely necessary for TQM and customer satisfaction.

Saying the customer is always right doesn't go nearly far enough by today's standards. Customers can be right and still not be treated with the respect and courtesy that should be reserved for someone who holds the fate of the organization in their hands. Many might not receive the quality service they deserve and therefore will not be a satisfied, long-term customer.

Customer satisfaction will not occur through a quick mention of the necessity for it, accompanied by a few signs posted in conspicuous places. Satisfaction must be incorporated into the training plan and every training session. Mentioning the importance of customer service and satisfaction without follow-through that incorporates that policy into every organizational action can cause considerable resentment and rejection. Talk without action signifies "another management fire drill that will be soon forgotten."

Internal Customer Relationships

Internal customers are discussed first because external customer care, service, or satisfaction will never occur until the internal customer is served. These internal customers are seldom considered as such in most organizations prior to their initiation of quality efforts. Instead, employees are just one more asset to be used in the effort to meet the goal. This discussion examines the things customers deserve in the way of training services from various teams or people within their organization.

The Training Team

Who are the training team's customers and what do they owe them? The "who" is pretty simple—it's everybody within the organization including training team members and the customers and potential customers external to the organization. "What" isn't much more difficult to answer. Customers deserve and expect professional, quality services that meet their needs, and this includes training services.

Customers must receive their just due and a little extra where possible. Training services are a reflection of the quality and professionalism of the organization as a whole. Therein lies a problem.

In many organizations the individuals who conduct quality training don't have the skills, knowledge, or experience required to provide the training necessary to support a long-term excellence program. The reasons are many. Trainers are selected for training duties in a variety of different ways: Some individuals are chosen to fill an opening without removing a person from production who is doing well, some are selected because they demonstrated a particular skill or knowledge on the job, and others are volunteers for training assignments. Seldom are people chosen to become trainers because they have both a solid training and job-related background with job skills being the most important.

There is a common occurrence that takes place when people are selected for new positions. Regardless of what the new position is or what their personal background has been, once in the new position they become the resident expert. Everyone, including those who were part of the selection process and know their background, almost immediately look to them for professional advice. Most trainers placed in this position feel obligated to provide the requested wisdom. That's what they are now being paid for, their knowledge of training. Things get worse when this advice is accepted as the gospel according to training without considering their true level of expertise.

This problem is compounded because most organizations don't have internal train-the-trainer programs to hone training skills continuously—initial training and go get 'em just won't do the job. This causes trainers to pick up their training skills on the job and through experience in training assignments supplemented by personal study on the subject.

The situation worsens when trainers are required to train on technical or quality subjects where they have little background. They must rely on material borrowed from other sources, material which they have not personally used in a work environment and have not received training on its use from someone who has. This situation occasionally occurs through necessity for all who involve themselves in training, but it must not become the routine way of doing business. Trainers must have a deeper understanding of their subjects.

In those cases where the trainer does not have deep-seated knowledge, much of the problem can be alleviated when each session is rehearsed and presented to other trainers and technically knowledgeable individuals before show time. Glitches are discovered before the actual training sessions, which minimizes problems and maintains the professional status of the training department. The customer deserves and should receive this type of preparation.

Training tends to be a thankless job in many organizations. Trainers are used as firefighters who are called on to solve the never-ending problems that occur in the reactive environments common to many organizations. In this mode, they are overworked and underappreciated as they struggle to meet commitments, borrow rooms for training, put training plans together, round up training aids and equipment, and secure cooperation from other departments. They tend to receive considerable blame and little support. This situation can be changed without a great deal of expense using the same "pick us up by the bootstraps approach" for the training department that is presented for the quality program in this series.

Management plan–The training team must be well managed. It is absolutely paramount that the person responsible for the training team act like a professional and ensures that professionalism permeates throughout the training group. Trainers must be looked up to and respected. Respect is earned not given and every trainer must put forth the required effort to ensure they are part of a respected team.

The training operation should report directly to an executive level so it becomes a direct part of the planning staff. This is essential since successful training plays such a major part in any long-term quality process. It provides the training department with the opportunity to serve its management customers in planning exercises to determine the training that best supports the organization's near-term and strategic goals. It also allows an input when the budget is developed, a necessity if training is to receive the support it should have.

Operating at this level integrates trainers into operations and provides them with an in-depth knowledge of other departments, how they are organized, and how they contribute to reaching the goal. This understanding of the organization, their market, and their customers, supports every aspect of training. It also assists trainers in their efforts to become truly customer focused because you have to know and understand your customers before you can satisfy their needs.

Training plan—The first requirement of the training plan is to include training for trainers. This can be internal training held by those with expertise in specified areas. Internal training is extremely important. It supports development and understanding of organizational culture, structure, and the goal, which must be included in the planning and presentation stages for all training activities. This knowledge provides a training fit to the organization and supports the long term organizational attitude toward performance improvement. These are criteria for all successful training programs.

Relatively low-cost supplemental training is possible for the training department through organizations such as ASTD. The members of these groups tend to be good samaritans of the training world and most of them readily offer assistance and material for fellow trainers. Some universities offer advanced degrees for training professionals. Penn State University offers such a masters program that is well attended and held in high regard. These longer programs offer a knowledge base that is virtually impossible to acquire through short-term programs.

Trainers should have individual self-study programs that supports their training efforts. It is not enough to wait for others to provide all the effort required to turn trainers into professionals. Most trainers appreciate help generating a self-study program. Those who decide not to take part in such programs set an extremely poor example for others, and they should be transferred to an assignment more suited to their lack of desire for self-improvement, if one could be found in a quality organization.

Self-training efforts by the training department can help some of the department's key customers. Internal train-the-trainer efforts should be opened up to internal customers. Groups that should be considered for invitation are the managers and supervisors who must continually provide training to their charges.

The training department's external customers also should be included when this can be accomplished in a professional manner. In fact, a close-knit relationship between supplier and customer training teams can significantly improve the professionalism of both groups while reducing the costs they must bear. It further cements the allegiance each organization has to the other, an extremely important criteria for long-term success in the global economy.

Technical experience—Trainers should be selected to participate in the introduction of new equipment and systems, and they must take part in the initial training evolutions. They must then immerse themselves into the operations which use these new products. It is likely that supervisors or a team of supervisors and trainers will do follow-up technical training. Trainers must know how these new additions fit into the operation so they can tie this information into other training efforts that are part of quality initiatives.

Change agents–Trainers provide extremely important service to the organization and their customers as change agents. Their customers must be prepared to change in many ways as the journey to excellence unfolds. Subjects such as organizational vision, the goal, benefits of performance improvement, and quality initiatives should be intertwined throughout every training program as a matter of course. It provides continual reinforcement to both the application and benefit of training initiatives.

Customer service–Training plays a major part in the transformation to a quality environment tuned to customer support and satisfaction. Trainers have influential ties to all other departments, something no other group below the executive level possesses. They are continually working with internal customers and hopefully external customers to an increasing degree. They tie executive-level culture and values to customer needs through training in marketing, manufacturing, shipping, receiving, and every other department to best meet customer expectations.

Trainers communicate news of performance improvement and customer satisfaction achievements through training evolutions. This helps participants understand that improvements are possible and occurring within their organization. Such information strongly supports training initiatives and the quality movement.

The Management Team

In one way or another, every person below the manager is a customer of the manager. The reverse also is true. Many managers have direct external customers who must be considered in all decisions. These relationships are established in Volumes I–III.

Managers owe their customers a great deal because without internal and external customers there would be no need for managers. The considerations of customer satisfaction must receive the level of importance due it since all of these individuals play significant roles in organizational transformation.

Leadership–The first thing managers owe their customers is visionary leadership. Each individual must have a vision of the future, how he fits into that future, and the benefits he can expect to receive when that vision becomes the present.

Working environment–Internal customers expect a supportive working environment that is conducive to performance improvement. A considerable part of all learning takes place on the job and will not occur in a hostile or unsupportive environment.

Skilled personnel with positive attitudes develop when the environment supports such development. The opposite also is true. Poor attitudes and even poorer work habits flourish where environmental support is lacking. Solid training comes to naught if the organizational environment doesn't support its use.

Training–Management owes its customers a well-trained leader who is personally working to become even better. Managers must train their subordinates to support the technical, quality, and customer service changes that must take place in their efforts to create a quality environment. Managers are responsible for much of their immediate subordinates training within a quality organization.

Training assets–Management also is responsible for supplying the assets required to operate a supportive training program. Some level of assets is available in every organization. The management team must work to build these assets to a level supportive of their quest for excellence as performance improvements pay off. Training cannot be ignored in the quest for quality or customer satisfaction. A greatly increased emphasis is necessary in most organizations in order to transform their operations to quality that satisfies both internal and external customers.

The use of training assets should be planned to best serve both internal and external customers. Trained personnel are better able to serve. As mentioned previously, there are numerous benefits of joint supplier/customer training sessions with few additional costs.

Customer service–Management must tune to the needs of all of their customers in order to improve the organization. External customers will not receive the service they deserve unless internal customer needs are first satisfied. Service by example is a most important aspect of the manager's leadership responsibilities. This service requirement includes solid communications of organizational successes, needs, and future plans. All customers must know where the organization is headed and the part they play in the future.

Supervisors and Their Customer

Every subordinate is a customer and supportive service to each of them is crucial to organizational success. Training requirements make up a considerable part of the supervisors' total responsibilities. Neglecting training has many consequences, all of which are negative. The results of poor training are immediately evident. Instead of performance improvement there are performance problems that continually frustrate the quest for process improvement. Problem-solving efforts are reactionary, firefighting efforts rather than proactive efforts to improve processes and customer satisfaction.

The supervisor who continually trains subordinates establishes supportive relationships, which induces others to cooperate with the quality and performance improvement efforts. Well-trained workers possess a positive self-image and self-esteem. They feel capable of contribution above the normal expected in the workplace because training has improved their skills, knowledge, and attitude. They are more supportive of team evolutions because they know their team members have received similar training and are capable of doing their fair share.

Well-trained supervisors benefit the organization in many ways. They know how to do things correctly and are continually involved in training others to do likewise. This supports the production of quality products and services because the supervisor knows how to meet and exceed minimum performance standards and continually trains others to do likewise.

The supervisor is on the job so she knows when problems are occurring and can step in at that point. No training schedule is required and no appointments have to be made—the trainer is the work team leader.

Internal customers in downstream processes immediately benefit from improved products and services. This tends to improve attitudes and work habits in follow-up evolutions. Workers who receive a quality product do not care to be known as the weak link that screwed up the works. Supervisors certainly don't care to be responsible for a poor product, and they don't want their people to find out they are not being trained and served as well as their next-door neighbors.

External customers also are well served. The product and service they receive is continually improved. The attitude of those with whom they deal also improves as the quality of their products improve and the complaints about products and services decrease. Organizational pride through quality products and services is something to behold. People take pride in their work and want to see their organization producing quality products and services that meet the goal. Their pride and professional life depend on it.

Several requirements are immediately evident if the supervisor is to become the training person just discussed. The training department must develop supportive programs to assist supervisors in several key areas.

Training skills–The supervisor will not become an effective trainer without interactive training skills. This requires the training department to develop and present appropriate train-the-trainer training programs for all individuals serving in supervisory positions.

Quality knowledge–Supervisors will undergo quality training as a part of management and work teams. They will receive stand-alone fundamentals training. To this they must add training to use these skills and knowledge properly in their work teams.

Customer-tuned training–Customer awareness, customer relations, and customer service training is extremely important. Supervisors must know and understand all their customers if they are to serve them properly.

Communications skills–Supervisors must be able to communicate need, commitment, and attitude to subordinates. They must develop listening skills so they can effectively communicate. They must know what their customers need and want if they are to satisfy them, and the only way that will occur is if they ask questions and listen.

Interpersonal relations–These skills are mandatory in their dealings with all customers. Learning them requires a genuine fondness for people and a sincere effort to do what is best for them. Telephone skills are important. The characteristics discussed must be developed to the point where they also come through over the phone.

Technical and product skills and knowledge–These elements are understood, but they are mentioned anyway. The supervisor must be a knowledgeable pro in both areas or there is no chance he will become a capable trainer who can lead performance improvement efforts.

The External Customer

The external customer is mentioned throughout this chapter. The needs of internal and external customers cannot be separated. They must become a working, if sometimes invisible, team. People who never meet during a working situation must, nevertheless, function as a team. Team members might not even speak the same language, but they must be a team. That is the way of the new world order that is upon us.

The organization tuned to the internal customer has an excellent foundation for external customer satisfaction. Well-treated workers who labor in a work environment conducive to excellence produce excellent products and services. Those who know people realize this is true.

Tuning to the External Customer

Every training session should consider the external customer and how service to the customer can be improved to increase customer satisfaction. Employees themselves are customers and they know what they like and don't like. They easily place themselves in the shoes of their customers and can produce significant improvements and benefits in this manner.

Workers must be able to understand how the product or service they help produce is used to support the customer's efforts. At times, products are used by people in remote locations where the work force never will be. How can they be expected to tune into the need of that customer if they have no knowledge of that organization or person?

Video equipment can reduce this distance to zero. Footage of equipment operating as intended at remote locations builds pride in the people who produce it. Interviews with satisfied operators builds pride in those who produce the product, which increases the value of such videos. There can be no better customer service training media than this. Such videos can be placed in lunchrooms and comparable locations to be watched at the worker's convenience.

At times, work supervisors and production workers can be assigned to installation teams as a cross-training effort. The experience gained from such efforts provides a great deal of support to internal customer service training efforts. People want to know how the product they produce supports the customer. When these individuals return to their normal job and serve in training evolutions, they show fellow workers what the customer needs, an improvement factor that would not otherwise occur.

Shared Training

The idea of shared training was previously mentioned, but its importance makes repetition worthwhile. Often the value of the improved relationships that occur is underestimated. Workers develop a greater appreciation of customers they know and want to serve them to a higher level. No one wants to be known by a friend in terms of the poor quality product or service they produce. This factor by itself tends to improve quality and service.

These training sessions also help the customer understand the product and the people who produce it to a greater depth. Instead of complaining about things they don't like, they share their concerns during training in a "how can we make this better" way. Customers often know what they want and how it can be made that way. Shared training usually supports efforts to make positive changes that are mutually beneficial.

Customers must know how to properly utilize new products to their intended capacity. Products loaded with features are of little use if no one knows how to use the features. In-depth training, rather than cursory training, supports the customer in his efforts to continue business efforts with you.

Customers stick with suppliers who are trying to help them in ways other than selling them good products and services. Often shared training can be the item that makes your organization more competitive than other similar organizations. As difficult as it is to cultivate and develop customers, no one can take the chance of losing good customers to competitors who willingly train them.

One of America's largest and most respected furniture manufacturers requires field sales personnel to train customer personnel on product, sales skills, and motivational subjects. One representative annually trained over 600 customer personnel in formal sessions alone. He also provided on-the-job training as required during each visit. Was it effective? Did he have time to sell? You bet the training was effective and he had time to sell. He was on the top 10 national sales list annually, two years he was number two, and one year he was number one. *The customer connection pays big dividends!*

Summary

1. It isn't enough for the customer to be right. Each internal and external customer must be treated correctly if an organization is to survive over in the long haul in the global market.

2. The training team's customers include individual members of the training department, members of all other departments, and the external customer.

3. The training department must develop an ongoing training program for use within their department to increase professionalism. No other training effort can be considered more important to performance improvement initiatives,

4. Trainers play a major role in the organization's transformation processes. They discuss quality, production, customer service, customer satisfaction, and progress that is being made in each area as a normal part of every training session.

5. Managers owe their customers visionary leadership, a supportive working environment, and excellent training. Supervisors share this same responsibility. Much of the total training load in a quality environment will be borne by these individuals.

6. Shared training between internal and external customers is a great way to develop solid working relationships, produce quality goods and services, and meet the goal.

Composite Bibliography

The resources used in the development of this project are a blend of the old and new. Some training ideas stand the test of time with few changes, others are constantly being updated, changed, and improved. These training books and other important training reference books can be found in your library located in the 650 section.

Every trainer must be aware of two important organizations that provide in-depth support for the quality training program: ASQC and ASTD.

American Society for Quality Control

The American Society for Quality Control (ASQC) is a premiere organization in the quality arena. Many of the ideas for this program obviously were generated from reading the material presented by this organization. More information on this organization or membership information is available from:

> American Society for Quality Control
> P.O. Box 3005
> Milwaukee, WI 53201-3066
> Phone: (414) 272-8575
> Fax: (414) 272-1734

American Society for Training and Development

ASTD provides ongoing assistance in the training and consulting field. They have other important offerings as well.

Train America's Workforce–ASTD recently developed this awareness program designed to communicate the extreme importance of training America's work force to all organizations. There is no other way if the United States is to remain competitive in the global market—training is crucial.

Speakers across America are presenting this informative program, Train America's Workforce, to all kinds of audiences. Like many others, I am a presenter for our local ASTD chapter. Most of the facts and figures presented in this book concerning training are presented in the material that accompanies that program.

More information on the program or ASTD membership is available from:

American Society for Training and Development
1640 King Street
Alexandria, VA 22313
Phone: (703) 683-8100
Fax: (703) 683-8103

Statistics Concerning Training Need and Status

Put Quality to Work–Train America's Workforce, Alexandria, VA: The American Society for Training and Development, 1991.

The Learning Enterprise, Alexandria, VA: The American Society for Training and Development, and Washington, D.C.: U.S. Department of Labor, 1991.

Workplace Basics: The Skills Employers Want, The American Society for Training and Development, and Washington, D.C.: U.S. Department of Labor, 1991.

Needs Assessment

Wedel, K. R. and Brown, G. *Assessing Training Needs,* Washington, D.C.: National Training and Development Service, 1974.

Objectives and Strategies:

Cassner-Lotto, J. and Associates, *Successful Training Strategies: Twenty-six Innovative Corporate Models,* San Francisco: Jossey-Bass , 1988.

Friedman, P. G. and Yarbrough, E. A. *Training Strategies from Start to Finish,* Englewood Cliffs, NJ: Prentice-Hall, 1985.

Mager, R. F. *Preparing Instructional Objectives,* 2nd ed., Belmont, CA: Fearon, 1975.

Program Design

Cooper, S. and Heenan, C. *A Humanistic Approach*, Boston, MA: CB Publishing, 1980.

Engel, H. M. *Handbook of Creative Learning Exercises*, Houston, TX: Gulf Publishing, 1973.

Pfeiffer, J. W. and Jones, J. E. *A Handbook of Structured Experiences for Human Relations Training* (Volumes I–VI). LaJolla, CA: University Associates, 1974–1979.

Rogoff, R. L. *The Training Wheel*, New York: John Wiley and Sons, 1987.

Materials Development

Abella, K. T. *Building Successful Training Programs*, Reading, MA: Addison-Wesley, 1986.

Kemp, J. E. *Planning and Producing Audiovisual Materials*, 3rd ed., New York: Thomas Y. Crowell, 1975.

Delivery

Broadwell, M. M. *The Supervisor as an Instructor*, Reading, MA: Addison-Wesley, 1970.

Carkhuff, R. R. and Pierce, R. M. *Training Delivery Skills, Part I*, Amherst, MA: Human Resource Development Press, 1984.

———. *Training Delivery Skills, Part II*, Amherst, MA: Human Resource Development Press, 1984.

Evaluation

Brinkerhoff, R. O. *Achieving Results from Training*, San Francisco: Jossey-Bass, 1987.

Davis, L. N. and McCallon, E. *Planning, Conducting and Evaluating Workshops*, Austin, TX: Learning Concepts, 1975.

Hamblin, A. C. *Evaluation and Control of Training*, New York: McGraw-Hill, 1974.

Kirkpatrick, D. L. *Evaluating Training Programs*, Madison, WI: American Society for Training and Development, 1975.

Phillips, J. J. *Handbook of Training Evaluation and Methods*, Houston, TX: Gulf Publishing, 1982.

On-the-Job Training

Broadwell, M. M. *The Supervisor and On-the-Job Training*, Reading, MA: Addison-Wesley, 1986.

Connor, J. J. *On-the-Job Training*, Boston, MA: International Human Resource Development Corporation, 1983.

Computer-Based Training

Kearsley, G. *Computer-based Training, a Guide to Selection and Implementation*, Reading, MA: Addison-Wesley, 1983.

General

Asionian, C. B. and Brickell, H. M. *Americans in Transition: Life Changes As Reasons for Adult Learning*, New York: College Entrance Examination Board, 1980.

Bienvenu, B. J. *New Priorities in Training*, New York: American Management Association, 1969.

Brinkerhoff, R. O. *Achieving Results from Training*, San Francisco: Jossey-Bass, 1987.

Campbell, D. D. *Adult Education as a Field of Study and Practice*, Vancouver: Center for Continuing Education, University of British Columbia, 1977.

Cohen, W. A. *The Art of the Leader*, Englewood Cliffs, NJ: Prentice-Hall, 1990.

Craig, R. L. (Ed.) *American Society for Training and Development, Training & Development Handbook*, New York: McGraw-Hill, 1976.

———. *Training and Development Handbook*, New York: McGraw-Hill, 1976.

Cross, P. K. *Adults as Learners*, San Francisco: Jossey-Bass, 1981.

Eitenton, J. E. *The Winning Trainer*, Houston, TX: Gulf Publishing, 1984.

Ellis, S. K. *How to Survive a Training Assignment*, Reading, MA: Addison-Wesley, 1988.

How to Teach Grownups, Canoga Park, CA: Practical Management Associates, 1979.

King, D. *Training Within the Organization*, London: Tavistock Publications, 1964.

Knowles, M. *The Adult Learner: A Neglected Species*, Houston, TX: Gulf Publishing, 1973.

————. *The Modern Practice of Adult Education,* New York: Association Press, 1970.

London, M. *Managing the Training Enterprise,* San Francisco: Jossey-Bass, 1978.

McLagan, P. A. *Helping Others Learn,* Reading, MA: Addison-Wesley, 1978.

Mitchell, G. *The Trainer's Handbook,* New York: American Management Association, 1987.

Odiorne, G. S. *Training by Objectives,* New York: The Macmillan Company, 1970.

Proctor, J. H. and Thorton, W. M. *Training: A Handbook for Line Managers,* New York: American Management Association, 1961.

Quality

Adam, E., Klershawer, J., and Rach, W. *Productivity and Quality,* Englewood Cliffs, NJ: Prentice-Hall, 1981.

Deming, W. E. *Out of the Crisis,* Cambridge, MA: Massachusetts Institute of Technology, Center for Advanced Engineering Study, 1982.

DiPrimo, A. *Quality Assurance in Service Industries,* Radnor, PA: Chilton Book Company, 1987.

Juran, J. M. *Juran on Planning for Quality,* New York: The Free Press, 1988.

Townsend, P. L. *Commit to Quality,* New York: John Wiley and Sons, 1986.

Articles

Broadbill, M. M. *Ten Myths About Instructor Training,* published in *Training,* 1990.

Training Programs

Attendance at U.S. Navy train-the-trainer programs provided the basis for many of ideas. Each chapter follows the outline of a training program developed by Quality America, Inc., of Mechanicsburg, Pennsylvania. Many of the figures, charts, forms, and questionnaires are taken from that program and used with permission.

Index